Choosing Intimacy

Chsing Intimacy

Exploring Christ's Model for
Mutuality *and* Deeper Relationships

Cindi J. Martin, LCSW

NASHVILLE

NEW YORK • LONDON • MELBOURNE • VANCOUVER

Choosing Intimacy

Exploring Christ's Model for Mutuality and Deeply Connected Relationships

Published in New York, New York, by Morgan James Publishing. Morgan James is a trademark of Morgan James, LLC. www.MorganJamesPublishing.com

Proudly distributed by Publishers Group West®

Berean Study Bible (BSB) scriptures taken from The Holy Bible, Berean Study Bible, BSB Copyright © 2016, 2020 by Bible Hub. Used by Permission. All Rights Reserved Worldwide.
Scriptures marked New Heart English Bible taken from New Heart English Bible © 2022 New Heart English Bible, Public Domain
NKJV scriptures taken from the New King James Version®. Copyright © 1982 by Thomas Nelson. Used by permission. All rights reserved.
NIV scriptures taken from the Holy Bible, New International Version®, NIV®. Copyright © 1973, 1978, 1984, 2011 by Biblica, Inc.™ Used by permission of Zondervan. All rights reserved worldwide. www.zondervan.com. The "NIV" and "New International Version" are trademarks registered in the United States Patent and Trademark Office by Biblica, Inc.™
NASB Scripture quotations and words of Jesus are taken or adapted from the New American Standard Bible, ® Copyright © 1960, 1962, 1963, 1968, 1971, 1973, 1975, 1977, 1995 by The Lockman Foundation. Used by permission.
NRSVA Scripture quotations are from New Revised Standard Version Bible Copyright © 1989, 1993 National Council of the Churches of Christ in the United States of America. Used by permission. All rights reserved worldwide.
TNIV scriptures taken from the HOLY BIBLE, TODAY'S NEW INTERNATIONAL VERSION®. TNIV®. Copyright © 2001, 2005 by International Bible Society. Used by permission of Zondervan. All rights reserved worldwide.

Morgan James BOGO™

A **FREE** ebook edition is available for you or a friend with the purchase of this print book.

CLEARLY SIGN YOUR NAME ABOVE

Instructions to claim your free ebook edition:
1. Visit MorganJamesBOGO.com
2. Sign your name CLEARLY in the space above
3. Complete the form and submit a photo of this entire page
4. You or your friend can download the ebook to your preferred device

ISBN 9781636982663 paperback
ISBN 9781636982670 ebook
Library of Congress Control Number: 2023941611

Cover Design by:
Rachel Lopez
www.r2cdesign.com

Interior Design by:
Christopher Kirk
www.GFSstudio.com

Morgan James is a proud partner of Habitat for Humanity Peninsula and Greater Williamsburg. Partners in building since 2006.

Get involved today! Visit: www.morgan-james-publishing.com/giving-back

This book is dedicated to Virginia Sloat
and
all who long for the deep connection of intimacy.

Table Of Contents

Acknowledgments

I extend a debt of gratitude to my friend Ronda Melendez, B.S., MBA, who, while harvesting produce with me in our Wellspring Charitable Gardens, listened to my musings, believed that this topic had merit, and encouraged me to write this book. My friend Lori Ransdell invested her brilliant, well-reasoned mind into a manuscript that was still just a jumble of unorganized ideas. I relied heavily on my friend and scholar of theology and ancient languages, Robert K. Brown, M.A., M.Div., whose meticulous mind informed my use of the Greek and Hebrew language, as did the wise and clear thinking of my longtime friend and theology scholar, Russ Herald, M.Div.

Professional readers of my original manuscript included Jinni Bradfield, M.Div., Meg Rusick, and Patricia Anders, who were invaluable in helping me sort out my target audience, which became broader than first envisioned. My dear friends and counseling colleagues, Susan Brumm, LPCC, and Marietta Huizenga, Certified Life Coach, both offered their love, support, honesty, and a word-for-word review of the final drafts from both a spiritual and psychological perspective.

I am also indebted to Jill Hubbard, Ph.D., and Steve Arterburn for supporting my work in numerous ways and offering their endorsements. A special thanks to Jill for laboring with me over early and late drafts and writing the foreword. Thank you to my daughter, Amanda Martin, and many faithful friends, including Nancy Berrens, Stephanie Hobbs, Julie Powers, LPCC, Brian Elliott, OD, Garrett Elliott, OD, Brandon Miller, JD, Paulette MacDonald, Jon Byron, Francie Byron, Hannah Brady, Jallen Rix, Ed.D., Cynthia McBeth, Robert Chin, MD, Ruth Brown, Claudia Kuypers, Naomi Kuypers, Sylvia Blickle, John Britton, Jenny Russell, Rebecca Tucker, LCSW,

Nancy Neufeld Silva, Ph.D., LCSW, Shirley Miranda, Michele Corgiat, LMFT, Rebecca McMahon, LCSW, Sherese Carter, Randy Carter, Janice Duncan, Bradford Chew, Susan Chew, and many other unnamed friends and family members for reading part or all of the earliest versions. Thank you to Kim Sarale, LMFT, for giving me courage to brave the social media world so much a part of the publishing industry today.

I am grateful to Deep River Publishing for introducing me to Terry Whalin and Morgan James Faith. Thank you to Arlyn Lawrence and Bill Watkins for their professional editing, and to Christopher Kirk for the graphic design of my Grief Map. Thank you to Shannon Peters, my Morgan James Faith author relations manager, along with the Morgan James Faith publishing team for walking me through new territory with such kindness and professionalism.

I celebrate the scores of unnamed clients who taught me the practical wisdom captured between the pages of this book. Though posthumous, I celebrate Jeanette Ricks for her love for Jesus and me, and her capacity for intimacy and spiritual wisdom, and also her brother Jallen, for demonstrating the power of love amidst existential differences. Finally, I owe my greatest debt of gratitude to my two favorite English teachers, my two most intimate friends, and my two most loving and honest critics: my husband, Keith Martin, and best girlfriend, Shelley Circle, for investing countless hours reading draft after revised draft and correcting errors in thought, theology, and English grammar.

I celebrate my soulmate and husband Keith for inspiring this book with the way he understood the power of mutuality in relationships at the young age of 23. His definition of intimacy as "the deep abiding confidence that someone knows you, cares for you, and desires and delights in your presence" has inspired my personal and professional life in profound ways. Finally, I give my highest praise to our Sovereign Lord and God for extending His invitation of mutual intimacy to all human beings.

Foreword

For the thoughtful Christian, *Choosing Intimacy* is a journey worth taking. It has been my privilege to gain entrance behind the scenes as Cindi has written her first book. She is gifted in her reflection of theological and psychological concepts and communicates clearly how the two weave together to give us a greater understanding of God's original seamless design for intimacy, not only with Him but also with others.

Cindi and I became acquainted with each other's work in the mid 1990s when I was the treating inpatient psychotherapist for one of her ongoing patients. As seasons of life, career, and ministry progressed, we had the unique opportunity to not only view each other's work via shared treatments but also come alongside one another to fill in the gaps during times of absence for maternity leaves or ministry seasons. Working from opposite ends of the state, we forged an out-of-the-box collegial relationship as clinicians.

Choosing Intimacy guides us beyond our limited capacities for closeness. It invites us to develop deeper, more enriching relationships where companions don't compete for position or power but rather share space that is expansive enough to encompass the best interests of both self and others. As we grow in personal insight and understanding of God's original design for our horizontal attachments, we can become more courageous, conscious, and intentional about deepening our connection with God and others.

Cindi's study and perspective of shared power as part of the divine path can have a healing ripple impact on those who are hurt when power is weaponized or one-sided, or where there is a lack of safe places to question authority. Both Cindi and I have supported men and women of all ages and stages who have been deflated and devastated by power differentials—worse yet, hurt when power has been abused within the Church. Even the most well-meaning Christians can be ensnared by cultural traditions seen through the lens of the Fall, shortsighted by familiarity, and with no allowance for deeper reflection.

God-given curiosity, critical thinking, and exploratory conversations about biblical assumptions and the ways they interface with day to day living are vital for spiritual and emotional growth. The freedom to express and work through questions about how to understand biblical authority or how to use power as Christ did is essential to our development and maturity. Yet, there is often no room for discussing our equality in Christ or how the use of power as New Creations differs markedly from worldly power in our Christian relationships. When writing my books about *Secrets Women Keep* or co-authoring *Forgiving our Fathers and Mothers*, I addressed the downside to hiding and subverting oneself for lack of a voice to freely speak out loud. Unanswered questions often go underground—fracturing relationships with God, within ourselves, and with others—and then manifest themselves in self-doubt, identity confusion, addictions, anxiety, and depression.

I believe God's desire for us is to live and love better. This means we lean into relationships, even when they are hard and messy, we question with honesty and humility, even when it's not customary, and we never settle or foreclose on our journey towards Christlikeness, even when the path seems elusive. We have the power to choose intimacy.

Thank you, Cindi, for giving us guidance, for showing us the value of asking tough questions, and for providing us with practical examples demonstrating how to achieve mutuality and deeper, more intimate relationships. I especially want to thank you for being vulnerable as you poured out your heart, expressed the joy and sorrow of your lived experiences, and shared what you have learned as a woman, wife, psychotherapist, and devoted disciple of Christ. May lives be healed and transformed by the power and Spirit of Christ and by following His model for intimacy.

Jill J. Hubbard, Ph.D.,
Clinical Psychologist, Author, and Co-host of New Life Live! *Radio Broadcast*

Introduction

I vividly remember the thrill of finding out that my maternal grandmother had invited me to spend the night with her. On the long car ride with my parents to her home in Santa Rosa, California, I contemplated questions I planned to ask her during my visit. Even at a young age, I was curious about my grandmother's childhood in the "olden days" and what she thought about when she was my age. I wondered if she had thought about what it was like to grow old and die.

We finally arrived and after unpacking the suitcase and saying goodbye to my parents, Grammie and I went for a walk on her country road. We had a delicious day of picking blackberries and making blackberry jelly in her tiny kitchen. In the evening, I snuggled comfortably next to her on an overstuffed sofa with kelly-green textured material and lace doilies pinned to the head and arm rests. Noticing her pin curled silver hair and beautiful tanned and lined face, I crossed my legs like she did and expected her to engage with me in an important conversation. I was seven years old when I wondered aloud, "Grammie, are you afraid to die?" I was certain that she would have some important wisdom to share with me. Instead, she was silent. Finally, after what seemed like an eternity to me, she said, "No, Cindi, I don't think I am afraid to die." Then she changed the subject.

The feeling of immense disappointment overwhelmed me. My stomach knotted. My face flushed with embarrassment. Where just moments ago there had been joy, warmth, and comfort in her presence, now there was a cold sadness and awkwardness, a tangible distance. I moved away from her, hugged the arm rest, stared at the T.V., and felt ashamed, as if by asking about her feelings, I had done something terribly wrong. I felt alone.

Looking back, I realize that I had just knocked on the door of my grandmother's heart, but she had not opened it. I could not have known it at the time, but I had ventured into an area of great vulnerability. When I asked if she was afraid of death, I expected her to not only answer my question, but also reciprocate by asking me similar questions.

I felt invisible that day, disappearing into her couch. I would have felt seen and heard if my grandmother had asked me something like, "Gee, what makes you ask that question?" Or, "Cindi, are *you* afraid of death?" Had there been reciprocity in the conversation, we might both have asked more questions of one another like, "What do you think happens after someone dies?" and, "Do you believe in God?" Had my grandmother opened this door to emotional and spiritual intimacy, we might have spent more time together and learned to know one another better. Perhaps we would have taken the risk of sharing more personal thoughts, feelings, and opinions about our life experiences. Had she lived long enough to know me as an adult, we might have become more than grandmother and granddaughter—we might have become deeply connected friends.

Though I did not understand it at the time, I was asserting the personal power of a seven year old and inviting my Grammie into a closer relationship. I wanted to get to know her better and share things about myself with her. Moving from picking blackberries to picking her brain, my heart was hoping for mutuality in our relationship. I did not know that she could use her personal power to prevent emotional or spiritual connection from developing further or that I could be disappointed by a lack of reciprocity. It was the wise sage King Solomon who aptly spoke the proverb, "Hope deferred makes the heart sick, but desire fulfilled is a tree of life (Proverbs 13:12, NASB 1995)." My heart was sad. My desire for intimacy was unfulfilled.

Intimate knowing, caring, desiring, and delighting are not limited to human beings. The stunning beauty and intricate complexity of our natural world can teach us about God, ourselves, and one another in surprisingly intimate and healing ways. For example, in 2004, I was trained in equine-assisted psychotherapy and had the privilege of watching traumatized veterans heal emotional wounds by building a relationship on the ground with a horse (as opposed to in the saddle).

Since horses are large animals of prey, they are wired with a highly sensitive fight-flight system.

James was a veteran having what are called dissociative episodes at home with his family. The first time this happened after returning from Afghanistan, James was eating a meal with his wife and children when suddenly he smelled something. He became hyper alert and agitated as if there were an imminent threat. Without warning, he turned over the kitchen table and began screaming commands for everyone to take cover. He had no awareness during this outburst, and he did not remember it afterwards. Dissociation is the mind's way of disconnecting from reality to cope with overwhelming thoughts, feelings, and traumatic experiences that would otherwise be intolerable. This was frightening to both James and his family, but he refused traditional talk therapy.

When James was finally offered equine-assisted psychotherapy, he eagerly engaged. It was not long before this same dissociative behavior occurred with me and Ginger, our therapy horse. It was a dusty, windy day when James became emotionally activated in the arena during a simple exercise of catching and haltering the horse. Suddenly, he unconsciously acted out in an aggressive manner toward the horse. Ginger responded immediately by turning her back side to James and felt sufficiently threatened to gallop away, kicking dust up with her hooves as she bounded over to the other side of the arena. The horse's behavior surprised James and jolted him into emotional and physical awareness, so we were able to process what he was thinking and feeling just prior to going blank.

James recalled a memory where he had been caught up in a dust storm and experienced an enemy attack while traveling with his unit across the desert. He realized that the wind had picked up and blown dust in his face when he was approaching Ginger with the halter. After that he had no memory until Ginger had bolted. Just talking about the incident activated James' human fight-flight system, making his heart race and triggering feelings of anger.

The connection between dust and his unit traveling through the desert opened up even more details about the traumatic aspects of the event that explained in part why he had become so aggressive. Dust was a trigger that could now inform him of a potential recurring episode. This knowledge became proactive power in the arena when Ginger was kicking up dust. He was able to practice remaining conscious and stroked Ginger's neck for comfort. This soothing touch helped him to settle and ground himself until his breathing and heart rate stabilized. Later, after much practice and repetition, he was able to transfer these skills to his home environment and significantly reduced the number of frightening episodes with his family. In fact, he soon figured out that the smell of burned toast had triggered the table-turning incident. His sense of smell connected him to the memory of a horrible vehicle fire in which he and two very good friends nearly lost their lives. He asked his wife and kids to bring his dog over when they noticed he was getting agitated, and this became a powerful non-verbal healing tool for the entire family.

Metaphors of Soil and Soul

Winston Churchill once said, "There is something about the outside of a horse that is good for the inside of a man." I had the privilege of loving and caring for our three beloved therapy horses (Ginger, Smokey, and Liberty) until I was diagnosed with a rare bone disease that threatened to paralyze me. Three cervical spine surgeries later, I faced giving up my horses, my equine-assisted psychotherapy practice, and my love of riding.

Each horse helped me to face my physical limitations and grieve the losses as I said goodbye to them and found them new homes. New hope grew from supportive friends and a skilled organic market gardener who turned the manure of our horse pastures into the rich, composted soil of a community-supported agriculture project (CSA). The sale of fresh produce in the form of weekly farm-to-table subscriptions would nourish our community families and the proceeds would help fund our counseling programs. Our staff and volunteers have a new quote to add to that of Winston Churchill, "There is something about the nature of garden soil that is good for the inside of human souls."

One of the first tasks our market gardener asks us to do when we begin preparing a new area for planting is to test the soil. The best soil is a rich, sandy loam which is a balance of sand, silt, and clay. Interestingly, even ideal soil needs to be amended or fed with organic matter containing microscopic bacteria, fungi, earthworms, and other beneficial insects. These creatures forge mutually rewarding partnerships with plant roots, making it possible for the plants to nourish themselves. The knowledge of this essential mutuality reminds me daily of the power of mutuality in close relationships.

As I contemplated my experience with market gardening and soil preparation, it occurred to me that soil provided the perfect metaphor for God's work on Earth and in the human heart. In Luke 8:4-15, Jesus explains the parable of the sower: God is like a farmer who sows the seed of His Word in different kinds of soil. The four soils represent various conditions of human hearts in preparation and responsiveness to the sown seed of the Word of God.

First, there is the soil of a well-traveled path. Seed is sown but is also easily visible to predators because of the hardness of the soil. Satan, like a ravenous bird, quickly eats the seeds before they can take root. The second kind of soil is rocky, where the seedling can quickly take root but then wilts because there is no depth of soil. This is the heart of someone initially excited about God's Word, but who quickly abandons it when living it out becomes difficult because of persecution or other hardship. The third type of heart is filled with thorns that choke out the tiny seeds and any growth. The thorns represent life's many distractions and worries that compete with God's Word. Finally, there is the heart that has been well cultivated and prepared. Good soil represents the heart ready to receive the seed and to bear the abundant fruit of hearing and doing the Word of God.

The choices we make in response to our life experiences can soften or harden hearts. The old, bruised, and dying plants of broken dreams and fractured relationships can eventually become the rich compost that amends and enriches us, allowing us to produce the fruit of the Spirit. Rather than allowing our hearts to remain hard, rocky, or thorny, we can choose to soften them and pursue a path of intimacy with God and others. This begins with a willingness to test the soil of our hearts, just as our gardeners test the soil of our fields. We are wise if we become students of the internal landscape of our souls. "Guard your heart with all diligence, for out of it is the wellspring of life (Proverbs 4:23, New Heart English Bible).

When Jesus told the parable of the sower, He would have been thinking of the Hebrew meaning of the word for heart, which is *lev*. The heart is the seat of our emotions (feelings), our minds (thoughts), and our wills (intentions). Yet many Christians have been taught to ignore and even suppress their emotions. We are created in God's image and our God, though much more, is also a feeling and thinking God.

As a lay student of the ancient languages, I was struck by the visceral, or deeply emotional, nature of the Hebrew language. For example, did you know that there are approximately 44 words for the variations on our one English word for grief? Among the meanings of the Hebrew words are "rage," "broken to pieces," "bitter," "sorrowful," "rubbed raw," and "writhed in a fetal position." We need both our heart and mind to inform our faith. We are often told not to trust or even pay attention to our emotions, but this is not a biblical perspective. Scripture teaches that we are to be informed by our emotions not controlled by them. We cannot be informed by what we are unable to access due to consciously suppressing or unconsciously repressing and denying our feelings.

How appropriate then, that God's Word speaks often of loving God as an integrative, whole-person process. We are told to love the Lord our God with all our heart, mind, soul, and strength. We cannot love God with our whole being when we do not take the time to know our inner thoughts, feelings, and intentions. Often the words of our mouths, meditations of our hearts, and the strength of our physical actions betray hidden desires, motivations, and intentions. The important spiritual discipline of self-examination and self-knowledge is often referred to as self-absorption and selfish preoccupation. However, healthy self-examination leads to healthier relationships with others.

In contrast, self-preoccupation is used as a substitute for intimacy with others. It is also possible to become obsessed with intellectual knowledge. For example, we can develop an insatiable need for intellectual learning without actually using the knowledge to develop emotionally honest relationships with God, ourselves, and others. We can use our intellect to distance and protect ourselves from the vulnerability of intimacy.

Neurological research on the brain illustrates our interconnectedness as humans. For example, we have learned that our amygdala, often referred to as the 911 center of the brain, is the integrative center for emotions, behavior, and motivation.[1] We now know that the amygdala triggers our fight-flight system, which can bypass our cerebral cortex, the thinking and reasoning brain. The amygdala is wired for our survival and will not respond to logical arguments when the body

---

1   Wright, Anthony, Ph.D. Department of Neurobiology and Anatomy. McGovern Medical School. October 10, 2020. Chapter 6.1. nba.uth.tmc.edu

senses emotional or physical danger. This is one of the reasons it is so difficult for us to make rational decisions when we feel afraid or threatened. Once the threat is passed, the vagus nerve, which is the longest cranial nerve and responsible for regulating breath and heart rate among many other functions (including mood), will allow the thinking brain back into harmony with its other parts.

Cultivating love and intimacy in relationships is an integrative process and requires whole person awareness and safety. Paul tells us in Romans 10:9–10 that is with the heart that humans believe in Christ, not simply intellectual assent. "…that if you confess with your mouth Jesus as Lord, and believe in your heart that God raised him from the dead, you will be saved; for with the heart a person believes resulting in righteousness, and with the mouth he confesses, resulting in salvation" (NASB 1995).

I have found that good psychology, literally "the study of the soul," is rooted in good theology, "the study of God." Consider the teachings of Jesus in Matthew 5:3–7 when He told His listeners to first take the log out of their own eye before attempting to take the speck out of someone else's eye. These concepts all originate in the need for self-awareness and the ability of someone to take personal responsibility for potentially hidden thoughts and feelings. Rightfully did David ask God to search him and know him and expose any hurtful way in him (Psalm 139:23–24). The ability to self-reflect, recognize, and manage potential blind spots can reduce our tendency to project or act out our unconscious wounds, needs, or desires onto others.

This concept is known in psychology as projection. Psychological projection involves superimposing our undesirable feelings or thoughts onto someone or something else, rather than admitting or dealing with our own feelings. It requires honest reflection, insight, and courage to admit when we are projecting our feelings onto others. For example, if a man feels ashamed of his attraction toward the wife of his best friend, he may accuse his wife of being attracted to another man. He would then be projecting his feelings onto her rather than taking responsibility for his own shame about desiring another woman.

Projections can become an obstacle to intimacy because they block our ability to see and know one another accurately for who they really are. Mutuality assumes that both people are learning to know themselves and advocating for one another in sharing their honest thoughts, feelings, needs, and desires. What is yet unconscious or unknown can become an area in the relationships for growth, curiosity, and discovery if we gently work together to understand our intense emotional reactions to one another. When people have conflicting needs—as we inevitably do in any relationship—there is a strong pull toward a power struggle about who is right or wrong or who has the authority to make decisions about certain resources. The generous nature of our triune God teaches us to share power rather than compete for it. The distinct and equal nature of the persons of the Trinity teach us to delight in mutually satisfying decisions that cultivate intimacy rather than crush it.

In fact, the Trinity of God shows us that persons, as God's image bearers, were created to be with other persons. We were designed for togetherness and belonging. God declared that the world and everything in it, including human beings, was very good. There was only one condition in the Garden of Eden that was decidedly not good—to be alone. Human beings were created to connect deeply with God, ourselves, one another, and all of creation. Yet many of us suffer from profound loneliness, whether in a crowd of people or even within our own families, marriages, and friendships. In many instances, we have reduced ourselves to "human *doings*" rather than "human *beings*." God told Moses that His name was I AM (Exodus 3:14). God is the Great I AM not the Great I DO. Many of us try to find our identity through the things that we do. In reality, our doing must flow from our being and who we are as God's unique creation. We are often unsure how to be in relationships. We struggle to cultivate intimacy with one another in ways that allow us to know and be known, to see and be seen, to hear and be heard, to understand and be understood for who we are rather than who others want us to be.

I have written this book to show how we can cultivate and enjoy intimacy in our relationships. As I will explain, intimacy begins with extending and accepting invitations to spend time together, share common interests and tasks, and eventually disclose intimate thoughts, feelings, and beliefs about ourselves and one another. We slowly build trust and confidence that we can become safe and trustworthy people who can care, desire, and delight in one another. Intimacy develops a mutual respect for individual differences, the responsible use of personal power, and the capacity to resolve conflict in mutually acceptable ways when expressing needs and desires in the relationship.

Structure of the Book

The structure of *Choosing Intimacy* is designed to provide a contextual and panoramic view of the Christian worldview as it relates to intimacy and the power of mutuality in relationships. I have divided it into four parts within four biblical and historical time periods which are: (1) the Pre-Fall Era, (2) the Post-Fall Era, (3) the New Creation Era, and (4) the New Heaven and Earth Era. In the Pre-Fall Era, we see that the nature of God is One and yet exists as three individual and equal persons of the Trinity. Humankind reflects this oneness, individuality, and equality in having been made in God's image, both male and female. Humans were created to reflect the image of God by enjoying Him, ourselves, one another, and all Creation. Our purpose is to glorify God by reflecting the cooperative nature of the Trinity and by harmoniously co-ruling the earth together as equal partners. We are to skillfully multiply and manage the earth's resources in ways that are life-giving and mutually beneficial to all of Creation.

In the Post-Fall Era, humans live with the curses and consequences of using our God-given freedom of choice to rebel against what is good, alienating ourselves from God, ourselves, and one another. Now sin and evil are known experientially, up close, and personal. Though humans still bear the image of God, albeit marred and distorted, we have fundamentally changed. Human beings, both male and female, now have a sin nature and no longer solely experience the intimacy of their God-designed nature. Our gifts and abilities are no longer only used in the service of love and nurturing. They do not exclusively generate the joy of mutually beneficial relationships that contribute to blessing, cultivation, and growth. Now men seek to rule over women for personal gain. Women desire to control men. Humans no longer share power and authority to steward resources for the mutual benefit of all creation. Men and women have become self-interested and compete for domination, which leads to further alienation, separation, decay, and death. In contrast to natural intimacy, belonging, and mutual delight of the pre-Fall world, there is now alienation from God and Creation. Relationships are exploited in an attempt to regain a sense of mastery over feelings of fear, shame and the constant threat of pain, suffering, and death.

In the new Creation, God's highest intention for human beings is realized through the birth, life, death, and resurrection of Jesus Christ. Human beings are redeemed and reconciled to God, finding new life and restored relationships with God, ourselves, one another, and all Creation through our Savior. We are not, however, completely rid of the post-Fall consequences of our sin. God's people still struggle to realize His highest intention for relationships due to our sinful human nature, our adversary, the devil, and the principalities of this world which are at war with the indwelling Spirit of God in believers.

Finally, the New Heaven and Earth Era is inaugurated by the Second Coming of Christ and the creation of the new heavens and the new earth. In this new era, God will usher in His highest intention and purpose for all of Creation, the *telos*[2] of God's eternal purpose. Christ as the Bridegroom will be united with all believers as His Bride. According to the Apostle Paul, the present tension of living a Spirit-filled life while existing in a "body of death" is resolved when death finally dies, and all things become new.[3]

In summary, God's vision for intimacy was compromised by the choice of humans to become intimate with evil. The knowledge of both good and evil resulted in a catastrophic distortion of God's highest intention for the exercise of authority and power. Humans have interpreted dominion as the opportunity to dominate and exploit the earth's inhabitants rather than exercise wise management and care. The privilege of sharing authority and power with other humans in harmonious and productive ways for the goodness of all Creation was corrupted by sin, corrected by the life work of Jesus Christ, created anew in the life of the Spirit, and comes to fruition in the New Heaven and Earth Era when Christ comes for His Bride and creates the new heavens and the new earth.

I now invite you to join me as a fellow critical thinker. Together we will re-examine passages that have both helped and hindered an understanding of the mutuality inherent to a sacred intimacy with God and others.

---

2   *Telos* is the ancient Greek term for an end, fulfillment, completion, goal or aim; it is the source of the modern word "teleology." Routledge Encyclopedia of Philosophy. https://www.rep.routledge.com/articles/thematic/telos/v-1
3   Romans 7:24; 1 Corinthians 15:55–58, NASB

PART I
Sacred Soil In The Pre-Fall Era

"In the beginning God created the heavens and the earth."
(Genesis 1:1, NIV)

CHAPTER 1

Sacred Vulnerability

"To love at all is to be vulnerable. Love anything, and your heart will certainly be wrung and possibly be broken. If you want to make sure of keeping it intact, you must give your heart to no one, not even to an animal. Wrap it carefully round with hobbies and little luxuries; avoid all entanglements; lock it up safe in the casket or coffin of your selfishness. But in that casket—safe, dark, motionless, airless—it will change. It will not be broken; it will become unbreakable, impenetrable, irredeemable..."[4]

—C.S. Lewis

As a professional Christian psychotherapist, I often tell my clients that two of the most problematic areas in relationships involve sex and finances. Why are sex and finances so problematic? They both offer an opportunity for intimacy but require the vulnerability of honest self-exposure and willingness to share power for mutual enjoyment. The Hebrew word for sexual intimacy, *yada*, means to know, to be known, and to be deeply respected. It can represent sex but also goes beyond that to signify a deep sense of vulnerability and connection between two people. In fact, this word, *yada*, "to know," is used over 900 times in the Old Testament.[5]

---

4   Lewis, C. S. *The Four Loves*. Harper Collins Publishers, 1960, p. 169.
5   https://jewish.shop/37787/abide-in-hebrew/

13

In his book *Connecting*, Larry Crabb said that, in connecting, there is power to change other people's lives. This is a transformational intimacy offered by God to us through Jesus Christ. This is a "profound meeting when the truest part of one soul meets the emptiest recesses in another and finds something there, when life passes from one to the other. When that happens, the giver is left more full than before and the receiver less terrified, eventually eager to experience even deeper, more mutual connection."[6] There is neither connection nor intimacy without honest knowing and being known. Jesus further develops the idea of this kind of intimacy in his statement, "Not everyone who says to Me, 'Lord, Lord,' will enter the kingdom of heaven; but he who does the will of my Father who is in heaven. Many will say on that day, 'Lord, Lord, did we not prophesy in Your name, and in Your name cast out demons, and in Your name perform many miracles?' "And then I will declare to them, 'I never knew you; Depart from me, you who practice lawlessness'" (Matthew 7:21–23, NASB 1977).

Vulnerability that leads to intimacy involves uncertainty, risk, and emotional exposure. According to researcher and professor at the University of Houston, Brené Brown, "To feel is to be vulnerable…Vulnerability is the birthplace of love, belonging, joy, courage, empathy, and creativity. It is the source of hope, empathy, accountability, and authenticity. If we want greater clarity in our purpose or deeper and more meaningful spiritual lives, vulnerability is the path."[7] Vulnerability is the bridge between intimacy and connection. It is the underlying and defining matrix that makes intimacy and connection realistic and attainable.

Spiritual Vulnerability

I was 15 years old when I began taking the risk of making myself vulnerable to a friend named Janet, whom I met in my high school gym class. She was dating a young man from her church and took the risk of talking with me about him and her faith in God. I still had questions about death that my Grammie had not

---

6   Crabb, Larry. *Connecting: Healing for Ourselves and Our Relationships: A Radical New Vision.* Nashville, TN: Word Pub., 1997. (25)

7   Brown, Brené. *Daring Greatly: How the Courage to Be Vulnerable Transforms the Way We Live, Love, and Lead.* New York: Avery, an Imprint of Penguin Random House, 2015. (33–34)

been able to answer, so I thought maybe she would be willing to talk about what happens after people die. We enjoyed many conversations about life, death, and the God of the Bible. The biggest obstacle to my faith in Christ was the idea that God wanted children to obey their parents.

As a rebellious teenager growing up in a home filled with conflict, I was not convinced that I wanted to get involved with a God who thought obeying my parents was a good idea. Janet emphasized God's love for me and encouraged me to delight and trust in Him. After much discussion, she finally said, "Cindi, what if you were to believe that God loves you and has your best interests at heart even if your parents don't? If you obey God, He will be faithful to you and provide for you." This was as pivotal as it was foreign to me, and I had no problem telling God how much I disliked the idea. At that point I still thought I was talking to the air. I remember trying to go to sleep one night and wrestling with this concept of obedience. I finally said, "Okay, God, I do not even know if You exist, but just in case You do, I will try this 'obey your parents' thing, trust you, and see what happens."

It was a mustard seed of faith, but the seeds of intimacy in my relationship with God and Janet were being sown. I felt seen, heard, and understood. Janet's willingness to listen without shaming me for my rather unorthodox approach to God paved the way for me to feel comfortable communicating directly with God about all my feelings, thoughts, and opinions, both positive and negative. As I trusted and obeyed God about speaking truth and obeying my parents, I also learned that any obedience to human authority had to be rooted in my faith in God, not in the human authority itself. If God were truly good, He would work on my behalf even if I believed the human authority was wrong or unreasonable.

By now I began to see God do amazing things as I submitted myself to His authority in my life. For a teenager accustomed to the adrenalin rush of lying and sneaking out to spend time with friends, I was rather shocked that I enjoyed the peace and comfort of speaking the truth. Surprisingly, obeying God and my parents did not make my life easier, though internally I was more at peace. One time when I apologized to my dad for coming home late after curfew, he yelled at me and said, "What is wrong with you? Why can't you argue with me like you used to. Are you a doper?"

My parents were not at all impressed with my newfound faith. My mom refused to allow me to read my Bible or play Christian music in our home and forbid me to see my friend Janet. My dad was hostile toward my faith as well. When he saw that I was exclusively dating young, Christian men, he became adamant about not walking me down the wedding aisle if I married a Christian. I was heartbroken to hear this, particularly because of the fallacious teaching about parental authority that I was under at that time. I was taught that if my parents did not give me permission to marry, that it was not God's will for me to marry until they did.

As you can imagine, this was the beginning of a new struggle between God and me. How could I reconcile God's Word, which taught that I was not to be unequally yoked with an unbeliever, together with yet another teaching that I must obey my parents? This was quite a conundrum for an 18-year-old who was dating a Christian man planning to become a pastor. We eventually broke up, but my confusion about how to reconcile my freedom in Christ with my seeming bondage to parental authority persisted. Fortunately, I had learned from Janet that the best way to handle my confusion was to argue and fight it out with God. I later learned that many of the prophets from Habakkuk to Jeremiah and Elijah regularly debated with God, and asked—

as I did—"Why?" questions, and lamented what God was doing in their lives. When a Christian friend once told me that my questioning of God was akin to heresy, I asked her if she planned an inquisition against Job, Moses, and the patriarchs as well! It was during these difficult times that I learned the importance of pressing into conflict with God and people rather than withdrawing. Intimacy requires the vulnerability of emotional and intellectual honesty and a willingness to work through conflict to find a mutually satisfying solution.

I met my future husband, Keith, in a psychology class when I was 21 years old. When our dating became more serious and we discussed the possibility of marriage, I explained my desire for my parents' approval and the challenge of my dad's refusal to support my marriage to a Christian man. To make things even more challenging, my dad had noticed that Keith walked with a limp and had scoffed at my interest in a man who was "a Christian *and* a cripple." Keith did, in fact, have a rare neurological disease called Spinal Muscular Atrophy, Type III. We talked very honestly about the challenges of a future together with a progressive and degenerative disease that would certainly place him in a wheelchair in the coming years.

With a great deal of hope and sobriety, we both believed that Christ could sustain our love for one another in the coming years, though we knew it would not be without struggle. Having decided that we wanted to be married, I asked Keith if he were willing to pray and wait on the Lord to confirm our plans and to work in my dad's heart to give us his blessing. Keith agreed and after a year and a half, he came to dinner at my parent's home and went out back where my dad was grilling chicken. Keith said, "I love your daughter and would consider it an honor if you would give us your blessing in marriage." My dad replied with a resoundingly indifferent, "Well, if that's what you want." We took that as a divine "yes" and were thrilled to become engaged to be married.

Keith and I never talked about what we would have done if my dad had declined his blessing, but by then I had moved out of my parents' home and may have come to the conclusion that, in this case, I was to obey God and not my parents. Yet even today, over 40 years later, many young Christian men and women I meet with in my office are being taught that obedience to the human authority of government leaders, pastors, husbands, and parents is the same as obedience to God. Our pastor of premarital counseling was about to challenge my conflation of human and divine authority and pave the way for God's highest intention for intimacy.

Mutual Vulnerability

The turning point in my understanding of the relationship between intimacy and the capacity to cultivate mutuality through shared authority, power, and control began formally when I was 23. Keith and I did our pre-marital counseling with a wise pastor and dedicated Bible teacher. The pastor introduced us to what I thought then (and realize now) was a revolutionary idea about how to understand the generous way men and women love and relate to one another in marriage. What made it even more amazing was that this concept came straight from a careful contextual understanding (*Sitz im Leben*)[8] of the Scriptures.

---

8   *Sitz im Leben* (literally "seat, place, or residence in life") is the German phrase used in biblical criticism for contextual consideration of the time, place, and circumstances in which the writing occurred.

As a young bride-to-be, I was anxious to prove my love for and fidelity to the Lord and my husband as we attended our premarital counseling sessions. Our pastor asked us to read and interpret 1 Peter 3:1–9 (NASB 1995), reflecting on the relationship between wives and husbands. That passage reads as follows:

¹In the same way, you wives, be submissive to your own husbands, so that even if any of them are disobedient to the word, they may be won without a word, by the behavior of their wives, ²as they observe your chaste and respectful behavior. ³Your adornment must not be merely external–braiding the hair, and wearing gold jewelry, or putting on dresses; ⁴but let it be the hidden person of the heart, with the imperishable quality of a gentle and quiet spirit, which is precious in the sight of God. ⁵For in this way in former times the holy women also, who hoped in God, used to adorn themselves, being submissive to their own husbands; ⁶ just as Sarah obeyed Abraham, calling him lord, and you have become her children if you do what is right without being frightened by any fear.

⁷You husbands in the same way⁹, live with your wives in an understanding way, as with someone weaker; since she is a

---

9   Personal Correspondence. Philip Payne. September 6, 2023. "The TNIV translates the participle 'dwelling together' as though it were an imperative, 'Live with.' Each of the three preceding sections, however, begins with a command to "submit" using the same verb, hypotassō:
-    "Submit yourselves for the Lord's sake to every human authority" (2:13)
-    "Slaves, in reverent fear of God submit yourselves to your masters" (2:18)
-    "Wives, in the same way [homoiōs] submit yourselves to your own husbands" (3:1)
So, when Peter writes in 3:7, "Husbands in the same way [homoiōs] …" the only command supplied by the context is "submit," and "submit" fits the context perfectly. "Husbands, in the same way submit to your own wives, dwelling together wisely." Furthermore, the close parallel between "Wives in the same way [homoiōs] submit yourselves to your own husbands" and "Husbands in the same way [homoiōs] …" naturally implies, "Husbands in the same way [submit yourselves to your own wives]." See Phillip Payne's Bible vs. Biblical Womanhood: How God's Word Consistently Affirms Gender Equality (Grand Rapids, MI: Zondervan, 2023), pp. 125–33."

woman; and show her honor as a fellow heir of the grace of life, so that your prayers may not be hindered. ⁸To sum up, all of you be harmonious, sympathetic, brotherly, kind-hearted, and humble in spirit; ⁹not returning evil for evil, or insult for insult but giving a blessing instead; for you were called for the very purpose that you might inherit a blessing.

After reading the text, I thought myself quite correct in my theological understanding. I had been taught to believe that in submitting to my husband without fear, I was also submitting to God's authority in my life. I was quite surprised when our pastor did not expound on the 1 Peter passage at all but rather opened the Bible and read aloud Genesis 1:26–28, which says,

> ²⁶*"Then God said, 'Let us make human beings in our image, in our likeness, so that they may rule over the fish in the sea and the birds in the sky, over the livestock and all the wild animals, and over all the creatures that move along the ground'. ²⁷So God created human beings in his own image, in the image of God he created them; male and female he created them. ²⁸God blessed them and said to them, 'Be fruitful and increase in number; fill the earth and subdue it. Rule over the fish in the sea and the birds in the sky and over every living creature that moves on the ground.'"*

> **(TNIV 2005)**

Our pastor challenged our notions of biblical submission as he emphasized the phrase "so that they may rule" in verse 26. He showed us that it was God's original intention to have Adam and Eve ruling together and sharing power in the administration of His creation in the Garden. As we will study in depth in Part II, it was sin, not the commandment of God, that corrupted authority in the human hands that wield it. It was sin, not God's highest intentions, that ushered in patriarchy and the power struggle between men and women that crushes intimacy.

Though I had read this verse in Genesis multiple times, I had never seen the phrase, nor considered the importance of these five words. Intellectually, I understood the principles of biblical hermeneutics, the importance of considering the whole context of Scripture, and the significance of the historical and cultural milieu of the text. Yet, there was a critical blind spot in my thinking exposed by this wise pastor during our premarital counseling. It dawned on me that I was not reading 1 Peter from the larger biblical perspective that began in Genesis and was brought to fruition in the book of Revelation. I had been building a narrow framework for biblical submission and reducing being a wife to a place on an organizational chart. God was at the top of the organization. Next in line was my husband, who was responsible for me to God, and I was responsible for obeying my husband.

The larger framework of God's original intention for the first couple to "exercise skilled mastery"[10] as co-rulers in the Garden, and the restoration of being equal, co-heirs in the new creation in Christ, was not something I had ever considered. The idea that in Christ, both my husband and I were free from the Fall that set up the worldly hierarchy of power and control, and that we could once again fulfill God's highest intention by ruling together as a married couple in mutual submission to one another and to God in Christ as our "head," was not something I had ever imagined.

Our pastor also challenged us to reevaluate the way we would make decisions in our marriage based on this creative, cooperative, and complementary nature and style of shared power under the lordship of Jesus Christ. I had always assumed that I would have input, but that my husband alone, as the leader, had the authority to make the final decision. I only later realized I needed new lenses, incorporating a clearer understanding of Pre-Fall, Post-Fall, New Creation, and New Heaven and Earth conditions, to better understand the Bible's overarching teaching regarding authority in the Bible and its relationship to men and women in marriage. This was critical to a fresh evaluation of the way I saw myself as a woman and a wife in all aspects of life.

Despite newfound insights on mutuality in marriage, on a practical level, I continued to view my husband as my leader and teacher. I can still remember, during our first year of marriage, when I asked Keith to disciple me. I thought this was the pinnacle of showing honor and respect to my husband as the leader of

---

10   Davis, Ellen F. *Opening Israel's Scriptures*. New York: Oxford University Press, 2019. (9)

our home and of me. I was shocked when he flatly refused. He looked at me quite incredulously and said, "No, Cindi. I will not disciple you. Jesus will disciple you." A discipleship relationship was popular in the 1980s and used to encourage young Christians to sit under the teaching of a more experienced Christian as the followers of Jesus sat under the teaching of Christ. These relationships were often instrumental in helping new believers form a solid understanding of Scripture, a strong bond with Christ, and other believers. However, they were also vulnerable to the abuse of power and were sometimes conflictual as the students outgrew their teachers or did not follow the instructions they were given by their leaders.

Keith understood that I was asking for a vertical (top-down) relationship with him, rather than a horizontal (mutual) relationship. He rightly saw that I was conflating the leadership of Christ with the leadership of my husband. My husband was correct however, in deferring to Jesus as our Lord. I was offering my husband responsibility, power, and control that he knew belonged to the Lord Jesus Christ alone. A less spiritually mature man would have eagerly accepted what I was naively offering. It took me years to understand how this shift in power improved our capacity to cultivate intimacy in our relationship and grow into the individuals God created us to be.

Keith understood on a practical level, even before I did, that in Christ we were joint heirs in Christ. This equality in Christ did not mean we were the same, but that we were not above or below one another in our position in marriage, our value as individuals, our access to resources (physical, financial, or otherwise), or our ability to make decisions. I stood contemplating his refusal to disciple me in the doorway of the wood-paneled den of the 1950s-style home in Sacramento, California, where we were housesitting. This was to be one among many lessons that my husband, in following Christ, would "teach me" without a formal "discipleship" relationship.

Keith did not view himself as my leader or teacher and would not try to direct, dominate, or control me but instead would encourage me to follow Christ as Savior and Lord. It would be in following Jesus as a couple that we would exercise our authority, power, and control to freely love one another, become more intimate, grow, and mature. This encounter with Keith suddenly flooded my heart, mind, and body with a powerful memory of his first love letter, written to me while we were dating in college. He captured my heart then with his prose, but now married, I remembered the lyrics of the Bruce Cockburn song "No Footprints" he had included in that first letter. Though I did not fully understand their meaning the first time I read them, I now see how the lyrics foreshadowed what God was teaching me about sharing power with my husband in Christ. There is a line in the song that says that the man wants to deeply touch a woman where she lives—not for power, but because he loves her. He then urges the woman to love the Lord, and in doing so, she will be loving him too. Together they will journey directly in the footsteps of Christ, leaving no footprints of their own behind.[11]

Absolute authority belongs solely to our holy and triune God. Power is God's ability to use and share His authority to accomplish His will. Control is God's capacity to choose how and when to exercise, restrain or release that power. Any authority, power, or control we have is a direct result of God's choice to share it with us for life-giving purposes. The capacity to choose intimacy means a willingness to submit to the sacred design of a mutual intimacy that is rooted in the nature of our triune God.

---

11 From the song, "No Footprints," on the *Dancing in the Dragon's Jaws* album (1979).

CHAPTER 2

Sacred Design Of Intimacy

"Intimacy is a deep abiding confidence that someone knows you,
cares for you, desires and delights in your presence."

—Keith F. Martin

The Imprint of Mutuality

Mutual intimacy is reflected in the nature of our triune Creator, who said, *"Let us* make human beings in our image, in our likeness" (Genesis 1:26, TNIV, emphasis added). All throughout nature, we see the imprint of God's desire for the *Let us* of intimate and reciprocal interactions that sing out the triune, "Holy, Holy, Holy is the Lord of hosts, the earth is full of his glory" (Isaiah 6:3, NASB 1995). We also read, "For since the creation of the world His invisible attributes, that is, His eternal power and divine nature, have been clearly perceived, being understood by what has been made so that they are without excuse" (Romans 1:20, NASB).

Creation illustrates the mutuality that God imagined for all His creatures. Scientists are now discovering the elaborate and mutually beneficial ways that trees and plants communicate and interact with one another and their environment.[12] In the past, we have seen all tall trees of the earth as

---

12 Grant, Richard. "Do Trees Talk to Each Other?" *Smithsonian Magazine*, March 2018, https://www.smithsonianmag.com/science-nature/the-whispering-trees-180968084/

having deep roots that create their own stability and strength. Today we know that the tallest trees in the world actually have a quite shallow root system. The strength of the California redwood trees comes from extending their roots horizontally over 100 feet from their base and intertwining them with the roots of other neighboring redwoods. The interdependence of this powerful partnership is the secret to their mutual stability during fierce winds and floods.[13]

The idea of fierce competition and survival of the fittest among species pales in comparison to the power of mutual cooperation that promotes a thriving ecosystem. Underneath the forest floor, intertwined with the roots of trees, is a fascinating microscopic network of fungi. We only recognize this vast underground "wood-wide-web" by its fruit, the mushroom. The greater fungal organism is composed of mycelium, or "threads of the greater fungal organism in the soil that wrap around and bore into tree roots."[14] Both organisms benefit as the fungi make it easier for the trees to get more nutrients and moisture from the soil. In return for the collaboration, the fungi get access to the sugars from the trees.

The Diverse Nature of Our Triune God

> *"Then God said, 'Let us make human beings in our image, in our likeness so that they may rule over the fish of the sea and over the birds in the sky, over the livestock and all the wild animals and over all the creatures that move along the ground. So God created human beings in his own image, in the image of God he created them; male and female he created them.'"*

(Genesis 1:26–27, TNIV)

---

13   California Department of Parks and Recreation, "About Coast Redwoods," California Department of Parks and Recreation CA.gov, 2023, https://www.parks.ca.gov/?page_id=22257

14   Holewinski, Britt. "Underground Networking: The Amazing Networking Below Your Feet," National Forest Foundation, 2023. www.nationalforests.org/blog/underground-mycorrhizal-network

Orthodox[15] Christians believe that the *us* in "Let us make human beings in our image," refers to the Holy Trinity. The doctrine of the Trinity holds that the Father, Son, and Holy Spirit are three equal and distinct persons existing as One unified Being. With the declaration, "Let us make human beings in our image, in our likeness, so that they may rule," we see that God's very nature is to share power as an intimate community. Where there is mutuality, there is intimacy.

Mutual authority is important to our discussion about intimacy because who God says He is as a community of persons—as *us*—directly relates to who God says human beings are, male and female—as *them*. In the very act of creation, God creates male and female to reflect the equal yet distinct and unified nature of the three-in-one. The magnificent and breathtaking "We Principle" of "Let Us create" was instituted by our sovereign God to reflect the beauty of His holiness. Our Creator did not say, "Let Me, *Father God*, create human beings in my own *Father God* image so that the male human may rule over the *female human*." Rather, He said, "Let *us* create human beings in *ou*r image, according to *our* likeness, so that *they* may rule…" (emphasis added).

Although God is eternally in perfect harmony and union in and among the persons of the Trinity, I like to imagine a lively discussion, even a delightful debate, about the ways in which these three persons work together as One. Perhaps there is internal dialogue about the infinite possibilities in which humans collaborate with God in managing the earth for further blessing. Perhaps the Father, Son, and Holy Spirit consider how the persons of the Trinity will respond to their foreknowledge of the human choice to gain knowledge of good and evil. This will require the Father, Son, and Holy Spirit, together as a community of distinct persons, to redeem humankind.

When we read that "God created human beings in his own image, in the image of God he created them; male and female he created them," it is reasonable to ask how the maleness and femaleness of humankind might reflect God's image. Just as God is one being in three distinct persons of the Father, Son, and Holy Spirit, so humankind is one, yet expressed in male and female persons. Reflecting

---

15   When I use the term orthodox, I am referring to those who, regardless of denominational affiliation, would in good conscience join together in a confession of faith as codified in the Apostles' Creed or Nicene Creed.

on this biblical truth, I began to consider how femaleness might be represented in the Trinity.

As I explored this in Scripture, a startling reality emerged: we actually see what some might consider traditional female characteristics revealed in each person of the Trinity. Please do not misunderstand me. I am not saying that God is female or male. God is spirit, according to Jesus in John 4:24. The hypostasis, the very Being of the triune God, however, contains all the perfections of both male and female characteristics. God created human beings, male and female, to reflect His diverse yet equal triune image. Let's consider what Scripture teaches us about the female characteristics of God the Father, God the Son, and God the Holy Spirit.

Father

There are many Old and New Testament examples in which God compares Himself to a mother. For example, Isaiah 66:13 says, "As a mother comforts her child, so will I comfort you; and you will be comforted over Jerusalem" (NIV). God also compares Himself to a mother bear protecting her cubs in Hosea 13:8. We see God speak of Himself like an eagle sheltering her young in her wings (Deuteronomy 32:11). In Isaiah 42:14, we read, "For a long time I have kept silent, I have been quiet and held myself back. But now, like a woman in childbirth, I cry out, I gasp and pant" (NIV). The metaphors in Scripture that refer to Him as both mother and father reveal the nature of the God as Creator who said, "Let us make human beings in our image... in the image of God he created them; male and female, he created them" (Genesis 1:26, 28, TNIV).

Son

In the Gospel of Matthew, Jesus said, "Jerusalem, Jerusalem, you who kill the prophets and stone those sent to you, how often I have longed to gather your children together, as a hen gathers her chicks under her wings, and you were not willing" (Matthew 23:37, TNIV). Jesus had no problem attributing (what in some cultures would be considered primarily maternal instincts) to Himself in His love for Jerusalem and by extension, the entire world.

The Apostle Paul and other New Testament writers repeatedly refer to the Church as the Bride of Christ. Revelation speaks of the Wedding Feast of the

Lamb, when Jesus and His Bride, the Church, are joined in marriage. "Let us be glad and rejoice and give him glory for the marriage of the lamb has come and his wife has made herself ready" (Revelation 19:7, NKJV). The head is not separate from the body, and yet as one they both retain their uniqueness. It is worth pondering how this metaphor might illustrate the male and female aspects of God in the Son.

Holy Spirit

Throughout Church history, some theologians have argued that the Holy Spirit is the feminine person of the Trinity.[16] Exemplified by Count Zinzendorf in Herrnhut, Germany, the Moravian Brethren have a well-established liturgy, prayer, and doctrine for the Holy Spirit as Mother.[17] Recent authors such as Juergen Moltmann and R.P. Nettlehorst have retained the masculine reference to Father and Son, but have used feminine language for the Holy Spirit.[18] Most orthodox Christians look to Jesus, who clearly refers to the promised Holy Spirit as *He*. In my view, trying to annex one person of the Trinity as the female representation of God does not fully capture the comprehensive nature of God.

Beyond Gender

God does, however, transcend our limited ideas of gender and has chosen to express masculine and feminine traits that belong to His image in the beauty and diversity of male and female human creation. Gregory of Nyssa, an early church bishop in Cappadocia from A.D. 372 to A.D. 376 and then again from A.D. 378 to A.D. 395, explored these complexities in his early church writings. Sarah Coakley, a professor of Divinity at Cambridge University, says that "the message

---

16   van Oort, Johannes. "The Holy Spirit as Feminine: Early Christian Testimonies and Their Interpretations." 2016. HTS Teologiese Studies / Theological Studies.www.academia.edu/63826092

17   Freeman, Arthur. "Gemeine: Count Nicholas von Zinzendorf's Understanding of the Church," The Durnbaugh Lecture, March 25, 1999, Young Center for the Study of Anabaptist and Pietist Groups, Elizabethtown, PA. Published 2002 in *Brethren Life and Thought*. https://www.moravianseminary.edu/sites/ms/files/files/documents/2017-04/Gemeine.pdf

18   Moltman, Juergen. *The Spirit of Life: A Universal Affirmation* (Minneapolis: Fortress, 1992), 157–158 and Pinnock, Clark H., "The Role of the Spirit in Creation," *Asbury Theological Journal 52* (Spring,1997), 47–54.

Gregory evidently wished to convey is that gender stereotypes must be reversed, undermined, and transcended if the soul is to advance to supreme intimacy with the trinitarian God; and the language of sexuality and gender, far from being an optional aside or mere rhetorical flourish in the process, is somehow necessary and intrinsic to the epistemological deepening that Gregory seeks to describe."[19]

When we reject the male and female characteristics of our human personality, are we not also potentially rejecting aspects of our triune God? C.S. Lewis made this moving comment about gender stereotyping upon reflecting on his own marriage in the early 1960s:

> "There is, hidden or flaunted, a sword between the sexes till an entire marriage reconciles them. It is arrogance in us to call frankness, fairness, and chivalry 'masculine' when we see them in a woman; it is arrogance in them to describe a man's sensitiveness or tact or tenderness as 'feminine.' But also what poor, warped fragments of humanity most mere men and mere women must be to make the implications of that arrogance plausible. Marriage heals this. Jointly the two become fully human. 'In the image of God, created he them.' Thus, by a paradox, this carnival of sexuality leads us beyond our sexes."[20]

Although we can argue about C.S. Lewis' views on women and whether or not marriage heals the sword between the sexes, Scripture clearly teaches that there was no sword before the serpent tempted Eve and Adam to choose the knowledge of good and evil over the wisdom of obedience to God. Choosing intimacy therefore involves a proper understanding of power relations between human beings regardless of gender, religion, race, social class, or any other distinction.

---

19   Coakley, Sarah. *Powers and Submissions: Spirituality, Philosophy, and Gender.* John Wiley & Sons, 2008, p. 128.
20   Lewis, C. S. *A Grief Observed.* London: Faber and Faber, 1961, p. 49.

CHAPTER 3

Sacred Connection Of Intimacy

The Lord God said, "It is not good for the man to be alone. I will make a helper suitable for him." Now the Lord God had formed out of the ground all the wild animals and all the birds in the sky. He brought them to the man to see what he would name them; and whatever the man called each living creature, that was its name. So the man gave names to all the livestock, the birds in the sky and all the wild animals. But for Adam no suitable helper was found. So the Lord God caused the man to fall into a deep sleep; and while he was sleeping he took one of the man's ribs and then closed up the place with flesh. Then the Lord God made a woman from the rib he had taken out of the man, and he brought her to the man. The man said, "This is now bone of my bones and flesh of my flesh; she shall be called 'woman,' for she was taken out of man." For this reason a man will leave his father and mother and be united to his wife and they will become one flesh. The man and his wife were both naked, and they felt no shame."

(Genesis 2:18–25, TNIV)

Not Good to be Alone

Whether we are talking about intimacy with God or human beings, being different together is clearly better than being the same alone. There was one thing about the human in the Garden that was not good. Aloneness. Even though God was right there alongside the human in the Garden, God signaled that there was an aloneness that neither God nor the animals could remedy: that of not having a suitable or corresponding human as a counterpart. God had the community of the Father, Son, and Holy Spirit. The animals belonged to one another as pairs. I find it intriguing that God allowed the human to experience this unique aloneness before intervening. God brought each creature to be named during the search for a suitable companion, "but for the human there could be found no helper corresponding to him (vs. 20)."

Who Is *Ezer*?

One of the best-kept secrets of biblical womanhood is the meaning of the word that Scripture uses in Genesis 2:18 to describe Eve. The Hebrew word *ezer* is translated into English as "helper", but a more accurate translation of *ezer kenegdo* is "a saving strength corresponding to him."[21] In a post-Fall world that prefers hierarchy to humility, the word "helpmate" or "helper" has been interpreted as meaning "subservient" to Adam. It may astonish some of us to learn that this is the same word used in Exodus 18:4 and Deuteronomy 33:29 to refer to God, the Helper and Deliverer of Israel.

God's use of this powerful word to describe Eve challenges the notion that a woman as *helper* is subordinate to man. In fact, the dignity of women is strengthened in light of Genesis 2:18. In these accounts, being a helper was not inferior, subservient, or subordinate. Eve was no more secondary to Adam than God was secondary or subordinate to Israel. Jesus also uses the term helper to refer to the Holy Spirit in John 14:26 (*parakletos*). A "helper" in this context is a powerful, creative, and active person. God created an *ezer* so that humans would not be alone. No wonder that God, through the person of Jesus Christ,[22] is our *ezer* in His promise to never leave us or forsake us (Hebrews 13:5, quoting Deuteronomy 31:6).

God gave Adam the command to not eat from the tree of the knowledge of good and evil before Eve was created. Indeed, God declared that it was not good for the human to be alone immediately after that first and only prohibition was issued in the garden. Was Adam especially vulnerable because of this aloneness, even though God was present with him in the Garden? This question is particu-

---

21 Personal Communication. Philip B. Payne. September 6, 2023. Payne, Bible, 3–4
22 See Deuteronomy 31:8; Matthew 28:20;n John 14:18

larly instructive in light of the Hebrew *ezer*, meaning "helper" in Genesis 2:18, which says, "The Lord God said, 'It is not good for the man to be alone. I will make a helper suitable for him (TNIV).'"

In his translation of the Old Testament, Hebrew scholar Robert Alter translates verse 18 in this way: "And the Lord God said, 'It is not good for the human to be alone, I shall make him a sustainer beside him.'" Humankind was designed to be male and female in order to enjoy the intimacy of the two becoming one flesh. Industry and productivity (being fruitful and multiplying) flowed from the fountainhead of being and intimacy (the two becoming one flesh), rather than the other way around. In other words, we were designed "to be" and then "to do." Like God, our identity is not in what we do or create but in who we are as image bearers of our Creator.

Yet it would be fallacious to believe that Adam could not exist apart from Eve or Eve apart from Adam. Adam clearly lived and breathed and worked in the Garden before the creation of Eve and we can assume that the same would have been true about Eve. Perhaps precisely because temptation was coming to the humans in the Garden, man and woman needed the power of a "we" to resist it. Male and female as individual persons together with the Creator would be that triune cord that would not be easily torn apart.[23]

In response to the declaration by God that it was not good for the man to be alone, He creates an individual woman whose complete parts fit together so perfectly with the complete parts of the individual man that their diversity becomes a unity. Belonging and togetherness dispel aloneness. Can you hear the exhilaration in Adam's exclamation that he has finally found someone like him?

> *"The man said, 'This is now bone of my bones, and flesh of my flesh; She shall be called Woman because she was taken out of Man. For this reason a man shall leave his father and his mother, and be joined to his wife. And they shall become one flesh. And the man and his wife were both naked and were not ashamed."*
>
> **(Genesis 2:18–25, NASB 1995)**

---

23   Martin, Keith F. "Couples Retreat," Oakdale, California, 2014.

When God builds the woman from Adam's side, the man awakens to find that God has fulfilled his unmet longing for corresponding strength and companionship. Although the word for "side" is often translated as "rib," the Hebrew term for "side" is actually an architectural term. It is used in the Old Testament to describe the Tabernacle of God, which has a corresponding side. No wonder that, upon seeing Eve, Adam was jubilant in the shout, "This time, she is it!" Co-equal together as man and woman in the Garden with God, Adam and Eve more accurately image the co-equal persons of our triune God.[24]

Equality Defined

The word "equality" is a socially and theologically freighted term. I have thoughtfully considered how to define equality without getting distracted by the varied theological and social scientific debates attached to this word.[25] I will define "equality" in light of the following orthodox Christian beliefs (See the Apostles' or Nicene Creed): First, in Christ there is inclusion regardless of gender, religion, race, social class, or other distinction (Galatians 3:28). Second, we have the same access to Christ and maintain our diversity and individuality without partiality or prejudice.

In my view, the strongest definition of "equality" is rooted in the doctrine of the Holy Trinity. According to a guest contributor on John Piper's website,[26] the Trinity "means that there is one God who eternally exists as three distinct Persons—Father, Son, and Holy Spirit." The author goes on to explain that these are not just three different ways of looking at God or ways of referring to three different roles that God plays, "because the Bible indicates that the Father, Son and Holy Spirit are distinct persons."[27] Likewise, the distinction of male and female is not simply the playing of roles, but the

---

24 I want to again emphasize that God's willingness to make humans in His image and according to His likeness does not mean that we are in any way equal to God.

25 For a more comprehensive discussion on the definition of equality, see Michelle Lee-Barnewall's book, *Neither Complementarian nor Egalitarian*. Baker Academic: Grand Rapids, Michigan, 2016.

26 www.desiringgod.com

27 Perman, Matt, Guest Contributor. "What Is the Doctrine of the Trinity?" January 23, 2006. https://www.desiringgod.org/articles/what-is-the-doctrine-of-the-trinity

existence of distinct and equal persons, made in the image and likeness of our triune God.

As human beings, we have equal worth and value, access to safety and life-sustaining resources, and the ability to make autonomous decisions free of oppression and tyranny. Adam and Eve both had equal access to God, one another, available resources, the capacity to choose, and temptation. Individual authority and freedom to exercise the power of choice makes intimacy with God and one another possible. It was and is by far one of the most powerful gifts our Creator gave to us as human beings. He did not limit our authority or power to make choices relative to gender. He expected His human creation to make responsible decisions and did not intervene or rescue us from their curses or consequences. We often ask God why He allows so much evil in the world. Perhaps we have not much pondered the alternative.

Vulnerability and Intimacy

> *"For this reason a man shall leave his father and his mother, and be joined to his wife; and they shall become one flesh. And the man and his wife were both naked and were not ashamed."*
> **(Genesis 2:25, NASB 1995)**

The capacity to be completely naked and unashamed means that we can safely expose ourselves to one another spiritually, emotionally, intellectually, socially, physically, and sexually. The ultimate in human intimacy is the ability to be vulnerable without fear of injury, and knowing that someone has your best interests at heart. The word vulnerable dates back to the early 17th century Latin word, *vulnerare*, meaning "to wound."

There are many definitions of intimacy but the one crafted by my husband captures the longing of my heart when I think about my desire for human closeness and connection. It touches and soothes the human ache for a deep sense of belonging with another human being.

Intimacy is a deep abiding confidence
that someone knows you, cares for you,
desires and delights in your presence.[28]

Naked and Unashamed

To deeply know another and be known on a spiritual, emotional, intellectual, social, and sexual level is breathtakingly fulfilling and mutually satisfying. To see and be seen. To know and be known. To care for and be cared for. To desire and be desired. To delight in and be delighted in. To be naked and unashamed. No fear of rejection or abandonment. This surely mirrors in part the intimacy of the Trinity. There is transparency. There is nothing hidden. There is no fear. There is knowing, caring, desiring, and delighting. There is love. There is mutuality. This is not a suffocating bond or attachment. There is freedom and room for separateness and differentness. There is no control, domination, or exploitation. There is healthy dependency and interdependency, which is the journey of the human experience from infancy to maturity.

As mentioned in the introduction section of the book, it is no coincidence that the Hebrew word for sexual intimacy, *yada*, actually means "to know, to be known, and to be deeply respected." Although frequently a euphemism for sexual relations, it goes beyond that to signify a deep sense of vulnerability and connection between two people. *Yada* is used over 900 times in the Old Testament, including instances that describe how God "*yada*" (knows and respects) us deeply."[29]

Psalm 139:1–2, for example, tells us that God has searched us and known us, that He knows when we sit down and when we rise. He knows our thoughts from afar, what we will say before we say it, is with us wherever we go. God created our innermost being, wove us in our mother's womb, and knows the length of each of our days on Earth. Throughout Scripture, we see God not only knowing and caring for us, but also desiring and delighting in the cultivation of mutual intimacy and friendship with us. This intimate knowing, caring, desiring, and delighting is reciprocal as the Psalmist also delights in the Lord (Psalm 37:4). When God says

---

28 Martin, Keith F. "Young Marrieds," 1998.
29 Jewish Shop. Yada. *Jewish Life Abide in Hebrew.* Jewish Shop, August 13, 2022, https://jewish.shop/37787/abide-in-hebrew

in Psalm 139:13 that God knit me together in my mother's womb, we see that intimacy, bonding, and attachment begin with God in the woman.

Today we know from the attachment research that indeed infant brain and body development are impacted by the in-utero relationship between mother and child in profound ways. According to developmental psychologists, "If the child's mother experiences hardship of any kind during pregnancy, her developing infant will bear neurochemical marks of her stress."[30] The gestational environment has long-term effects on brain development. "Stress-related biological processes can affect the way in which nerve cells grow, survive, differentiate, and communicate with one another. Specifically, they can alter availability of protective neurotrophic growth factors, synapse (neuron junction) development, neurotransmitter (chemical signal) levels, myelination (sheathing of nerve fibers), and even adult neuron production."[31]

Many adults are not aware of how the environment of their biological mother or early years of childhood may have impacted their own ability to develop close relationships. The great news is that God created our human brains with phenomenal plasticity, which is the ability of the brain to heal itself. We can learn the skills of intimacy with proper support, training, time, and practice.

The Skills of Intimacy

Jude Cassidy, a professor of psychology at the University of Maryland, describes four key skills required for intimacy, including the ability to seek care, the ability to give care, the ability to feel comfortable with an autonomous self, and the ability to negotiate.[32] Another definition of intimacy by Sobral, Teixeira, and Costa[33] is "the capacity to exchange thoughts and feelings of personal significance with

30 Call, Casey, Ph.D., Purvis, Karen, Ph.D., Parris, Sharri R., Ph.D., Cross, David, Ph.D., "Creating Trauma-Informed Classrooms." *Adoption Advocate* No. 75, September 2014.

31 Buss, Claudia, Ph.D., Sonja Entringer, Ph.D., Swanson, James M., Ph.D., Wadhwa, Pathik D., M.D., Ph.D., *The Role of Stress in Brain Development: The Gestational Environment's Long-Term Effects on the Brain*, PMC PubMed Central: Cerebrum, Published Online April 25, 2012. https://www.ncbi.nlm.nih.gov/pmc/articles/PMC3574809/

32 Cassidy, Jude. "Truth, Lies, and Intimacy: An Attachment Perspective." *Attachment and Human Development.* Vol 3. No. 2. September, 20011. (121–155)

33 Aristone, Carolynn. "Fear of Intimacy: Do You Have a Fear of Intimacy?" Center for Intimate Relationships, Accessed July 9, 2023. https://myintimaterelationship.com/fear-of-intimacy/

another individual who is highly valued and to depend on them while also experiencing healthy autonomy."

Interestingly, we see these skills operating within the Trinity during the creation of humans, and between God and humans thereafter. We may not be privy to the conversation that went on before and after God said, "Let us make humankind in our image (Genesis 1:26, NRSVA)," but we do know that each of the persons of the Trinity highly value one another and have the agency (similar to the autonomous self Jude Cassidy describes) to act as their own persons. The Father, Son, and Holy Spirit are not controlled by one person of the Trinity, but act in concert, not in competition, with one another. Throughout Scripture, we see that the relationship God has with Himself and with His creation exemplifies the ability to seek care, to give care, to be whole and separate persons, and to negotiate (see God and Moses in Exodus 32:9–14) and the Father and the Son in Gethsemane (Matthew 26:36–56).

God is worthy of worship. He is our sovereign and awesome Lord and God. Yet, throughout Scripture, God invites humans to come and talk to Him in a personal and familiar way. God walked with Adam and Eve in the Garden (Genesis 3:8). Enoch faithfully walked with God (Genesis 5:22–24, TNIV). Both Abraham and Moses were called friends of God. Abraham entered into negotiations with God multiple times on behalf of the righteous people living in Sodom and Gomorrah. God even agreed to Abraham's changes to the original plan. Job, Jeremiah, Gideon, and Habakkuk are among others in the Old Testament who ventured into serious conversation or negotiations with God. They were not afraid to ask God, "Why?" They asked God for what they wanted and even complained about things they thought were unfair. Hezekiah even asked God to prolong his life and God granted him 15 more years of life (2 Kings 20:2–6, TNIV).

These interactions reflect a mutuality and intimacy with God that does not in any way diminish or compromise the authority or power of God. If God grants us as humans such mutuality in relationships, how much more does He delight in our mutual sharing of authority with one another as humans? In the New Testament, God comes to us in an even more familiar way as the infant Son of God. The incarnation of God in Christ brings God even more near to us and, through His sacrifice for our sins, we now enter boldly into his presence (Hebrews 4:16).

Jesus cared for people but also asked for care such as when He asked the woman at the well to give Him something to drink (John 4:5–7). He often talks with His Father, making requests on behalf of others and himself. In the Garden of Gethsemane, Jesus asks the Father three times whether or not the cup of suffering might pass from him. Unlike Hezekiah, Jesus is not granted His request. In this case, there is no other way to reconcile the world to God and Jesus submits saying, "Thy will not mine be done." This was the choice of our Savior, not coercion, threat, or control by the Father.

God does not negotiate with respect to what is good and evil and He expects the boundaries placed around his holiness to be respected. Yet we do see God continually make adjustments in his relationship with humans. Sharing power through negotiations and adjustments is a gift from God to humans which in no way puts them on equal footing with Him nor in any way undermines God's sovereign authority.

If we return to the earlier passage in Genesis, we see that to become one flesh without losing individuality and distinctness was the cause for Adam's ecstatic delight. But such intimacy would also require the ability to leave loved ones for the purpose of a new family unit. A curious statement is tucked into this passage, "For this reason a man will leave his father and mother and be united to his wife, and they will become one flesh" (Genesis 2:24, TNIV). Before the Fall, leaving was a path toward growth and gain rather than grievous loss and pain.

When I view this passage from a psychological perspective, I see the ancient layers of wisdom for human couples packed tightly within the last verses of the Pre-Fall Era. There is the delight of connection, the joy of taking leave, and the resulting intimacy and oneness between husband and wife. Adam and Eve experience the wonder of being fully exposed, seen, and known without fear or shame. In my experience, few humans have the privilege of growing into the kind of connection with another human that allows for this intoxicating and satisfying kind of mutuality; when it does occur however, it is deeply satisfying.

Psychologists of all theoretical orientations have developed theories about human development. John Bowlby and Mary Ainsworth's attachment and bonding theories, along with Ainsworth's development of a protocol to test secure attachments between children and their caregivers, have been significant to the bonding and attachment literature.

Other development models include Harry Stack Sullivan's interpersonal model, Margaret Mahler's separation-individuation theory, Erik Erikson's epigenetic model, and Heinz Kohut's psychology of the self. Bonding and attachment theory is credited as being one of the few developmental theories that is eminently researchable.[34] As previously mentioned, breakthrough research in neuroscience is confirming what bonding and attachment theorists have long believed. Bessel VanderKolk, Peter Levine, Dan Siegel, Regina Sullivan, Karyn Purvis, David Cross, and Laurence Heller, among others, are at the forefront of research and treatment approaches that address bonding, attachment, and the wounds of early developmental trauma on our capacity to form and maintain healthy bonds and attachments. Authors Milan and Kay Yerkovich have written on the way couples love one another based on early bonding and attachment experiences.[35]

A powerful example of the way that bonding and attachment develops in childhood can be seen in the Still Face Experiment available on YouTube.[36] In 1975, Edward Tronick and colleagues described the three-minute interaction of an infant with her mother. When the mother is mirroring and engaging with smiles, laughter, language and vocal cues, the child responds with similar smiles, laughter and non-verbal engagement. However, after three minutes with a non-responsive and expressionless mother, the child becomes physically and emotionally distressed and makes attempts to recover the reciprocal pattern. When repeated attempts fail to re-engage this parent-child mutuality, the child turns body and face away instead of toward the mother with a "withdrawn and hopeless expression."

In adult relationships, John Gottmann and Julie Schwartz Gottman call this process "bidding for connection."[37] A bid for connection can be anything from sitting down next to a person, to making a casual remark while watching TV, to as subtle a communication as a sigh. The question is whether or not that bid for connection elicits a response from the person to whom it is pitched. In their

34   Brandell, Jerrold R. "Contemporary Psychoanalytic Perspectives on Attachment, Psychoanalytic Social Work," 17:2, 2010, 132–157, DOI: 10.1080/15228878.2010.512265

35   Yerkovich, Milan, and Yerkovich, Kay. *How We Love: A Revolutionary Approach to Deeper Connections in Marriage.* Colorado Springs, CO: WaterBrook Press, 2006.

36   The Research: The Still Face Experiment. The Gottman Institute. www.gottmann.com

37   Gottman, John Mordechai, and Gottman Julie Schwartz. *The Love Prescription: Seven Days to Connection, and Joy.* New York: Penguin Books, 2022. (3)

book, *The Love Prescription: 7 Days to More Intimacy, Connection, and Joy*, the Gottmans describe three potential responses: "turning toward (the partner gives a positive response, acknowledging the other person and engaging with their attempt to connect), turning away (the partner gives no response, either actively ignoring or not noticing the attempt to connect), or turning against (the partner responds with anger or irritation to actively shut down their partner's attempt to connect)."[38] Their longitudinal study of 130 newlywed couples showed that the couples who stayed together had turned toward one another 86 percent of the time while those who divorced returned their partner's bids for connection only 33 percent. In 1992, John Gottmann was able to predict with 93.6 percent accuracy which couples would eventually divorce. Highly successful couples can manage a 5:1 ratio of turning toward one another even in the midst of conflict.[39]

Kari Rusnak says this means that couples who had five seconds together in a positive or neutral emotional state for every one second of a negative emotional state were more likely to stay together than those with less than a 5:1 ratio. Outside of conflict, the ratio for couples who stayed together was 20 positive interactions for every one negative interaction. Negative interactions that increase a negative emotional state include defensiveness, criticism, contempt, and stonewalling.[40] Positive interactions that increase a positive emotional or neutral state include beginning with something you appreciate about your partner, validating your partner's opinion without necessarily agreeing with them, and showing compassion and empathy for the pain they are feeling regardless of whether or not you believe you caused it. Conflict that does not resolve into true win-win solutions results in perpetual power struggles that crush intimacy.

Human individuality becomes a solitary island without the shared power that can create a mutually positive connection. God created the ideal conditions for intimacy to thrive in the Garden of Delight: autonomy (in the sense of having the freedom to exercise individual authority through power of personal choice, Genesis 2:17a), safety (clear expectations and boundaries with the forewarning

---

38 Ibid. New York: Penguin Books (5)

39 Klemz, Joseph. "How Dr. Gottman Can Predict Divorce (with 94% Accuracy)." *Real Life Counseling*. 2017. reallifecounseling.us.

40 Rusnak, Kari. "The Magic Ratio: The Key to Relationship Satisfaction." The Gottman Institute. gottman.com

of consequences, Genesis 2:17b), hearing, vision, and voice (the capacity to hear, see, and speak, Genesis 2:19, 3:2–8), and unique complementarity and connection (the joy of fitting together and belonging, Genesis 2:21–24). Without freedom of choice and individuality, authority becomes suffocating and abusive; the relationship becomes robotic and degrades into a coercive and corrosive bond that controls, dominates, and destroys closeness. The demand for merging and sameness replaces the invitation to enjoy diversity in unity.

Separate and Connected

"For this reason a man shall leave his father and his mother,
and be joined to his wife; and they shall become one flesh."
(Genesis 2:22–24, NASB 1995)

For what reason is separation from parents necessary? Separation is required to form a new and more intimate bond. Leaving and cleaving enlarged humanity as Adam now delighted in his newly created, uniquely designed, and perfectly fitting wife, Eve. They were not two incomplete halves but two whole persons, just as the Trinity is not composed of three incomplete thirds but three whole persons. This blessed and intimate union was meant to continue multiplying and growing the generosity of God among all of Creation. "Leaving" in the Pre-Fall Era was not disconnection from but further extension of relationships through growth and generativity.[41] The capacity to separate from parents and caregivers in healthy ways is vital to healthy future bonding and attachment with companions and partners. This important relational skill will be explored more thoroughly in Chapter 18.

God's expression of intimate relationships within the community of the Trinity (Father, Son, and Holy Spirit) and between Creator and His human creation illustrates God's desire and provision for loving relationships that build upon healthy bonding, attachment, and human development. This open, transparent, mutual, and joyful union reflects God's good intention for the delightful, loving union of humans.

---

41   Merriam-Webster Dictionary, "Generativity," Merriam-Webster Dictionary, 2023, https://www.merriam-webster.com/medical/generativity#:~:text=noun,contribute%20to%20the%20next%20generation

CHAPTER 4

Sacred Authority Of Intimacy

"Mutual intimacy grows from the rich soil of personal responsibility.
Blaming others sabotages our sacred authority and makes us powerless victims."
—Cindi J. Martin

I ntimacy and authority seem mutually exclusive without a nuanced understanding of related words like "rule," "subdue," and "have dominion." In
the modern vernacular, they understandably carry the connotation of the
exploitative perpetrator, imperialist, colonialist, and all manner of forced submission, domination, control of resources for personal gain, and the destructive
enslavement of people. While it is true that the words of authority in Genesis 1
have been used for millennia to justify both the dehumanization and slavery of
countless human beings and the exploitation of the earth and its resources, it does
not follow that the words themselves are intrinsically evil and promote abuse of
authority, as some scholars suggest.

As an example of beautiful authority, let us imagine a garden planted without
the authority of a vintner who controls growth through the nurture and care of
the grapevines. What quickly unfolds before our eyes is unbridled growth into a
jungle-like environment in just a few seasons. In contrast, the grapevine that has
been well managed by pruning, shaping, and trellising is more productive for
human consumption than a wild grapevine. This is not a judgment against wild

grapes and natural ecological systems or a value statement about the superiority of cultivated grapes. The world is, after all, large enough to experience both forms.

Our English word for "authority" originates from Latin, Old French, and Middle English. The Latin word, *auctor*, means "originator, causer, doer, or founder." It can also mean "Creator, God, Author, Seller, or Vendor." Other words related to authority are the Latin words *augeo*—which figuratively means "to exalt, praise, spread, expand, increase, and lengthen"—and *auctoritas*—which carries the meaning of "influence, authority, prestige, power conferred, and responsibility." Today, the English word "authority" is defined as "a person accepted as a source of reliable information on a subject, the power to enforce rules or give orders, a person in command or a government agency which runs a revenue generating activity."[42] Merriam Webster defines "power" as "implying possession of the ability to wield force, authority, or influence," and "control" as the ability to "exercise restraining or directing influence over" in the sense of regulating or controlling one's anger.

It is important to see how our definitions of authority have developed over time, and the biases and blind spots that develop when we limit our definition to our current culture. As we will see, personal responsibility is related to authority, power, and control. Intimacy requires us to take full responsibility for who we are, what we want, and how we go about getting those things in a way that is mutually beneficial and satisfying.

Beautiful Authority

The authority, power, and control that God has given to humans was meant to beautify, nourish, maintain, and multiply the goodness of God on Earth. While it is true that humans are often limited in their God-given expression of freedom because of the systems of cultural, economic, and political oppression they are born into, it does not automatically follow that God or the use of the words are responsible for this injustice. We actually do ourselves a great disservice by surrendering the meanings and exercise of authority, power, and control to those who abuse them, rather than reclaiming them as they were designed to be used

---

42   Authority etymology, https://etymologeek.com/eng/authority/21139455

in the most creative and life-giving forms. We abdicate our God-given, inherent, personal power of choice by the wholesale rejection of these terms; we become victims. In contrast, when we choose intimacy with God and others, we take responsibility for our freedom to exercise our God-given, personal authority. We respect boundaries. We have the opportunity to grow, share our power with others, and demonstrate self-control in life giving ways.

The Dignity of Creative Control

As mentioned before, the Hebrew word for Eden means "delight." As long as humans respected the one boundary set by God around the tree of the knowledge of good and evil, there would only be the unbounded joy of creative control and the skillful management of growth. As we shall see in the next chapter of Part II, disrespect for God's loving boundary results in the growth of thorns and thistles that compete with the lush vegetation meant to sustain and nourish us.

As a market gardener of three acres in our post-Fall world, I have experienced on a micro level the value of weed management. I have dominion over and subdue the weeds. The weeds will always be with me in the garden and farmers have not been able to completely eradicate them. Attempts at eradicating weeds have not only done violence to the earth, but humans are suffering from cancer now known to be related to certain herbicides. Our micro market gardeners do not use harsh pesticides or herbicides but must have control over invasive weeds naturally in order to ensure that the other garden plants are adequately nourished and grown. In this way, we have learned to skillfully manage weeds for the purpose of increasing productivity so we have enough quality produce to share with the CSA (community supported agriculture) subscribers of our Wellspring Charitable Gardens.

On a macro level in 2020, we experienced the capacity (and in some cases the incapacity) of world leaders to manage a pandemic called COVID-19. Our world, national, and local leaders made decisions that restricted our freedom and movement. We can argue about whether these measures were truly life-giving and in our best interests, but whatever we think, the reality was that they subdued and exercised dominion over the choices we made when it came to work, travel and gathering in large groups. Many submitted to these laws and decrees, while others protested and some chose to disobey the injunctions. Most Americans understand civil disobedience and choose to exercise it when they believe it is necessary and are prepared to pay the consequences of that disobedience whether it means going to jail, paying a fine, or losing a job.

There are many other examples we can use, from controlling our bowels to controlling the motor vehicles we are driving. We can rename authority, power, and control and employ euphemisms to avoid modern negative connotations, but it does not change the reality that every human being can, does, and must exercise some measure of responsible, life-giving, and life-sustaining power and control over their own lives to stay safe, even in our post-Fall world. In the pre-Fall world, God's highest intention was to generously share creative authority with male and female humans equally so we would reflect His triune glory. The intimacy of God's own divine community is still the bedrock of healthy mutuality, interdependence, and diversity in unity.

The Delight of Sharing Responsibility

Over time, Keith and I realized that many Christian couples do not enjoy the kind of intimacy that is built on husband and wife sharing power and responsibility for decision-making in marriage as God originally designed. Much of this is based on the idea that, in order for the husband to fulfill his God-given responsibility and role as the spiritual leader of his home, he alone must bear final responsibility for decisions made as a couple. Rather than sharing mutual responsibility as co-heirs in Christ, many couples become trapped in artificial roles and worldly top-down models of leadership and power struggles that are more akin to the Fall than to the New Creation in Christ.

Years ago, Keith and I designed a couples retreat where he introduced the "We Principle of 'Let Us'" based on Genesis 1:26–27, which though quoted in the previous chapter, warrants repeating here:

> *"Then God said, 'Let us make human beings in our image, in our likeness so that **they may rule** over the fish of the sea and over the birds in the sky, over the livestock and all the wild animals and over all the creatures that move along the ground. So God created human beings in his own image, in the image of God he created them; male and female he created them.'"*
>
> **(Genesis 1:26–27, TNIV, emphasis added)**

The "We Principle" of "Let Us" is rooted in the nature of God and His original design for husband-and-wife to co-rule in a way that reflects the very nature of our triune God's generosity, shared power, and mutual intimacy. When operating, the "We Principle" cultivates shared responsibility. There is an understanding that the *me* of a distinct person impacts the *we* of us as a union or community. This vital aspect of mutuality in decision-making was not threatening, difficult, or conflictual before the Fall. The challenge of each partnership is to pray and seek not simply *my way* or *your way*, but *our way* in Christ.

Today, the word "responsibility" carries a variety of meanings and is associated with words that were previously defined such as "authority," "power," and "control." Merriam-Webster defines "responsibility" as "moral, legal, or mental accountability" and as "reliability or trustworthiness."[43] In an article called "Responsibility and Authority in Quality Management,"[44] responsibility was defined first as "the state or fact of having a duty to deal with something or having control over someone." The second definition was "the state or fact of being accountable or to blame for something." The third definition was "the opportunity or ability to act independently and make decisions without authorization." Each of these definitions is a sobering reminder of the relationship between responsibility and human creative power and authority. The willingness to risk making a decision and to accept the credit for good decisions and responsibility or blame for bad decisions is both unique and inherent to human agency.

When the triune God made humans male and female in His image, He knew that His Garden of Delight could only be maintained if they respected His beautiful authority. He defined goodness and required that His one prohibition be respected. No knowledge of evil would be tolerated. Still, obedience was invited not coerced Even in modern terms, a responsible landlord is required to prepare a lease agreement with clear occupancy guidelines, expectations, and the consequences of failure to comply. God certainly outlined in advance the advantages of living in His Garden and the severe penalty of

---

43 Merriam-Webster Dictionary, "Responsibility," Merriam-Webster Dictionary, 2023, https://www.merriam-webster.com/dictionary/responsibility
44 Udoka, Naemeka. "Responsibility and Authority in Quality Management." December 22, 2015.linkedin.com

death for those who chose to eat of the tree of the knowledge of good and evil. Adam and Eve bore the responsibility to respect those boundaries individually and as a couple. For the modern couple, the "and let them rule" of shared responsibility is still God's highest intention. Marital decision-making looks immeasurably different when a husband and wife see the "We Principle" operating in and through their respective gifts and talents under the sovereign Lordship of Christ.

The "We Principle" of shared responsibility in decision-making also applies to singles and couples in friendships, at work or in ministry. Mutuality is the mark of our Creator's highest intention for human design, whether at home, at church, or in larger society. We can aspire to God's pattern for mutuality and personal responsibility and in so doing, cultivate intimacy.

The Shared Weight of Responsibility

"Now the serpent was more crafty than any of the wild animals the Lord God had made. He said to the woman, 'Did God really say, "You must not eat from any tree in the garden"?'

The woman said to the serpent, 'We may eat fruit from the trees in the garden', "but God did say, 'You must not eat fruit from the tree that is in the middle of the garden, and you must not touch it, or you will die.'"

'You will not certainly die,' the serpent said to the woman. [5]'For God knows that when you eat from it your eyes will be opened, and you will be like God, knowing good and evil.'

When the woman saw that the fruit of the tree was good for food and pleasing to the eye, and also desirable for gaining wisdom, she took some and ate it. She also gave some to her husband, who was with her, and he ate it.

Then the eyes of both of them were opened, and they realized they were naked; so they sewed fig leaves together and made coverings for themselves."

(Genesis 3:1–7, TNIV)

In this passage, the "Let Us" of Genesis 1:26 gives way to the "Let me" of Genesis 3:6. There is no evidence of any dialogue with anyone else here except between the snake and the woman. The man does not enter into the discussion as far as we can see, nor is God invited into the decision-making process. The serpent challenges, twists, and casts doubt upon the words of God and mocks the wisdom of heeding God's related warning. Influenced by the serpent, the woman made the decision herself. The titillating temptation to become like God, knowing good and evil, is presented as preferable to what the male and female already possessed: being made in the very image of God and according to his likeness. As with nearly every offer of temptation, the charlatan represents what one already possesses as defective or lacking so that the counterfeit, although ultimately toxic, can be presented and accepted as preferable. Grievously, the woman does not seek the support of her God or her husband as she considers the serpent's offer.

> "Then the man and his wife heard the sound of the Lord God as he was walking in the garden in the cool of the day, and they hid from the Lord God among the trees of the garden. But the Lord God called to the man, 'Where are you?' He answered, 'I heard you in the garden, and I was afraid because I was naked; so I hid.' And he said, 'Who told you that you were naked? Have you eaten from the tree that I commanded you not to eat from?' The man said, 'The woman you put here with me—she gave me some fruit from the tree, and I ate it.' Then the Lord God said to the woman, 'What is this you have done?' The woman said, 'The serpent deceived me, and I ate.'"
>
> **(Genesis 3:8–13, TNIV)**

The experiential knowledge of evil results in, first and foremost, the loss of intimate connection between the Creator and humans. Evil conceives and births fear, shame, and alienation. Shame develops a fear of exposure. Fear and shame grow with hiding and blaming attitudes and actions to avoid punishment. Hiding and blaming, rather than the taking of personal responsibility, perpetuates a cycle of disconnection and loss of intimacy in the form of spiritual and physical death.

God, not the humans, initiates reconnection. This is fleshed out brilliantly in Genesis 3. God wisely and carefully allows the humans to take full responsibility for their particular actions and bear the related consequences. Even God takes responsibility for the part the Trinity will play in restoring and reconciling creation to Himself by dealing with the serpent, pain, death, and resurrection that will be related to it. God gave the humans the capacity to freely choose obedience or disobedience in the Garden of Delight. Their choices would set in motion a series of events that would be cataclysmic for themselves, other human beings, and the rest of Creation for generations to come.

Tragically, this gifted and powerful woman, created in the image of God, whose Hebrew descriptor is *ezer*, did not fulfill her purpose to be like God in helping Adam withstand temptation and overcome evil; instead, she became the very conduit for evil. Acknowledging the reality of this opportunity and the failure of this woman does not make her sacred femininity cursed or evil. God did not curse the woman. There is no evidence to suggest that the male human would not have been deceived had the serpent approached Adam before Eve, though perhaps some theologians have made this argument. Whether deceived or willfully disobedient, God clearly did not curse His human creation.

I wonder what might have been the result if Eve had called upon God and Adam to join her in a debate or discussion with the serpent about the idea it was proposing? What if Eve had asked God if death would have truly been the consequence of eating of the tree of the knowledge of good and evil? Consider yet another scenario: Eve offers the fruit to Adam, and Adam simply tells his wife, "No, thank you." Might the two of them have had a good, healthy debate? Might the entire course of history have been changed because they eventually came to an agreement about the wisdom of following or not following the serpent's suggestion? If they hit an impasse, what would have happened had Adam called out to God for help and wisdom? Instead, Adam takes and eats.

The New Testament states that our sin came through Adam (and Eve, 2 Corinthians 11:3; 1 Timothy 2:14) our salvation through Christ, the second Adam (Romans 5:12–18; 1 Corinthians 15:45). Both the man and the woman fail to honor God's command, regardless of the beguiling of Eve by the serpent. God calls out to Adam and asks, "Where are you?" Adam begins with identifying his fear, and then in further conversation, blames both God and his wife for his decision. Next, God asks the woman—and she promptly blames the serpent for deceiving her. At this point, God begins to hold each party responsible.

First, God curses the serpent, then promises a battle or "enmity" between the seed of the woman and the seed of the serpent, as well as a triumph over the serpent. Next God explains the consequences of sin for Eve and Adam and, finally, he curses the soil. God holds all involved in this incident responsible for their behavior but he does not curse Adam or Eve. Life on this earth will never be the same.

Conclusion of Part I

In Part I, we explored the nature of God and the way that humans reflect oneness, individuality, and equality as male and female image bearers of God. Human beings glorify God and reflect the cooperative nature of the Trinity when we harmoniously co-rule the earth together as equal partners. We discovered that God's highest intention for sharing His authority with humans is to skillfully manage the earth's resources in ways that are life-giving and mutually beneficial to all Creation. Finally, we learned some practical ways to cultivate intimacy in our relationships.

As we move into Part II of this book, we will examine massive changes of the Post-Fall Era that result from humans choosing to know good and evil. The curses and consequences of the Fall will be explored along with their impact on our perceptions, identity, and relationships. We will also look at how sin, rather than God's intention for mutuality, is responsible for the creation of a patriarchal power structure governing interaction between humans and the natural world. Without mutuality, alienation replaces intimacy. Adam and Eve now become subject to hundreds of oppressive rules instead of one life-sustaining rule that safely ensures intimacy with God, themselves, one another, and all Creation. Mutuality is swallowed up into grasping power for personal gain. Finally, we will discover how defining marital relationships through the lens of the Fall has robbed couples in Christ of God's highest intentions for marital intimacy.

PART II:

Contaminated Soil In The Post-Fall Era

"Fear is the great enemy of intimacy. Fear makes us run away from each other or cling to each other but does not create true intimacy."
– Henri Nouwen

CHAPTER 5

Contaminated By Curses
And Consequences

*"So the Lord God said to the serpent, 'Because you have done this,
'Cursed are you above all livestock and all wild animals! You will crawl
on your belly and you will eat dust all the days of your life. And I will
put enmity between you and the woman and between your offspring and
hers; he will crush your head and you will strike his heel.'*

*"To the woman he said, 'I will make your pains in childbearing
very severe; with pain you will give birth to children. Your desire
will be for your husband, and he will rule over you.'*

*"To Adam he said, 'Because you listened to your wife and ate
from the tree about which I commanded you, 'You must not eat
of it,' 'Cursed is the ground because of you; through painful toil
you will eat of it all the days of your life. It will produce thorns
and thistles for you, and you will eat the plants of the field. By the
sweat of your brow you will eat your food until you return to the
ground, since from it you were taken; for dust you are and to dust
you will return.' Adam named his wife Eve, because she would
become the mother of all the living.*

*"The Lord God made garments of skin for Adam and his wife
and clothed them. And the Lord God said, 'The man has now*

become like one of us, knowing good and evil. He must not be allowed to reach out his hand and take also from the tree of life and eat, and live forever.' So the Lord God banished him from the Garden of Eden to work the ground from which he had been taken. After he drove them out, he placed on the east side of the Garden of Eden cherubim and a flaming sword flashing back and forth to guard the way to the tree of life."

(Genesis 3:14–24, TNIV)

Contaminated soil is often referred to as "polluted soil," and is caused by a variety of conditions—some naturally occurring but more frequently the result of human activity. Land degradation caused by industrial activity, particularly the improper disposal of waste and agricultural products, can transform rich soil teeming with life into a dead wasteland. What we commonly call "dirt" is dead and devoid of air, water, minerals, and organic matter, while "soil" is alive with these elements, which together create a hospitable environment for plant growth. Anytime our garden volunteers dig in the soil of our gardens and find earthworms or other living creatures, we are encouraged that the soil is healthy.

In the Garden of Eden, the healthy soil—fresh from its creation— was still vulnerable and could be contaminated by human choice. In that Garden of Delight, Adam and Eve were told to abstain from eating the fruit of only one tree. God made it clear that this was not an arbitrary rule of no consequence. On the contrary, God explained that eating of the fruit of the Knowledge of Good and Evil meant certain contamination—death.

The generous privileges and enjoyment given to humans in the pre-Fall Garden came with equally generous responsibilities. I find it intriguing that God made a definitive and far-reaching distinction in this Genesis 3 passage between curses and consequences. This distinction is rarely made in discussions about original sin and the Fall. Neither the man nor the woman were cursed. Humans were pre-warned that the dire consequences of their choice to know evil would result in death. Both humans were told specifically how the knowledge of evil would change their relationships (as a woman vis a vis childbirth) and for the man (vis a vis the soil), to one another as a couple (vis a vis authority and power), and to God as Creator and Lord of the Garden (vis a vis the need for a Redeemer).

The Hebrew word for sin, *hata*, literally means "to go astray." This is where the doctrines of "the Fall" and "original sin" were born. Like a genetic mutation or defect, this sin nature would now appear in each successive generation of humanity. Our internal battle with sin is intensified by the external battle between God and our fleshly inclination toward sin, the world, and the devil. This unrelenting adversary tempts us to sin and seeks to steal, kill, and destroy us as he accuses us day and night before the throne of God.[45]

But let us not miss the reality that God cursed the serpent and soil, not His children. It is difficult to understate the impact of this omission of biblical truth in relation to the way humans perceive the worth of themselves and one another. In reality, despite our sin and the corruption of both soul and body, human beings have great value, bear the very good imprint of our Creator, and are worth redeeming. God wants to restore intimacy between Himself and His human creations and between human beings, themselves, and the natural world.

Evil in the form of internal struggles, external conflict, and interpersonal strife plague humankind as individuals and communities. Yet God so valued humans that He would leave the Garden of Delight to go with them to where the serpent and soil were cursed and contaminated and where death would ultimately claim His own incarnated life. God's love made Him vulnerable to suffering and death. Jesus literally became both the sin of the world and the sacrifice required to reconcile us with God (2 Corinthians 5:21). Our Creator would stop at nothing to redeem, restore and ultimately resurrect His beloved human creation. In the Post-Fall Era, we see God moving through history with Israel toward faith in Christ, that all humans might once again enjoy fellowship with Him.

Degradation of *Ezer*

In Chapter 2, we learned that God's solution to Adam's aloneness was the creation of a corresponding human and co-ruler of the Garden of Eden. In the post-Fall

---

45   See Matthew 4:3; John 10:10; Revelation 12:10

world, however, *ezer* was now viewed through the lens of evil, which easily subordinates women to her male counterpart. Bible teachers for millennia have used the word "helper" to convey the idea that women are most fulfilled when they are "helpers" of men. According to this way of thinking, wives are encouraged to see their role in marriage as helping their husbands to accomplish whatever it is that God designed for the husband to do. Rather than helping one another to identify their unique callings, gifts, and talents as individuals and partners, post-Fall women have often been subjugated to a role that was and often still is solely defined by those in authority over them such as parents, husbands, ministers, and priests rather than by God. There is no emphasis on the truth that both men and women are whole and distinct persons in and of themselves and in relationship to one another and to God, just as the three persons of the Trinity are whole and distinct persons, yet united as One.

Mutuality, which is a keynote of intimacy, has been severely damaged by our human penchant to lord authority over one another, rather than to see one another as having individual power for the purpose of helping and strengthening one another to be the best that God created us to be. Until women of every tongue, tribe, and nation take their God-appointed place as equal partners alongside men in our world, the body of Christ will continue to suffer great loss of intimacy, power, and purpose in displaying the great love of our Triune God to our broken world.

Alone, Naked, and Ashamed

The Post-Fall Era ushered in intensified aloneness. There was already something in the Garden that God declared "not good." We understand how sin and the curse intensified aloneness, feelings of rejection, and a sense of utter abandonment within the human soul. It is ironic therefore, that Eve, created by God to actually improve the one thing that was not good in the garden before the Fall (human aloneness), would now be tempted by the serpent to act alone. And in so doing, this very good woman that God designed for the joy and delight of mutual intimacy became the target of first the serpent and then other humans who delight to deceive, manipulate, dominate, control, humiliate, degrade, demean, and enslave both women and men at every opportunity for personal pleasure and gain.

The Pre-Fall Era was a time when nakedness was the glory of human intimacy. Exposure, authenticity, openness, and vulnerability led to the joy of connection and closeness. The pleasure of mutual seeing, hearing, and understanding was the climax of human engagement on every level: spiritual, emotional, intellectual, social, physical, and sexual. The creative, cooperative, and complementary dance of male and female human beings on the world stage that God created for them must have been like the thrill of ballet dancers in perfect synchronization with one another and the symphonic music of their Creator.

Imagine the searing shame of coming into a harsh and bright spotlight that no longer showcased beauty and strength but now exposed weaknesses and mistakes for the purpose of shame and humiliation rather than praise and applause. Shame thrives on secrecy and keeping things in the dark. The two humans who became a unity of one without losing their separate identities were disconnected and torn asunder. The raw and exposed flesh now sought to hide from prying eyes. The fear of shame and punishment fueled anger and blame. With the experiential knowledge of good and evil, there was now profound loneliness and alienation for the first time since Creation. Where gender differences were beautifully designed for male and female to complement one another, fit together, and add creativity and beauty to humanity, now gender stereotypes and hierarchy would rob women and men of wholeness and mutuality.

Anita

Anita was a single woman and recent college graduate who had attended her church since childhood. She worked as a public high school teacher and was looking for ways to serve at church. She began singing in the church choir on Sunday mornings and attended practice on Monday nights.

Soon her Music Minister began inviting her to sing solos with the choir, which required an additional evening of rehearsals. When her minister also selected her to be part of the youth worship team, which rehearsed on Wednesdays, she was flattered but called him up to discuss this additional responsibility. Anita explained that although honored by the opportunity, she needed to decline because an extra rehearsal night would stretch her too thin. She was developing some important friendships within her small group at church and wanted to invest in these friendships on the evening of the extra rehearsal.

Anita was taken off guard when the minister suggested that she give up her "friendship-building activities" unless she was seriously dating someone or engaged to be married. Since she was unmarried and serving in the church, he reasoned, she must come under his spiritual authority as her leader. When Anita became defensive, he accused her of attacking him. He told her she had a responsibility to submit to him as her leader according to Hebrews 13:17, which states, "Obey your leaders and submit to them, for they keep watch over your souls as those who will give an account. Let them do this with joy and not with grief, for this would be unprofitable for you." Anita felt angry, confused, and trapped. If she refused to follow his direction, she feared she would gain a reputation for being unsubmissive to authority and lose the opportunity to serve in other ways in the future. If she stayed, she would be allowing this man to define her character and control her behavior.

Christian women like Anita often stay and acquiesce or leave these situations to avoid confronting leaders who lord authority over them. Over the years, I have heard countless stories about the way leaders in various ministries, whether vocational or lay leaders, sometimes wield the power of their position to pressure people into serving in their programs. I have heard leaders diminish and disparage ministry outside of the organized church (even the ministry of Christian parachurch organizations) in order to pressure their church members to make a choice that the leader defines as more spiritual or more profitable. Church members, and especially new believers, may be particularly vulnerable to this pressure if they do not have people in their lives who can give them the emotional support they need to stand up against the pressure.

Distorted Identity

If we are to enjoy intimacy with God and one another, it is important to ask ourselves if we are viewing a passage of Scripture through the lens of the Fall or through the lens of God's highest intention for humans. For centuries, men have dominated theology and the interpretation of the creation story and the Fall. Many men and women have been taught that the consequences of sin, such as men ruling over women, were by God's design when He simply described the damage that was done to all Creation as a result of their choice to know good and evil. From a human viewpoint, it is certainly to the advantage of men to assume an identity that places them in a superior position over women. As we have clearly seen in the Pre-Fall section of this book, God's highest intention in the Garden, however, was that humans rule together in a cooperative way that beautifies, benefits, and blesses all concerned.

I do not believe that God ever intended for humans to live as if the consequences of sin actually defined their identity. Let's take an example from family life. Imagine you have a daughter. You have explained that your home has a water heater and that if she is not careful, and touches the area that protects the pilot light, she will be burned. Imagine she ignores your warning and is badly burned. You tell her she will experience intense pain at the burn site and that a skin graft might be required and will leave an unsightly scar. Although the wound will heal, she will not have much sensation at the burn site.

Now imagine that the same child interprets the consequences you describe to her as actually defining her identity and worth as a person. Her life now revolves around the trauma of being severely burned. Her focus is on the scars and numbness where the skin graft took place. Every decision she makes centers around her identity as a burn victim. She is told that she deserves this life of victimhood because she did not listen to you. She does not seek to live up to her potential but lives only as defined by the consequences of her disobedience. What kind of development do you imagine would be possible for a child under this impression?

The desire of God for men and women to mirror the marvelous beauty of the Holy Triune Image did not change with the human choice to sin. What did change was human nature and the ability and ease with which humans, male and female, can live into the identity He originally created and called "very good." You may be asking the question, "Do we still have the freedom to choose, now that we have been marred by sin?" This question has been debated as long as humans have contemplated the ideas of free will and predestination. Perhaps Newtonian and quantum physicists are not so different from Calvinist and Arminian theologians or our deterministic and humanistic psychologists. It is human to ask these questions. The nature-or-nurture dilemma is related to this debate and an either-or approach to the question is being challenged by non-dualist thinkers who, like quantum scientists, see the world with a complexity that linear thinking simply does not allow. God is the Master of Paradox and transcends our simplistic ways of resolving tension by choosing between the extremes.

The difference between the freedom to choose in the garden with ideal soil and the freedom to choose in a garden of contaminated soil, is that with contaminated soil, humans begin with a huge deficit. In ideal soil, it is not difficult for the gardener to plant new things. It is complete and ready to receive new seeds. It is simply a delight and does not involve testing the soil or breaking it with the sweat of one's brow. This became obvious to me on this very day as I was out in our Charitable Garden. I observed one of our volunteers with a full wheelbarrow of heavy rich dirt that she carried several hundred feet back and forth multiple times from a compost pile to amend the new beds of hard clay soil before planting. It was already over 80 degrees in the Central Valley heat of California this morning at 10:00 a.m. Male or female, our volunteers were sweating at this necessary but labor-intensive task.

Similarly, the soil of the human heart was contaminated and hardened by sin. Rather than inclining naturally to do what is good, we find it easier to do the wrong thing: to be greedy instead of generous, to seek to control others rather than practice self-control, to be competitive rather than cooperative, divisive rather than diverse, to hoard things for ourselves rather than share them with others. It is without effort that a child throws tantrums, breaks things, or hits others with anger. But it takes lifelong practice to exercise productive self-control when expressing anger. It takes no effort to blame others, while it takes great effort to humbly take personal responsibility for mistakes.

As a result of this contamination, rather than men and women delighting in the individual gifts endowed to them by their Creator, roles have become prescribed by the prevailing culture, which can crush creativity and inhibit intimacy. Yet God is famous for working outside of expected conventions, like in the cases where the Moabitess Ruth and the harlot Rahab became key women in the birth line of the Messiah Jesus. Whether in marriage, society, or in the Church, God's will and creativity is not constrained by our rigid ideas of what it means to be a man, woman, or leader. Throughout Scripture, God works through myriad personalities, genders, races, religions, and social standings to accomplish His plan to bless and redeem His people.

Women are not the only ones who suffer from rigid roles defined by the consequences of the Fall rather than the freedom of God's highest intention for mutuality in marriage. It is not uncommon for women to come to my office and complain that their husbands are not fulfilling the role of a good spiritual leader in their home. This can range from a perceived lack of interest in spiritual things to not making enough money so the wife can stay at home with the children. Ironically, men who share the leadership of the home with their wives or encourage their wives to develop their gifts and pursue a career outside the home can also be judged by other men and women as not being willing to take full responsibility as "leader of his home." Here, too, intimacy is profoundly compromised by an inability to choose *relationships* over rigid *roles*.

Stan and Evelyn

Stan was a man in his forties who made an appointment for counseling with me at the request of Evelyn, his wife. He entered my office with hunched shoulders and eyes fixed on the ground. When I asked him what brought him to my office, he could not look at me when he answered, "My wife says I need to work on being a better spiritual leader. I guess I am not a good provider." He went on to explain that he wasn't making enough money to support his family, even though he was working two jobs. "Evelyn is afraid that she is going to have to get a job outside our home to help pay bills. We want to have more children. I promised her when we got married that she could stay at home and raise our children." When Stan and Evelyn met with their pastor as a couple, the pastor asked if Stan was spending daily time in the Word and leading the family in devotions. He had to admit that he was not consistent in his own time with God and felt intimidated about leading his family in devotions. "Is that really what God expects from me?" he asked miserably. "Am I failing my responsibility as a husband and leader of my home if my wife has to work, or we have to wait to have more children?"

While not responsible for Stan's depression, narrowly defined biblical roles of manhood and womanhood do significantly impact the well-being of both husbands and wives. Strict gender-based roles have frequently stripped men and women of their God-given, unique, and individual personalities, gifts, and talents unrelated to gender. There is little room to discover the unique identity of a couple when they are given a preformed mold by well-meaning spiritual leaders, pastors, and teachers. The pressure to conform to these roles within certain evangelical churches can be enormous. Stan later revealed to me that he believed his family would be better off without him, had contemplated suicide, and needed to be evaluated for potential hospitalization.

Eventually, Stan and Evelyn both allowed the Holy Spirit to bring healing to them, but it was a long journey of recovery and discovering the "We" of mutuality in their marriage so that both could find joy in their uniqueness as individuals and as a couple. In Chapter 6, we will look intently at how the Fall has distorted God's clear design for mutuality between women and men. We will see examples of how viewing each other through the lens of the curses and consequences of sin has deprived humanity of the intimacy that reflects the "Let Us" of our triune God.

CHAPTER 6

Contaminated Design

"Two are better than one because they have a good return for their labor. For if either of them falls, the one will lift up his companion, But woe to the one who falls when there is not another to lift him up. Furthermore, if two lie down together they keep warm but how can one be warm alone? And if one can overpower him who is alone, two can resist him. A cord of three strands is not quickly torn apart."

(Ecclesiastes 4:9–12, NASB 1995)

God's Design for Three-Dimensional Vision

God created humans in His image, male and female. I like to think about physical vision as a metaphor for the choices women and men can make to coordinate and work together as a team rather than attempt to dominate and suppress a partner. Both the female and male perspectives are essential to seeing God, one another, and our world accurately, making room for each to see a slightly different image. Our Creator, through the power of His Holy Spirit, blends these two human perspectives, male and female, into one cohesive and powerful view of intimacy.

Binocular Vision: Seeing with Both Eyes

I am continually amazed at what the natural world can teach us about the nature of God. In this metaphor, the capacity for two eyes to work together for optimal vision seems to reflect the cooperative nature of our triune God. According to Marsha Sorenson, OD, and Timothy C. Hain, MD,[46] binocular vision "refers to how the eyes work together to produce a three-dimensional perception of the world. The visual system must converge (turn eyes inward) and diverge (turn eyes outward) to maintain a clear, single, three-dimensional image. The American Optometric Association describes binocular vision in the following: "Eye coordination is the ability of both eyes to work together as a team. Each of your eyes sees a slightly different image. Your brain, through a process called fusion, blends these two images into one three-dimensional picture."[47]

Monocular Vision: Seeing with One Eye

The symptoms of dysfunctional binocular vision include eye strain, double vision, blurred vision, visual fatigue, and headaches. In order to avoid double vision, the brain will completely shut down the use of an eye that is being dominated in a process called suppression. If caught early, it is possible to engage in vision therapy exercises to retrain both eyes to coordinate and work together as a team to prevent the dominant eye from engaging in monocular or one-eyed vision. Vision therapy focuses on binocularity and requires frequent *suppression checks* because the person with an eye turn loses the capacity to even recognize when the eye has turned off.

In a conversation I had with Garrett Elliott, O.D.,[48] I learned that humans also have two eyes for the purpose of depth perception, which is lost when one eye is not fully functioning. Simple tasks like catching a baseball or judging steps on stairs become significantly more difficult. As one eye continues to dominate the other, the person begins to lose the capacity to see out of the dominated eye. This loss of vision

46   Sorenson, Marsha, OD and Hain, Timothy C., MD, "Binocular Vision Dysfunction
       (BVD)", Dizziness-and-balance.com, last Modified May 2, 2023, https://dizziness-and-
       balance.com/disorders/visual/binocular.html
47   The American Optometric Association, "Eye Coordination," American Optometric
       Association, Accessed July 9, 2023, https://www.aoa.org/healthy-eyes/eye-and-vision-
       conditions/eye-coordination
48   Garrett Elliott, Telephone and Text Communication, July 11, 2020

is then referred to as amblyopia, or in the vernacular, a lazy eye. The brain wants two equally clear images from both the eyes, so if one image is compromised by domination, the brain begins to reflexively suppress the dominated eye. If the brain did not suppress an image in this scenario, you would have a case of "double vision."

Treating a lazy eye is difficult; it often requires forcing the dominated eye to work at seeing again. *Patching* is the term used when a person purposefully closes their dominant eye, i.e., with an eyepatch, to make the brain rely only on the lazy eye. Through time and enough exercise, the brain gradually *re-learns* how to use the lazy eye. It is worth noting that when patching, the dominant eye should not be patched indefinitely. Patching is done in small increments throughout the day to encourage the weaker eye, while not debilitating a person by obstructing vision in their *good eye*. If the dominant eye is constantly patched, it is possible for it to become a lazy eye itself while the original lazy eye becomes dominant. The goal is equal but distinctive use of both eyes.

The penchant for one eye to dominate the other, both literally and figuratively, is what gives us a distorted view of God's magnificent Creation. It is as if the male eye has dominated the female eye for centuries, and as a result of excluding her, humankind has often lost half of its visual field. Though this is now changing, for thousands of years, most of what has been written about the Bible has been written by men and described through a male lens.

A History of Monocular Male Vision

Although there are notable exceptions, a historical look at the writings of male biblical scholars, theologians, and clergy reveals a perspective that presents men as the dominant eye and even as the superior eye. In contrast to men, women have been underrepresented in their ability to study, teach, or preach theology. Though notable exceptions exist, here too, they do not by any means balance out the male-dominated perspective, even today. There are still some denominations, evangelical biblical teachers, and pastors who find it difficult (and some impossible) to even read theological work done by a woman, much less employ them as pastors, based on the belief that women are not allowed to teach Scripture to men.[49]

---

49   For more on the topic of women teachers and pastors, see McKnight, Scot. *The Blue Parakeet: Rethinking How You Read the Bible.* Grand Rapids, MI: Zondervan, 2018.

First published in 1890 and largely unchanged even today, the 1978 edition of the *Strong's Concordance* still stated that the definition for male, *zakar*, means "a male (of man or animals, as being the most noteworthy sex)." As a lay person studying Scripture, I have relied heavily upon James Strong for learning about the meaning of ancient Hebrew and Greek words. In this case, women like me have been misled to believe that Scripture and even the original language of Hebrew support this man's opinion that men are the most noteworthy sex.[50]

Despite such blind spots and injustices throughout the history of Christianity as it relates to women, God's choice to refer to Himself as "He," and as a father, is significant. I reject the idea of simple gender equivocation because it doesn't allow me to explore the important and meaningful reasons God had for choosing to use relational terms like Father and Son to describe Himself to our fallen world. Jesus clearly called God His heavenly Father, not His heavenly Mother. This does not mean that God does not act in maternal ways. Even the idea of being born again in Christ brings with it the image of a spiritual womb, nursing on the milk of the Word, and developing into mature adults who can be nourished on the meat of sound doctrine.

Calling God my Mother and my Savior a Daughter does not, in my estimation, do anything to resolve the theological gender conflicts between men and women. I prefer to ask the question, "What might a good, loving, and just God, whose very nature is revealed in the distinct but equal creation of men and women, want to reveal to His Creation about Himself and the way He relates to us through His choice of gender-specific albeit culturally and politically incorrect terms?" I do not have any hope that a matriarchal society would be superior to a patriarchal society. This view exchanges a male monocular vision for a female monocular vision. It does nothing to cultivate the depth perception available when both male and female views are valued and promoted. Inequality and the abuse of power and control are not intrinsically pre-Fall gender issues but a post-Fall sin issue, which will be addressed thoroughly in the next chapter. Although I reject gender equivocation, I fully accept, embrace, and urge a more thorough exploration of God's nature as revealed in the feminine gender. God cannot create

---

50 Strong, James. *Strong's Exhaustive Concordance of the Bible: Hebrew and Chaldee Dictionary.* Nashville, TN: Abingdon, 1978.

humans in His own image, both male and female, and not have both masculine and feminine attributes that are part of His nature. We must, therefore, be careful not to minimize, understate, or dismiss the female aspect of God declared to be present in the godhead. Still, the bigger issue is mutuality, whether in relation to humans or to God.

Throughout historical Christianity, we have been taught to think of God in a vertical, top-down manner. Our orthodox trinitarian background reminds us that God is One and that the persons of the Trinity, though distinct, are equal. At the Council of Nicaea in AD 325, a group of important religious and political leaders, including church bishops and Emperor Constantine, rightfully argued that the Father, Son, and Holy Spirit exist as One in three distinct and equal persons.[51] Nevertheless, they unwittingly introduced a subtle but powerful bias of ordering and ranking that reinforced their own top-down, worldly authority structures. Even today we refer to God the Father as the first person of the Trinity, the Son of God as the second person of the Trinity, and the Holy Spirit as the third person of the Trinity. We do not find this linear, numerical, or top-down definition of God in Scripture.

Still, the dominant approach by Christians in society has been to legitimize the top-down authority of humans over other humans as sanctioned by God. Some of the most egregious sins against humanity have been done in the name of God as servants of "king and country." Regardless of the need for order and submission to governing authorities, we must never forget that human authority over other humans was created by the Fall, not by God's design. Even the human authority that we are urged to obey by Paul in Romans 13:1–7 (TNIV) does not reflect God's highest intention for His beautiful, shared authority but is merely a shadow of the beautiful authority of God.

Worldly leaders and governments have a place for keeping order and peace in our fallen human society and citizens have a place for expecting accountability and limiting authority when authority becomes abusive. Peter and the other apostles made a case for civil disobedience when they challenged the limits of Roman

---

51 Pelikan, Jaroslav. *The Christian Tradition: A History of the Development of Doctrine.* "The Emergence of the Catholic Tradition" (100-600). Chicago, IL: University of Chicago Press, 1975. (201)

authority. They clearly stated that they would submit to God above human authority (Acts 5:27–32). Submission to human authority, whether parents, husbands, the Sanhedrin, or kings, is not always submission to God. Jesus completely redefined leadership for the believer. When we think of the responsibilities given to church leaders, husbands, or anyone else, whether male or female, we are not to think in terms of worldly, top-down authority, power, and control over others. Instead, we are to use our authority, power, and control to love and care for others with the character and serving style of Christ. The Apostle Peter tells elders to "shepherd the flock of God among you, exercising oversight not under compulsion, but voluntarily, according to the will of God; and not for sordid gain, but with eagerness; nor yet as lording it over those allotted to your charge, but proving to be examples to the flock."[52]

The principles of hermeneutics require students of the Bible to consider the vital role of contextualization when interpreting a passage of Scripture. Yet when it comes to understanding the authority structure God intended for humans in general and male-female relations in particular, it seems as though tradition trumps truth. By truth, I mean the example of generous sharing of authority and power within the godhead during the creation of human beings, male and female, and the generous sharing of authority and power by Jesus Christ with His followers, male and female, while on Earth. By tradition, I mean the long Church history of legitimizing the exclusive and often unquestioned and legally binding authority of husbands, parents, masters, church leaders, caesars, and governments over those entrusted to their care. The power structure of a top-down hierarchy was decidedly not the one modeled by Jesus Christ as He interacted with government officials, religious leaders, His disciples, and the crowds of people.

In the 16th century, it was Martin Luther[53] who identified the fallacious belief within the Roman Catholic Church that to obey those in authority was the same as obeying God. He exposed this heresy when he challenged the Pope and other Roman Catholic leaders to support their decisions with more than a few proof text verses that urge Christians to obey their leaders. In fact, this doctrine did not

---

52   1 Peter 5:1–2, NASB 1995.
53   Metaxas, Eric. *Martin Luther*. New York: Viking, an Imprint of Penguin, Random House, 2017.

align with the whole of Scripture. How is it, then, that this doctrine continues to subvert the ways of Christ in male-female relations? It is still alive and well in both Roman Catholic and Protestant churches today. It's time we realize that this path leads away from love and intimacy that is mutually nourishing. Instead, it leads toward power and control that demands from others what it wants under the guise of legitimate authority.

A thorough review of Church history demonstrates the habitual ravaging of the Bride of Christ (believers) when the politics of government aligns itself with the politics of the organized church. How might authority, power, and control be redefined if, instead of viewing them through the monocular lens of the Fall, with men ruling over women (or the more powerful humans ruling over more vulnerable humans, regardless of gender), we viewed them through the complex lens of the Pre-Fall, New Creation, and New Heaven and Earth Eras as well? How might our homes, communities, and nations thrive if we emphasized mutuality and the generosity of sharing power and authority within and among them? Binocular vision gives us the advantages that God had in mind when He created humans, male and female.

Acknowledging Blind Spots

It is impossible to miss the parallels when it comes to generations of loss that continue to go unrecognized in the theological community because of monocular male vision. What rich treasures have gone undiscovered because the eye of the female mind has been so thoroughly shut down. Would not suppression checks be in order on a theological level? It is not uncommon for the eye of a male reader to dismiss and disregard a female biblical scholar or theologian when looking for commentaries and exegetical wisdom. Assumptions are made about the kind of biblical orthodoxy the reader will find in the book or article written by a woman before her work is even read. What would happen if a woman's perspective were actively sought out by pastors and seminary professors and explored with an expectation of being enriched?

As a woman, I want to explore and claim more fully the ways in which God expresses His image through women and in the female characteristics of God, without compromising biblical integrity and orthodoxy. I also want to recognize the male gender bias and the lens through which so much theology has been filtered. If the Latinization of Scripture kept laypersons from understanding Scripture in their own languages, so has the masculinization of Scripture kept women from seeing Scripture through their own feminine eyes. As in the case of binocular vision, God created male and female to work *together* as a team in understanding the nuances of Scripture.

For example, as a young woman, I had never noticed my own biases when reading the Genesis account of the creation of humankind. I grew up reading the New American Standard Version of the Bible (NASB 1978), which was purported at the time it was first published as being a more literal translation of the ancient languages. Not only had I never noticed the words our premarital counseling pastor pointed out ("let *them* rule" instead of "let the *male* rule") in Genesis 1:26, but neither had I the sophistication to notice that the Hebrew word *adam* in verse 26 clearly refers to humankind, and is not the same word used for the singular Hebrew word for "male."

I wrongly assumed that "Let us make man in our image" meant "Let us make the male Adam in our image." Hebrew scholars point out that the more accurate translation of this word in 1:26 is clearly referring to humankind. Genesis 1:26 (TNIV) reads: "Then God said, 'Let us make humankind (Heb. *adam*) in our image.'" The Hebrew word *adam* is both a proper name, Adam, and a word meaning "humankind," including both male and female. Here humankind is clearly in view, as the plural "let them rule" makes clear. The introduction of the plural pronoun "them" and the explicit reference to both male and female here clearly point to translating *adam* as the human being or humankind (referring to both genders).[54]

If this error unwittingly shaped my thinking as a female reader, then, it has tremendous implications for my identity as an intentional and critical-thinking Christian woman and wife now. It is important to have a nuanced understanding of the Hebrew text and of how a casual reading of the English translation sets the stage for misunderstanding God's good intentions for humankind, both male and female. John H. Walton[55] has argued in many of his books that biblical languages

---

54   Personal communication with Robert K. Brown, April 16, 2021.
55   Walton, John H. *The Lost World of Scripture: Ancient Literary Culture and Biblical Authority.* Downers Grove, IL: IVP Academic, an Imprint of InterVarsity Press, 2013. (7)

are not simply disembodied words on paper that can be translated in the abstract. He notes, "Language assumes a culture, operates in a culture, serves a culture, and is designed to communicate into the framework of a culture. Consequently, when we read a text written in another language and addressed to another culture, we must translate the culture as well as the language if we hope to understand the text fully."

Translators must consider culture, and so must readers. Each of us as readers of Scripture brings our own cultural biases around gender to Scripture. I bring a particular perspective to the Bible as a modern American woman. As a thoughtful reader, I hope you are not only looking for evidence of my biases but are also examining your own biases as you read things that seem startling or strange. The question is not whether we bring biases to our reading of the text (which we inevitably do), but whether we allow those biases to be challenged and transformed by a careful listening (with the help of the Holy Spirit) to what the text is saying. How might they either illuminate or obscure our understanding? Although I strive to be as conscious of my own personal and cultural biases as I can in order to see the biblical text as clearly as possible, I am inevitably still vulnerable to these challenges. Sometimes our bias is what C.S. Lewis called chronological snobbery or "the uncritical acceptance of the intellectual climate of our own age and the assumption that whatever has gone out of date is on that count discredited[56]."

Acknowledging the Blind Eye of Abusive Authority

The failure of Christendom to properly see women and men as our Triune God originally intended has perpetuated the abuse of authority, which is a barrier to intimacy, ironically as much for men as for women. After 45 years of following Christ, I continue to be stunned, though no longer surprised, by the commonly held beliefs about authority that legitimize abuses of power within evangelical homes, churches, and other Christian organizations, sabotaging intimacy. What follows is one example of the many ways I have been challenged to think deeply about how a distorted understanding of biblical authority and power destroys

---

56 Lindsay, Art. *C.S. Lewis on Chronological Snobbery*. C.S. Lewis Institute. A Teaching Quarterly for Discipleship of Heart and Mind (Knowing and Doing) Spring 2003, https://www.cslewisinstitute.org/webfm_send/47.

lives and God's highest intention for human beings. My work counseling hurting people as a missionary, church leader, and professional psychotherapist has almost exclusively involved some dimension of the misuse or blatant abuse of authority and power in the lives of the children, women, and men who have come to me for help and healing. What follows is an example I assumed would be a rare exception in my counseling office but in fact found to be devastatingly common.

Sexual Abuse in Marriage—Rachel and Christopher

I will never forget the first time I encountered a spiritual leader who believed that all sexual behavior in the privacy of a married couple's bedroom was sanctioned by God. Rachel and Christopher were a young married couple who had come to my office for counseling. Christopher told me his wife was having trouble submitting to his authority in their sexual relationship. As I spoke with this timid, quiet, and fearful woman, I learned that Rachel felt incredibly guilty for not enjoying the "games" her husband wanted to play in the bedroom during their times of sexual intimacy. She asked me if I could help her get over being a "prude" and let loose and just enjoy playing the victim tied up to the bedposts of the marital bed. She told me that when they "made love" during this game, that he liked to put an unloaded gun to her head and, at the point of completion, let it click on her forehead.

If you are sickened by this example and feel it is nearly inappropriate for print, then imagine my horror as I listened to the response of the spiritual leader with whom the couple had asked me to speak. With the couple's permission, I made an appointment to speak with the pastor at his church office. At this point, the couple did not want to be included in my meeting with the pastor. When I asked him what he knew of this "sexual game," he immediately put his open palm up in the air, signaling me to stop talking and quickly told me he didn't need to know the details. He said that the couple simply needed to watch a marriage video series and read a Psalm and a Proverb each day. When I showed him the release of confidential information I had, and urged him to understand what was being done to the wife under the guise of sex play, he told me it didn't matter because she had a responsibility to submit and satisfy him or she would be responsible for his looking elsewhere for what he needed. When I challenged this, he ordered me out of his office with the assurance that he would never refer another couple for counseling to me again.

I can hear some of you making the argument that this is an exception. Every therapist who hears these stories knows that such an example does not characterize the pastorate in general. In no way are such examples included to demean men or degrade the honorable vocation of pastoral ministry. However, I cannot say in honesty that this is a rare and infrequent experience among women in homes, churches, and communities. It is not helpful or healing to the Body of Christ to mindlessly exonerate the men who perpetuate such beliefs in the name of biblical authority. We need to hold one another accountable for such abuses in truth and grace. We must also be willing to look beneath the symptoms of such abuse to the beliefs that perpetuate the behavior. Neither women nor men are well served by such denial that minimizes, justifies, or refuses to deal with the reality and frequency of this behavior.

In addition, this pastor's view of male leadership works contrary to genuine intimacy. It is traumatizing for the wife, and the husband who emotionally manipulates or physically forces his wife into sexual behaviors that are odious to her is also doing violence to himself. This is an often-neglected consequence of domestic violence. There is great suffering in men who abuse their power in relationships, and they often have been victims of abuse themselves. While this in no way excuses or legitimizes the behavior, we must not be under the mistaken impression that men who abuse power are unscathed by it. Christopher was taught by this pastor that his wife was to blame for any future infidelity if she did not comply with his demands, regardless of her desires. This is the antithesis of Paul's metaphor of a husband loving his wife as Christ loved the church in Ephesians 5:25–28. This kind of coercion and manipulation in the name of spiritual authority is steeped in the Fall, not in the freedom of Christ.

Oneness of husband and wife is not meant to usurp the freedom to make individual choices. Suffocating oneness does not obliterate differences. Oneness with God or in marriage becomes bondage rather than bonding when improperly interpreted. Misunderstanding the idea of becoming one flesh in marriage has been as catastrophic for women as the concept of being created as a subservient helper to men. In both cases, women have often lost their individual identity, voice, and personhood under the guise of biblical submission to their husbands. If we return momentarily to the example of a husband demanding particular sexual behaviors from his wife (even if they are not as dramatic as those mentioned in the previous example), we see how both are deprived of genuine intimacy.

The freedom to admit differences in sexual desires, preferences, and frequency and the ability to respect those differences in our spouse despite our hurt and disappointment is the foundation upon which a satisfying mutuality is built. One of the great tragedies of sexual addiction among us is the way short-term gratification promises the thrill of ecstasy, only to dissolve at times into the long-term incapacity to be physically satisfied. Some cases of male erectile dysfunction have been linked to chronic masturbation and pornography.[57] It may be counter intuitive, but I have seen couples develop greatly heightened levels of spiritual, psychological, and sexual intimacy in their relationship despite erectile dysfunction. This has also been true with couples in which a woman is experiencing vaginismus. Both of these conditions can become an opportunity for increasing intimacy when communication is enhanced, compassion is shown, needs are honestly expressed, and mutually satisfying solutions are discovered. Sexual intimacy is far more than the capacity to experience orgasm or coitus. When partners take the time to know and respect one another on a spiritual, emotional, and physical level, there is often heightened arousal and sensitivity as couples deepen their capacity to bond rather than see one another as simple objects of gratification.

---

57   Park, Brian Y., Wilson, Gary, Berger, Jonathan, Christman, Matthew, Reina, Bryn, Bishop, Frank, Klam, Warren P., and Doan, Andrew P. "Is Internet Pornography Causing Sexual Dysfunctions: A Review with Clinical Reports," National Library of Medicine: National Center for Biotechnology Information, August 6, 2016. https://www.ncbi.nlm.nih.gov/pmc/articles/PMC5039517/

CHAPTER 7

Contaminated Authority

"Power tends to corrupt and absolute power corrupts absolutely...
There is no worse heresy than the office sanctifies the holder of it.
That is the point at which...the end learns to justify the means."[58]

—Lord Acton

I n the Garden, we humans exchanged loneliness for intimacy, equality, diversity, and the knowledge of goodness for inequality, divisiveness, and the knowledge of both good and evil. Beautiful authority that created life became corrupt authority that destroyed it. Using freedom to choose evil instead of good severed the unity and diversity of connection. The clear, clean waters of cooperation became polluted with the waters of competition, leading to a distortion of God's original design and ultimately to death.

If we follow the path that led from the ideal soil of the Garden of Eden to the contaminated soil of the Post-Fall Era in the Bible, we follow a path strewn with the pain of broken relationships characterized by hiding and blaming, competition and domination, violent murder and death. Yet our Creator understood this change in human nature and knew that the only path out of this cursed soil would be to stay in a close and intimate relationship with the triune God.

---

58 Acton, John. "Acton-Creighton Correspondence," OLL, 1887. https://oll.libertyfund.org/title/acton-acton-creighton-correspondence

Knowledge of Evil Corrupts Authority

God greatly values love and intimacy that is freely given and received. He created humans capable of choice and gave them clear expectations and consequences to inform their decision rather than attempt to coerce, manipulate, dominate, or control them. Even today, modern child psychotherapists encourage parents to give children clear expectations and logical consequences in advance in order to promote healthy development and the self-regulation skills necessary for responsible adulthood.

Literature in every generation tells stories about what happens when a child's love is coerced by parental authority through threats and bribes. Coercion and manipulation do not produce the fruit of genuine love. Responsible parents eventually have the painful job of allowing their children to experience the consequences of their own actions. Though we may do all we can to teach them, motivate them, and prevent them from making costly and life-destroying decisions, in the end, the child must choose for themselves if they are ever to mature into healthy adults.

Perhaps God allows humans to do it our own way so we can experience our inability to reverse the Fall, regardless of our inexhaustible human cleverness, creativity, determination, will, and resilience. God is willing to suffer with us as we learn for ourselves that His authority truly is safe, reliable, and good. The alternative, the lack of freedom to choose, is unthinkable, abject slavery. This is completely contrary to the nature of God.

Human Rejection of God's Preference for Intimate Relationship

It is easy to forget that, according to the Hebrew Bible, God interacted with humans for hundreds if not thousands of years on a personal and individual level before the nation of Israel and the Mosaic Law was instituted. God continually sought the pre-Fall relationship of walking with humans, even though the humans now wandered on cursed soil, hearts forever changed to incline toward evil. Indeed, the mark of the curse on the soil and the consequence of a sinful human nature is evidenced even before Adam and Eve exit the Garden. In preparation for life outside the hospitable climate of the Garden, God provides the fur coats of animals to protect them from exposure to the elements, not even a consideration before the Fall. Adam and likely Eve knew these very animals by name. Is it possible that this is the first indication of what the knowledge of good and evil would cost humans and the Son of God (the sacrifice of the beloved) in order to redeem humankind?

Afterwards and until this very day, the animals who were once the beloved and safe companions of the humans became prey for food and clothing. We are told that all Creation groans to be clothed with the imperishable flesh that never decays and never dies. Even the Old Testament prophet Isaiah foresaw the day coming when the distinction between prey and predator would forever be set aside:

> *"The wolf will live with the lamb, the leopard will lie down with the goat, the calf and the lion and the yearling together; and a little child will lead them. The cow will feed with the bear, their young will lie down together, and the lion will eat straw like the ox. Infants will play near the hole of the cobra; young children will put their hands into the viper's nest. They will neither harm nor destroy on my holy mountain, for the earth will be filled with the knowledge of the Lord, as the waters cover the sea."*
>
> **(Isaiah 11:6-9, TNIV)**

In the Post-Fall world however, the inclination for the man to rule over the woman would extend to a preference for male over female children and a history counted through the male line. There would be competition rather than collaboration between tillers of the soil and keepers of flocks, just as there was competition between Cain and Abel. Cain was the tiller of cursed soil who killed Abel, his brother, a shepherd of flocks—perhaps once again foreshadowing the battleground between the Serpent and the Good Shepherd. Later in the same chapter, we see the first evidence of both domestic violence and polygamy, in which Lamech threatens his two wives by saying, "Listen to my voice, you wives of Lamech. Give heed to my speech, for I have killed a man for wounding me and a boy for striking me. If Cain is avenged sevenfold, then Lamech seventy-sevenfold" (Genesis 4:23–24 NASB 1995). Bravado and boasting aside, these women would have known the terror and violence of such a husband.

Interestingly, Genesis 5:1 (TNIV) echoes the language of a Pre-Fall Era to validate God's highest intention once again for humans: "This is the written account of Adam's family line. When God created human beings, he made them in the likeness of God. He created them male and female and blessed them. And when they were created, he called them 'human beings.'" Unfortunately, we see a change of focus in the language from being made in the likeness of God to being born in the likeness of Adam. This is a significant if subtle change in the post-Fall language. "Genesis 5:3 (TNIV) records a significant shift in focus from seeing humans made in God's likeness to being made in his own male likeness: "When Adam had lived 130 years, he had a son in his own likeness, in his own image; and he named him Seth." If patriarchy has been defined "as a social organization marked by the supremacy of the father in the clan or family, the legal dependence of wives and children, and the reckoning of descent and inheritance in the male line,"[59] then it is certainly the language of the Fall together with its curses and consequences. It isn't long before the precedent set by the Fall of men ruling over women and women seeking an unhealthy desire for their husbands (including the desire to control them) spreads like gangrene to the rest of domestic life.

Despite the curses and consequences of the Fall, God continues to desire an intimate relationship with humans. From Adam to Noah, Noah to Abraham, and Abraham to Israel, God is recorded as walking with them, talking with them, providing for them, protecting them, directing them, and blessing them. Long before slavery in Egypt or deliverance by Moses, the writing of the Ten Commandments and the institution of the male priesthood and Mosaic Law, God longed for the humans to stay in direct relationship with Him. The more the people of God rejected a personal relationship with Him, the more they subjected themselves to the rule of human authority instead of God's own authority. In fact, God called Himself "the Creator" and "the Lord God" until the Exodus, when He commissioned Moses to deliver the people of Israel from Egyptian slavery as a father delivers his children. Prior to that, God sought to be the God who walks, talks, and leads His people as an intimate friend.

---

59   www.merriam-webster.com

Human Preference for Patriarchy Rather than God's Authority

"But when they said, 'Give us a king to lead us,' this displeased Samuel; so he prayed to the LORD. And the LORD told him: 'Listen to all that the people are saying to you; it is not you they have rejected, but they have rejected me as their king. As they have done from the day I brought them up out of Egypt until this day, forsaking me and serving other gods, so they are doing to you.'"

(1 Samuel 8:6–8, TNIV)

Patriarchy was not God's idea. This thread of truth runs through each of our chapters and biblical eras. We are continually reminded that patriarchy and the abuse of power by humans began in the Garden when both Eve and Adam chose the knowledge of good and evil over the goodness of God. In ancient Israel, humans gravitated toward, and even preferred, human power structures and rules to genuine relationship with God. Do you remember what happened when Israel traded a living relationship with God in exchange for leadership modeled after the curses and consequences of sin? In 1 Samuel 8, we are privy to a conversation between God and the prophet Samuel about Israel's demand for human authority in the form of a king.

It seems Samuel perceived himself to be responsible for Israel's failure and was personalizing the people's demand for a king in place of God's direct leading. God reassured Samuel that the people were not rejecting him but God. The people wanted the kind of authority they saw operating in the world. God willingly listened to Israel's demand. Ultimately, He allowed Israel to choose an earthly king, with all the rules and domination that would accompany this choice. Just like in the pre-Fall Garden of Eden, God outlined what the outcome would be if Israel persisted in choosing a king like the other nations, rather than being a holy people ruled by God Himself. God wanted to make sure Israel understood the consequences of their choice. The penchant for post-Fall thinking was so great that they were drawn to kings that would rule over them rather than to a God who longed for an intimate relationship with them.

> *"'Now listen to them; but warn them solemnly and let them know what the king who will reign over them will do…This is what the king who will reign over you will do: He will take your sons and make them serve with his chariots and horses, and they will run in front of his chariots…He will take your daughters to be perfumers…He will take the best of your fields and vineyards and olive groves and give them to his attendants. He will take a tenth of your grain and of your vintage and give it to his officials and attendants…He will take a tenth of your flocks, and you yourselves will become his slaves.'…But the people refused to listen to Samuel. 'No!' they said. 'We want a king over us.'"*
>
> **(1 Samuel 8:9–19, NASB)**

God warned Israel against this decision because He knew how all humans, having a sin nature, are inclined to abuse authority and power. But He allowed it and worked within the structure.

I can't emphasize enough how God's willingness to work with us in our evil choices in no way legitimizes the choice or the abuse of power that comes with it. God does not contaminate Himself or compromise His character by walking with us but rather continues to work in the midst of our corruption. As we learn, evil has rules of its own that God will eventually overturn completely—first with the coming of the Messiah, Jesus Christ, and finally, in the second coming of Christ in the era of the new Heaven and Earth. During the New Creation Era (Part III) and the New Heaven and Earth Era (Part IV), we will see the intimacy of the Bridegroom Jesus and His Bride, the Church, restored and transformed.

The Law of Moses Was not God's Highest Intention for Humans

Neither the Law, nor the prophets and judges, nor an earthly king, was God's highest intention for humans. We abandoned the mutuality of an intimate relationship with God and one another in favor of the rules set up by our own rebellion and then blamed God for allowing the consequences to follow. This was not His highest intention for His people then, any more than it is His highest intention for the misuse of authority among different races of men and women, husbands and wives, slaves and masters, or parents and children today. Old Testament Law may showcase the impact of sin upon God's original design, but it in no way legitimizes it.

I readily acknowledge that I am disturbed by the patriarchal system set up in the Old Testament. I openly decry a system terribly vulnerable to abuse and inferior to God's original design. It was sin, not God's desire for humans, that perpetuated to this very day the curses and consequences of knowing evil. One of the greatest mistakes we can make is to read the entire Old Testament through the lens of the Fall and assume that the Mosaic Law made to breach the gap between God and humans on a cursed earth was His highest and best for them. The Law was not meant to legitimize patriarchy but to expose what happens to humans who choose human authority over God's authority.

The Law constantly reinforced that humans lived under a destructive curse with dire consequences resulting from a choice to know good and evil. With each successive generation, it became increasingly clear that human effort was insufficient to restore humans to God's original design. The Law became more and more oppressive in the hands of the priests and teachers who interpreted it and added to it. If anything, the Law demonstrates just how destructive sin and the Fall were and the violence done to humans in general and women in particular. The Law could not save humans from their depravity. The best it could do was to become a tutor[60] that would lead us to the conclusion that we were sinners in need of a Savior who was both God and human: a Savior who would choose God's definition of good over evil every time He was tempted.

Interestingly, the Old Testament prophets who proclaimed the day of the Lord also prophesied a coming day when the destructiveness and grief caused by the Fall would be overthrown. The sinful disparities based on gender, age, race, and social status would be overturned. In Joel 2:28–29 (TNIV) we read, "And afterward, I will pour out my Spirit on all people. Your sons and daughters will prophesy, your old men will dream dreams, your young men will see visions. Even on my servants, both men and women, I will pour out my Spirit in those days" (see Peter's sermon in Acts 2:14ff.).

---

60   Galatians 3:24

This was God's heart and holy intention. Women need not accept a shred of inferiority or the diminishing of power as females. We are members of a unified body of Christ, which does not distinguish itself by ethnicity, social class, or gender (Galatians 3:28–29, TNIV). We (male and female) are co-heirs and co-rulers with Jesus (Romans 8:17; Revelation 5:9–10 and 20:4 (TNIV). The fact that Eve, Adam, and all their descendants exchanged beauty for ashes and created the destructive fires of uncontrolled and unrestrained sin, and that we have marred the beauty of being made in the image of God for the horrors of knowing both good and evil, are human sin issues, not gender issues.

Choosing to forsake a mature adult relationship with God and an interdependent relationship with one another, humans became immature and disobedient children. As a result, God became less and less Creator and Friend and increasingly a Father to them—not the God and Father of adult mature children but the Father of young children, children who aren't mature enough to think of others, children who hurt themselves and are vulnerable to being hurt by others.

The Fall was not the punishment of a mean father, but the direct result of our human invitation of evil into the world. As we have seen, Adam attempted to blame God for the gift of Eve and tried to hide the shame of his naked disobedience from God when he chose to sin. I am convinced that the choices of both Adam and Eve have resulted in a terribly distorted image of God as well as what it means to be male and female.

Our inclination to blame the wholly good and kind God who loves us is by far one of the most violent and life-depriving aspects of our sinful nature. I also believe that humankind has suffered bitterly in every conceivable way for the choice to know both good and evil, and that these consequences cannot be eradicated by human effort, though now in Christ and through the power of the Holy Spirit we can live transformed lives that reflect God's original design. As such, we must walk in the Spirit and bear the fruit of the Spirit, which leads to a communion of true freedom, equality, forgiveness, mercy, grace, and love among saints and in the world.

In summary, humans in ancient Israel gravitated toward, and even preferred, human power structures and rules to genuine relationship with God. Israel rejected God as King in exchange for a top-down leadership structure modeled after the curses and consequences of sin. On the surface, rules tend to be simpler and more clear-cut, if harsh. How many children in generations past have told parents they preferred a consequence to a lecture? "Let's just get this over with," says the child.

In contrast, our loving God says, "Come now, let us reason together."[61] He wants the reciprocity of dialogue. We see this acted out in Genesis, when God pursued Adam after that fateful moment when both Eve and Adam ate the fruit of the tree of the knowledge of good and evil. God's question to Adam was, "Where are you?" God knew exactly where Adam was hiding. But God wanted a conversation, a coming clean to restore the relationship and intimacy. We see God negotiate with His leaders as if they have power to influence a holy God, and they do. From Abraham to Moses, from Job to Gideon, and down to you and me, we see God willing to reason and listen to His beloved. He gives us the dignity of mutuality that does not diminish His authority or exaggerate our own.

---

61   Isaiah 1:18 (TNIV)

CHAPTER 8

Contaminated Intimacy

"The temptation of power is greatest when intimacy is a threat. Much Christian leadership is exercised by people who do not know how to develop healthy, intimate relationships and have opted for power and control instead."[62]

—Henri Nouwen

Genuine relationships offer shared power, mutuality, and intimacy but are also unpredictable, complicated, and messy. They require dialogue, self-examination, self-knowledge, and humility. There is a need to wrestle, to ask questions, to risk offense, rejection, and to summon the courage to expose our weaknesses to another person. The reward can be great when the result is resolved conflict, more freedom, trust, and connection.

Recognizing Genuine and False Intimacy

What distinguishes false intimacy from genuine intimacy? The answer in part is found in the way we view people and our response to unmet needs and desires. Individuals experiencing false intimacy view people as objects to gratify their own needs and desires. When needs go unmet over time, we tend to become

---

62   Nouwen, Henri J.M. In the Name of Jesus: Reflections on Christian Leadership. New York, New York: The Crossroad Publishing Company, 1989. (79)

more demanding and abusive or withdraw. In contrast, genuine intimacy allows us to expose our vulnerable emotions, needs, and desires to people who can comfort us, which increases a sense of closeness. In either case, when a relationship is not meeting our needs and we cannot or will not negotiate a mutually satisfactory solution, a person unable to tolerate genuine (mutual) intimacy can become anxious, depressed, angry, and dependent upon objects within their control. It is not uncommon for food, alcohol, drugs, pornography, and gambling (to name just a few) to be used to meet unconscious needs without respect to the healthy needs of self and others. In some cases, a more reliable substitute for a caring relationship might include a gang of criminals, stealing from others, sexual abuse, and involvement with sexual slave trafficking. But it can also mean achieving high levels of success and status in businesses of all kinds, including seminaries, universities, church ministry, and missionary service. Sin has predisposed us to preferring to meet our own needs in unhealthy ways, both unilaterally and superficially.

In contrast, individuals cultivating genuine intimacy view both people in the relationship as having their own legitimate needs. When we take the risk of asking for what we want or need, we reveal vulnerable feelings, thoughts, and desires. When our partner cannot or will not give us what we are hoping for, we may feel hurt, frightened, or angry. We may be tempted to self-medicate in any number of unhealthy ways. Even though we may initially withdraw, blame others, or lash out, we can (but often do not) eventually reach back to our loved one and restore the relationship through communication, clarification, and, when necessary, an apology. This does not mean that people cultivating genuine intimacy do not struggle with addictions. The difference is that there is a willingness to be open and honest about our needs and struggles directly with our partner, ask for professional help outside the relationship when needed, and bring any temptations or lapses into addiction into the open with our partner. There is power in the light but bondage in what is hidden in the dark.

Pastor Jack: An Example of False Intimacy

Jack was a charismatic pastor of a growing megachurch in the Midwest. A recently licensed counselor, Janelle, was new at her church and looking for ways to serve others using her counseling and recovery skills. She set up an appointment to meet with Pastor Jack. His secretary greeted her with a friendly smile and invited her into his spacious office, which was well organized and displayed a number of Bibles and several leadership books he had authored.

Pastor Jack greeted Janelle with a warm smile. He wore a crisp dress shirt and slacks, both freshly ironed and creased. His hair was carefully groomed, and nails manicured, his manner friendly and engaging. Throughout the conversation, however, Janelle noticed that, despite the broad smile, Jack's eyes seemed distant and detached even though he was looking directly at her. He avoided questions about himself. He seemed both distracted and focused at the same time. Each time she began to share something about a potential counseling and recovery ministry, he changed the subject. When she tried to describe the emotional needs of Christians and how lay and professional counseling could help, he suggested that she get involved in the Women's Bible Study ministry, which he felt was sufficient counseling help for believers.

Within a few years, Janelle began to hear reports of verbal abuse, public humiliation of church members, and the sexual harassment of staff. Not long afterward, Pastor Jack's use of pornography on church computers was exposed and it was revealed he had been having sex with young men and women involved in a sex trafficking ring. He was arrested and court ordered into psychotherapy.

Like Janelle, you may have wondered why prominent people like Pastor Jack and other priests, political leaders, and businesspeople often find themselves embroiled in sex scandals involving prostitution and pornography. Although each situation is unique and extraordinarily complex, trauma and the difficulties connecting intimately with others are common underlying themes. Sex crimes are primarily about the abuse of power, not about sexual relations or genuine intimacy, both of which require the sharing of power and respect for the needs and choices of others. Highly successful men and women often use achievement as a substitute for genuine bonding and attachment. At the beginning, the abuse of power can be subtle manipulation, which escapes the notice of others. Eventually, though, the inability to share power and engage in meaningful reciprocal relationships can escalate into destructive and even criminal behavior.

The Importance of Understanding Our History

It is not at all unusual for men like Pastor Jack and women in similar situations to enter my office and tell me that there is no reason to look into their past history. They remind me that according to 2 Corinthians 5:17 (NASB), they are new creations in Christ and therefore the old is gone. When asked the reason they might read the books of the Old Testament, they begin to see that I am not asking them to dig up dirt from the past for the purpose of mudslinging at parents or getting stuck in the mire of past sins, but for the purpose of learning. "For whatever was written in earlier times was written for our instruction so that through perseverance and the encouragement of the Scriptures we might have hope" (Romans 15:4, NASB). I remind them that we all have an Old Testament in our lives that we can allow the Holy Spirit to illuminate for the purpose of healing and growth.

Whenever we are resistant to looking at our history, there is likely something disturbing under the surface. If we do have a painful past, we may believe that sharing this information with others could be a blight on our testimony for Christ. Yet Scripture tells the real and raw histories of men and women without apology or fear. We do not get redacted or revised versions of the lives of Moses, Miriam, or Aaron. The truth about their lives, both good and bad, informs us of mistakes common to the human race. The revealing of David's secret sins reassures us that God's love is not based on putting our best foot forward but in admitting when our feet are broken. We must stay the course of healing even when it is painful.

Sadly, it is not unusual for gifted leaders like Pastor Jack to have unconscious and unresolved traumatic wounds in their background that have been buried and unattended for years. When symptoms or incidents arise, they are spiritualized away, emotionally minimized, and even completely denied. A profound sense of shame keeps many bound in an internal prison where they are unable to expose their own abuse of authority to anyone, including their closest friends and family members. They often deny any knowledge of such offenses experienced as children by adults or offenses they have perpetrated against others. "The stress of these family issues creates a loneliness that creates vulnerability. When vulnerability leads to sexual sin, we face the opportunity to heal."[63]

---

63 Earle, Ralph H. Jr. and Laaser, Mark R. *The Pornography Trap: Setting Pastors and Laypersons Free from Sexual Addiction.* Kansas City: Beacon Hill Press, 2002. (34)

These unacknowledged wounds interfere with their ability to cultivate genuine and intimate relationships and lead to deep internal loneliness and isolation that fuels addiction, despite the appearance of having numerous friends and acquaintances. In many cases, unacknowledged abuse transforms itself into self-abuse or another form of abusing personal power over others, even if it is not the same kind of abuse. A man who was physically abused by his father and witnessed violence against his mother may vow to never hit his future wife, only to use excessive discipline with his children that crosses the line into verbal, emotional, physical, or sexual abuse. Someone with a history of substance abuse may stop using illicit drugs only to exchange it for another powerful prescription drug addiction without ever exploring the legitimate needs that fueled the past and present use of drugs and medication.

Participating in Treatment

If there is to be healing in us as leaders in the Body of Christ, it is essential to understand the connection between abuses of power perpetrated against us and those against whom we have perpetrated abuse. Pastor Jack lived five decades before discovering wounds from his past related to his most recent criminal behavior that robbed him of genuine intimacy. It is my experience that church leadership is often tempted to use bandages with bleeding clergy when tourniquets and surgery are needed. They fear besmirching the name of Christ, losing membership, and being fired from their jobs. The prophet Jeremiah said it this way, "From the least to the greatest, all are greedy for gain; prophets and priests alike, all practice deceit. They dress the wound of my people as though it were not serious. 'Peace, peace,' they say, when there is no peace" (Jeremiah 8:10b–11, TNIV).

It is not within the scope of this section to give extensive attention to the important topics related to a person like Pastor Jack. My purpose is to briefly illustrate some of what is often underneath the stubborn, sinful, and destructive behaviors that defy a leader's past attempts to master them. God asked Cain why he was angry with his brother Abel. The pivotal question of our wonderful Counselor God was an invitation to intimacy that could have begun with Cain's willingness to first self-reflect, then expose his vulnerable feelings to God, and finally to master the sinful rage that could escalate into murder. We see that Cain did none of these life-giving tasks. He did not engage in self-reflection or any dialogue with his Creator but instead chose to express a murderous rage against his brother Abel.

In the beginning of the therapeutic process, Jack was unable to remember large chunks of his childhood. He revealed that his father was a well-known pastor in a large Midwest church and was known for passionate preaching against premarital sex, adultery, and homosexuality. As he began to reflect on his relationship with his father, he described behavior that was abusive and humiliating. Under the guise of wise parenting, Jack's father had exposed him to pornography at an early age. His father claimed he wanted to teach Jack about his sexuality before other ungodly influences could corrupt him. When he and Jack went on private spiritual retreats, his father brought illicit pornography with pictures of men acting out sexually with other men, women, and children.

As an adolescent, Jack was confused about sexuality and tried to share his guilt about these experiences with a trusted adult who was also an elder at his father's church. The elder had a legal, moral, and ethical responsibility to report this behavior to the authorities and to protect this young man. Instead, the son was told by the elder to forgive his father and not to share this with anyone or he would be responsible for his father losing his job in the ministry, leaving the entire family destitute.

This kind of lie has ravaged the lives of countless victims and allowed untold numbers of clergy to escape conviction for crimes against children and adults. I also believe this is a crime committed against the clergy themselves. It has prevented genuine repentance on the part of the offender and interfered with the opportunity for treatment that could bring genuine healing. Such behavior must have severe consequences unmitigated by any amount of forgiveness by the victims or those to whom the perpetrators are accountable.

The process of professional psychotherapy often exposes the abuse of authority that many men and women have experienced in their own lives at the hands of trusted loved ones. It allows them to see how they have gone on to use people and substances to medicate their wounds and avoid the healing pain necessary for true long-term recovery. Legitimate explanations, however, do not excuse abusive domestic and criminal behavior, nor do they mitigate the damage caused by such behavior. Taking responsibility in open and honest ways, though painful, releases the toxic shame that hiding, denying, and blaming store up to continue poisoning both the offenders and victims for generations to come.

It may be difficult and at times feel impossible to imagine having compassion for someone like Pastor Jack. Others who are close to such leaders will find it difficult and nearly impossible to take this information about a beloved leader to the civil authorities. For this reason, it is essential to reach outside the synod, church, or school system in order to get professional help to navigate this treacherous water. There are professional Christian psychotherapists and psychologists who specialize in walking with governing bodies of such churches, schools, and organizations through this process. Without professional intervention, the blind spots of any person—even a mental health professional who attends that church—interfere with and prevent an objective assessment of the situation and necessary action and accountability. The Life Model Works founded by Dr. Jim Wilder is an example of one such resource.[64]

For those who have been abused, it is possible to learn slowly, over much time, and for their own well-being as well as the perpetrator's, how to forgive atrocities without forgetting, minimizing, excusing, or even trusting such a person ever again. There is a vast difference between offering forgiveness and extending trust.[65] It may take years, but it is possible to let go of the hurt, anger, and pain of abuse and also maintain healthy boundaries that prevent further abuse.

While it is true that we experience forgiveness from God the moment we repent of sin, the wounds of sin committed by us or against us rarely heal in relationships without a long and arduous process of restoration. There is much written about abuse of power within the Church and society. Others have written sensitively about the topic of forgiveness. Diane Langberg's books, *Redeeming Power* and *Suffering and the Heart of God*[66] are two excellent resources. On a societal scale, Desmond Tutu has written on forgiveness from the point of view of those who suffered from the abuse of both the government and individuals who

---

64   www.lifemodelworks.org
65   Cloud, Henry. *Trust: In Life and Business.* New York, New York: Worthy Books. 2023.
66   Langberg, Diane. *Redeeming Power: Understanding Authority and Abuse in the Church* and Langberg, Diane. *Suffering and the Heart of God: How Trauma Destroys and Christ Restores.* Greensboro, NC: New Growth Press. 2015.

supported apartheid in South Africa.[67] There are other excellent books available that treat both of these topics with the careful, thoughtful attention they deserve.

It is important to not only treat the symptoms of contaminated intimacy, but to prevent the conditions that make us vulnerable to it. If we look at one another through the lens of the curses and consequences of sin, we will continue to believe that God's highest intention for humans involves exercising authority over one another rather than sharing authority with one another. This belief system contains a subtle attitude of entitlement that delights in having authority and power over others rather than a humility that invites rather than demands mutually satisfying relations. Are we willing to do a fierce moral inventory of our own theological and characterological blind spots and the ways we try to control others to get our needs met rather than doing the hard work of taking personal responsibility for ourselves and engaging in mutual negotiations? In the next chapter, we will look at how relationships are also contaminated by reducing one another to prescribed roles rather than allowing God to develop the vast and diverse humanity He created.

---

67 Tutu, Desmond. *The Book of Forgiving: The Fourfold Path for Healing Ourselves and Our World*. New York, New York: HarperCollins Publishers. 2015.

CHAPTER 9

Contaminated Relationships

"When anyone outside of Jesus Christ is allowed to define us, we become a slave to human ideas rather than God's Holy Spirit. A theology that rigidly defines identity according to the curses and consequences of the Fall is more concerned about a law of gender roles, stereotypes, and a worldly force of power than the grace of expressing the beauty and diversity of a person's unique gifts and talents."

—Cindi J. Martin

I ntimate relationships are God's priority for all of Creation. Yet without a nuanced understanding of God's highest intention for human relationships, our fallen human nature defaults into living the curses and consequences of the Fall. We unconsciously merge the language of the Fall, such as ruling others, with the worldly language of leadership, such as following a chain of command. The rules and roles of organizational survival quickly replace the responsiveness and reciprocity of living relational systems that understand the necessity of shared authority and mutual responsibility.

Relationship and Roles

Post-Fall humans easily conflate roles with relationships. While it is not wrong to use the word "role," we must be aware of some of the inherent dangers of defining

93

people primarily through this particular lens. Who we are as persons transcends the role a man or woman takes on. Being the beloved daughter or son of God is not just a role; it is our personhood, at the very core of our existence.

Throughout much of the Church's history, its theologians and leaders have taught that women are equally saved but intrinsically unequal to men. Many in Church history have believed that women are less intelligent and less capable than men, as well as more prone to instability and deception.[68]

In 1977, George Knight III wrote a book introducing the idea of "equal" but "different" roles for men and women. This kind of language raises immediate suspicion in light of those who suffered from similar language under Jim Crow laws that continued to discriminate against black Americans even after the Civil War. "In legal theory, blacks received 'separate but equal' treatment under the law—in actuality, public facilities for blacks were nearly always inferior to those for whites, when they existed at all. In addition, blacks were systematically denied the right to vote in most of the rural South through the selective application of literary tests and other racially motivated criteria."[69]

Like in the case of "separate but equal" for Black Americans, this idea of "equal" but "different" roles for women is another distortion of truth that robs them of their freedom, power, and authority in Christ. It continues to gain popularity among evangelicals who support the subjugation of women but crushes the kind of marital mutuality and intimacy promoted by Jesus and the apostles throughout the New Testament.

In 2004, a group of theologians moved from the idea of "equal with different roles" to the idea that the Trinity supported the subjection of wives to husbands because Jesus subjected Himself to the Father. According to Terran Williams, other trusted theologians came together in 2016 and successfully challenged those who were moving in the direction of Wayne Grudem's Eternal Functional Subordination theology. According to Terran Williams, this position "veers in a similar direction to, though not going as far as, the ancient heresy of Arianism in

---

68 Langberg, Diane. *Redeeming Power. Authority and Abuse in the Church*. Grand Rapids, Michigan: Brazos Publishers. A division of Baker Publishing Group. 2020.

69 Williams, Terran. "Subordinating Jesus and Women (and How Influential Evangelical Teachers Led Us Astray)". Priscilla Paper 36/3 Summer 2022.cbeinternational.org (10)

which the Son is in eternal essence less than the Father."[70] Williams quotes Liam Goligher's statement during the debate: "To say that there is a real primacy of the Father or subordination of the Son within the eternal trinity is to have moved out of Christian orthodoxy."[71] This debate among evangelicals illustrates how far some will go to maintain a post-Fall hierarchy of roles within marriage rather than support the shared authority and power that cultivates mutuality and intimacy in marriage and all Christian relationships.

The New Testament uses the metaphor of a body and living organism to describe both the Bride of Christ and the mysterious marriage of the Bridegroom Christ to His Church. The exclusive or primary use of the word "role" is problematic because it is a word borrowed from 17th century French theater. It means the "the part played by a person in life," and was literally the actor's part in a play written on a "roll" of paper.

Sadly, many women and men are taught to play a rigid role as it is found in a few selected verses in New Testament Epistles. Instead, a survey of Scripture from Genesis to Revelation teaches us that God transcends our limited cultural contexts for gender and leads us in bold and expansive ways of becoming all He imagined us to be as unique, complex, and talented persons made in His image. It is therefore important to reevaluate the use of the word "role" as it relates to both men and women, whether in the marital relationship or within the general Body of Christ.

First and foremost, a role primarily describes how we "act" and is more about behavior than genuine personhood. Men and women, husbands and wives, can be best understood as whole persons with unique differences. Outside the sphere of theater and play acting, a person told to play a role that is inconsistent with who they are as individuals not only crushes the spirit of their personhood but also quenches the unique and creative work of the Holy Spirit. While it is true that I can interact differently with others as a wife, mother, daughter, and friend, I interact primarily as a person within these relationships, not as a role with a prescribed set of particular behaviors. Humans, male and female, were made in the image of

---

70   Williams, Terran. "Subordinating Jesus and Women (and How Influential Evangelical Teachers Led Us Astray)". Priscilla Paper 36/3 Summer 2022.cbeinternational.org (10)
71   Williams, Terran. "Subordinating Jesus and Women (and How Influential Evangelical Teachers Led Us Astray)". Priscilla Paper 36/3 Summer 2022.cbeinternational.org (13)

our triune God who is One God in three persons, not One God in three roles. We must resist the temptation to conform to roles that reflect worldly facades, even when wrapped in biblical language. It was Satan who used Scripture to tempt Jesus in the wilderness on the eve of His earthly ministry (Matthew 4:1–10).

There are many biblical stories in which both men and women did not fit the stereotypic male or female behavior of their particular time in history, so we see God often working outside the particular cultural descriptors of a woman or man. Our relationships to God, ourselves, and others are compromised when we are not allowed to develop the gifts and talents we were given by God. Intimacy is sabotaged by trying to be someone we are not and by indeed acting out a role that we think others may expect of us. It is further compromised by the fear that, in revealing our true selves, we will be rejected and abandoned by those with whom we seek closeness and connection.

Rigid Gender Stereotypes

One such example is that of the Old Testament judge and warrior, Deborah (Judges 4:4). It is most egregious to hear some pastors dismiss the person and work of Deborah as an anomaly on God's part. It has been said that God only allowed Deborah to be a judge in Israel because He could not find a qualified man to do the job. (As if God's preference is always a man for a leadership role, but He will settle for a woman when He must.) Examples of outstanding female leadership in Scripture are more frequent than we are taught; female leaders are in no way inferior to male leaders. This premise is truly dishonoring to God, women, and men.

Deborah was among women prophetesses named in the Bible including Miriam (Exodus 15:20, AMP), Huldah (2 Kings 22:14; 2 Chronicles 34:22, AMP), Noadiah (Nehemiah 6:14, AMP) and an unnamed prophetess from Israel (mentioned in Isaiah 8:3, AMP). In the New Testament, Anna is named a prophetess (Luke 2:36, AMP), Mary and other women prophesy according to Acts 1:14 and 2:17, and the daughters of Phillip are called virgins who prophesy (Act 21:9, KJV).

Leslie and Bill

"Is it wrong for me to want to work outside my home?" asked Leslie in tears during her first counseling appointment. She felt guilty for her daydreams about returning to school to finish her teaching credential. She felt herself slipping into depression and wondered if she needed to be on medication. She also felt irritable and was snapping at her children more than usual. When she brought up the subject with her husband, Bill, he insisted that her job was as wife and helper to him and then as a mother to their children. He could not see how she could get everything done around the house and pursue her own "selfish ambitions." "After all," he insisted, "I am the one who pays the bills so you can stay home and care for our family. I am not going to pay for you to get an education that will take you away from us. Maybe when the kids are out of the house, you can go back to school."

Leslie's situation is a familiar one in many Christian families, and yet it is difficult for many couples to approach this sensitive issue. When conflicts such as these result in mental or physical health symptoms, we would be wise to listen to clues that carry a message about what we may be feeling, thinking, and experiencing on an unconscious or subconscious level. For example, her guilt, depression, and irritability may be alerting her to conflicts that she is unable to confront within herself and her marriage for fear of the losses they represent.

If Leslie is honest about how much she wants to go back to school and work as a teacher, she may lose Bill's approval and affection. She may be accused of being selfish, or of not loving God, her husband, or her children enough. If she believes that going against her husband is tantamount to disobeying God, she may even experience some hidden anger toward God. This can activate feelings of doubt about the legitimacy of a faith that puts her husband in control of decisions that impact her life in such fundamental ways. I have often seen such thoughts cascade into a crisis of faith. When a married woman struggles with these kinds of thoughts and feelings, it is critical that she find safe spiritual companions, friends, and counselors with whom she is allowed to express doubts and questions rather than be compelled to either maintain the status quo or make a complete break from her faith or marriage.

Leslie and Bill will need some time to sort out the meaning of these conflicts and both will have to learn some tools to engage with one another in redefining what marriage means to them. As discussed in Chapter 3, when God said He would make a "helper" or "helpmate" corresponding to Adam, God did not use a word that meant Eve was to be Adam's subordinate or domestic servant. Instead, God used an expansive word for helpmate that reveals the kind of intimate companionship that God himself offers to humankind.

Leslie's situation can help to shed light on God's highest intention for women and couples. As previously discussed, we are *ezer*, made in God's image, and endowed with expansive gifts and talents that bring glory to God. There are many and diverse combinations of family life. Some women are most fulfilled using their gifts and talents within their homes while others combine marriage and family with a career. If you or your spouse have encountered conflict around this topic, I hope you will consider seeking out professional help to find a mutually satisfying agreement. An openness to our Lord's creative way of *We* in marriage can increase intimacy by healing wounds, resolving conflict, and developing your gifts as individuals and as a couple to the glory of God.

Certainly, women have been primary wage earners and have provided for their families in countless ways for millennia and have worked and sweated alongside men, whether on the land, in factories, or in homes. At times they have become forced labor in their own homes and in some countries are still sold into slavery for the benefit of their husbands. But before the Fall, the division of labor was not related to gender, pain in childbirth, domination, strength to subdue those weaker, or the stamina to endure physical labor. Before the Fall, women and men ruled together, shared tasks, and managed the earth's resources together. God created us human beings, male and female, to live and work as one.

Dorothy L. Sayers, a contemporary and friend of C.S. Lewis wrote a collection of 21 essays in 1947 called *Unpopular Opinions*. In one essay entitled, "Are Women Human," Sayers writes, "A woman is just as much an ordinary human being as a man, with the same individual preferences, and with just as much right to the tastes and preferences of an individual. What is repugnant to every human being is to be reckoned always as a member of a class and not as an individual person…What is unreasonable and irritating is to assume that all one's tastes and preferences have to be conditioned by the class to which one belongs. That has been the very common error into which men have frequently fallen about women—and it is the error into which feminist women are, perhaps, a little inclined to fall about themselves."[72]

---

72   Sayers, Dorothy L. *Are Women Human? Astute and Witty Essay on the Role of Women in Society.* Grand Rapids, Michigan, Wm.B. Eerdmans Publishing Co, 1971 (24–25).

Mutuality and Interdependence

Modern science is constantly proving what the Apostle Paul understood spiritually when he described the metaphor of a mutually submissive and interdependent human head and body (1 Corinthians 12, NIV). Today, research continues to reveal the interconnectedness of the human brain and body, so much so that the stomach is now being called the second brain. Scientists call this the enteric nervous system (ENS). This consists of "two thin layers of more than 100 million nerve cells lining your gastrointestinal tract from esophagus to rectum."[73] The mental health community has long suspected that there is a connection between anger, depression, and anxiety with digestive and gastro-intestinal problems. The mutual submission of the mind and body and its collaborative nature is supported by continuing studies that show a higher-than-normal percentage of people known in medicine as Irritable Bowel Syndrome (IBS) and functional bowel problems who also develop depression and anxiety. Today gastroenterologists are prescribing antidepressants and mind-body therapies to help these two brains talk to each other. In addition, "it may also show up as high blood pressure, rapid heart rate, shallow breathing (overstimulated sympathetic nervous system), insomnia, fatigue, and possibly even autoimmune diseases."[74]

In Ephesians 5:21, we find this key to understanding human relationships among all believers: "Be subject to one another in reverence to Christ." This command is not a worldly, top-down hierarchy of roles, but a vitally interdependent relationship of mutual submission. Have you ever dropped something on your toe? Have you noticed that your head cannot think of anything but your toe when it is hurting? Have you noticed how mutually submissive your toe and head become in an attempt to bring healing and restoration to the body? Even if we think of the husband as the head and the wife as the body, we very quickly recognize the mutual and complementary ways that husbands and wives interact by submitting to one another in love. The idea that the head does all the leading even in the human body is a fallacy. The head and the body work together in myriad ways and are most effective when each system is listening and responding properly to the other systems.

---

73 John Hopkins Medicine. "The Brain-Gut Connection," *Health*, 2023. https://www.hopkinsmedicine.org/health/wellness-and-prevention/the-brain-gut-connection
74 Dr. Robert Chin. Personal Communication. April 20, 2023.

Failure to honor the shared power and authority of the various systems of the body is done at our own peril. It is my understanding, for example, that with cancer, a healthy cell begins to multiply uncontrollably. The feedback loop that keeps the number of cells in a healthy balance is disrupted, almost as if it is not listening to the other parts of the body. It is as if these cells begin to act unilaterally outside the balance of the rest of the body. Eventually those extra cells become tumors and can block or otherwise inhibit healthy bodily functioning. It is even more dangerous when part of the tumor breaks off and begins to make tumors in other places in the body. This breaking off and appearing elsewhere is what we commonly call metastasis. This can often lead to death because the cells refuse to be in mutual submission to the rest of the body's signals about where and how many cells to produce.

Conclusion of Part II

We have spent a considerable amount of time here looking at the curses and consequences of the Fall. We have seen how a legitimate desire for "knowledge that makes one wise" was distorted by the serpent's temptation to indulge in the human "Me Principle" rather than intimately abide in the divine "We Principle." Like all who initially sow the seemingly necessary seeds of independence, Adam and Eve reaped in their disobedience an unexpected harvest of human horror: inequality, division, domination, control, patriarchy, identity loss, shame, profound loneliness, destruction, and death.

For many who read the Bible, it seems the Old Testament portrays a great many examples of these human horrors. Much of God's instructions in the Torah are understood to promote patriarchy. Commands that involve capital punishment (among many other commands and instructions) appear primitive or unjust to modern readers. It is commonly assumed in the culture at large (and often in the Church) that the nature and character of the Old Testament God seems to be diametrically opposed to the nature and character of the New Testament God in Christ. Yet a more careful and comprehensive reading of the Bible reveals that this is not the case. It is the nature and character of evil and sin that have changed the human condition and it is the way God interacts with Creation rather than the nature and character of God that has changed. Throughout Scripture, God demonstrates that He is a God who is loving, merciful, and gracious, desiring an intimate relationship with His children.

If we draw our picture of God solely on the basis of the harsh and brutal consequences of sin reflected in the Old Testament and the Mosaic Law and disregard His willingness to walk out of the Garden and into the Wilderness with His children, we will have misunderstood the greatest love story of all time. He did not reject or abandon us. God shows incomparable love for His people despite constant rejection and disregard for His goodness in our lives throughout history. God is not the source of patriarchy. We must be careful not to conflate the consequences of sin with the character of God.

As we come to the end of Part II, we have now seen the massive changes that resulted from humans choosing to know evil. We explored the curses and consequences of the Fall, along with its impact on our identity and relationships. We also looked at how sin, rather than God's highest intentions for humans, is responsible for the creation of a patriarchal power structure governing interaction between humans and the natural world. Despite God's warning, rules replaced intimate relationships and communal harmony, which was God's intended end for His people. Finally, we discovered how the post-Fall way of defining marital relationships has robbed couples of personhood and replaced it with rigid roles, devoid of the creative power of mutuality that leads to deep intimate connection.

PART III:

Transformed Soil
In The New Creation Era

"'Not by might nor by power, but by my Spirit,'
says the Lord Almighty."
(Zechariah 4:6, NIV)

CHAPTER 10

Transformed Social Relationships

"Therefore, if anyone is in Christ, the new creation has come; the old has gone, the new is here. All this is from God, who reconciled us to Himself through Christ and gave us the ministry of reconciliation: that God was reconciling the world to himself in Christ, not counting people's sins against them...God made Him who had no sin to be sin for us so that in Him we might become the righteousness of God."

(2 Corinthians 5:17–18, 21, NIV)

In staying with our soil metaphor, it is as if the life, death, and resurrection of Jesus became rich organic, composted material that amended and transformed dead, contaminated soil, and brought it back to life. The fruit of the Holy Spirit can replace the spoiled fruit of sinful flesh. Believers in Jesus are gifted not only with a New Creation nature, but also the power of the indwelling Holy Spirit to live out God's highest intentions for humans on this earth. Practically, there will be tribulation and trial. Nevertheless, we have been transformed and are invited to live into this new Spirit-led life with one another.

In the New Creation Era, the incarnated Son of God does for His heavenly Father on Earth what Adam and Eve and the rest of humanity could not do: consistently choose good over evil and overcome sin and death. As a result, the curses and consequences of the post-Fall world are crucified with Christ and the magnificent pre-Fall design for humans is matched and even surpassed in the resurrection and eschatological reality of Jesus Christ.

We encounter Christ as He invites humans into a relationship with God that not only gives humans victory over the Fall but goes far beyond it to make us like Him through His indwelling Holy Spirit. Christ rises above the Post-Fall Era by demonstrating how to respect human authority while challenging and reversing it. We consider how social relationships, intimate friendship, and even grief are transformed as we live our lives as new creations in Christ.

We will also learn that in order to enjoy the benefits of Christ's victory, we must reevaluate the ways in which we have misunderstood biblical authority and rationalized it for power and control over others. We can choose to enter into the joy of intimate communion with our triune God and one another. The Body of Christ can demonstrate the beauty of shared authority and power in Christ and live incarnationally for the benefit, blessing, and growth of all Creation.

In the New Creation Era, both women and men, singles and couples, and people of every social status, tribe, tongue, and nation have the opportunity to become equal, diverse, and united members of the Body of Christ without partiality. They joyfully enter into the intimate knowing of God, themselves, and one another in order to share power and control that once again blesses and nourishes all of creation. Humans are to responsibly manage natural resources with their power and authority rather than exploiting it or ruling over fellow humans. They are to enjoy the mutual responsibility of building a world together that reflects the love and creativity of their Creator's original intention, and they are to invite all without distinction to repent of sin, believe in the risen Christ, and join the family of God.

Rising above the Fall

Since Jesus ushered in the New Creation Era on Earth, we must look to His life to see how we are to walk in the power of His Spirit. We need to see what God's highest intention for humans on earth looks like practically, where human evil continues to battle for supremacy on a daily basis. We need an example of God's hope for the new Creation despite our weaknesses, flaws, and penchant toward indulging self-interest in all the ways of the Fall. Jesus shows us how to rise above the Fall by His interactions with people and Creation.

Competition and Cooperation

John the Baptist, a cousin of Jesus, was a powerful figure in Jesus' life. John's purpose was to prepare the way for Jesus the Messiah. At the beginning of Jesus' public ministry, a competitive spirit arose between Jesus' disciples and those of John the Baptist. The disciples of John were worried that so many of his disciples were leaving the Baptist to follow Jesus. In response, John quickly established God's sovereign authority and his own humility as supreme:

> "A person can receive only what is given them from heaven. You yourselves can testify that I said, 'I am not the Messiah but am sent ahead of him.' The bride belongs to the bridegroom. The friend who attends the bridegroom waits and listens for him, and is full of joy when he hears the bridegroom's voice. That joy is mine, and it is now complete. He must become greater; I must become less."
>
> **(John 3:27–30, NIV)**

John was declaring that there were differences between himself and Jesus, but that these differences would combine rather than divide them and their ministries. John used this Bridegroom-Bride metaphor to illustrate their solidarity, his unique purpose, as well as his intent to cooperate with the purposes of God rather than compete for notoriety among humans. This is significant in understanding the metaphor of bridegroom and bride when used both to describe the relationship between Christ and His Church and later the relationship between husband and wife—differences made to combine, not divide. Humans want to exploit differences to empower themselves or enslave others, whereas Spirit-led disciples of Christ want to complement one another and collaborate for a greater purpose.

This encounter between Jesus and John the Baptist reveals the strong character of both of these men, an understanding of their own individual identities apart from one another, a unity of purpose in cooperating together in relation to one another's unique calling, and their ability to support one another. They were able to do this in loving, affirming, humble, yet truthful ways, even when tempted by a crowd of peers who were competing for notoriety. A secure identity is the best antidote for a competitive spirit. This is a portrait of mutuality between a humble God and man in an intimate, Spirit-filled, New Creation relationship. Even though God has supreme authority in the person of Jesus Christ, He wields that power not by lording it over John, but by generously sharing it. This is the example we want to follow whether we are friends, roommates, ministry partners, or marital spouses.

Breaking Down Gender, Racial, Religious, and Socio-Economic Barriers

The Gospel of John also provides rich examples of how Jesus interacted with people who were diverse in personality, purpose, gender, ethnicity, religion, and social class. Although Jesus was God, He did not rule over women in the spirit of the Fall or the culture of His day. In fact, the next encounter recorded in the Gospel of John (after the incident with John the Baptist's disciples) is with not only a woman, but a *Samaritan* woman. It is no mistake that Jesus, a Jew who normally had no dealings with ethnic Samaritans, quickly turned issues of gender, race, and religion upside down by stopping in Samaria to talk theology with a woman. This woman was amazed that Jesus knew about the details of her marital history and surmised that he was a prophet (John 4: 4–19, NIV). This was a culture where women were not allowed to study theology or even sit with men in a synagogue. Yet Jesus took time to know her intimately, care for her, and teach her. She took his message to the men and women of her village and became one of the first to spread the message about Christ as the promised Messiah. Jesus elevated the dignity and status of women, men, and children in every encounter He had with them during His earthly ministry.

If the soil of our hearts has truly been transformed and we are indeed new creations in Christ, then why have many orthodox[75] Christians lived so long as if relations between men and women are still defined by the curses and conse-

---

75 When I use the term orthodox, I am referring to those who, regardless of denominational affiliation, would in good conscience join together in a confession of faith as codified in the Apostles' Creed or Nicene Creed.

quences of the Fall? What prevents us from living out the New Creation values of equal and shared power between men and women modeled by Jesus and reflected in our triune God's Creation design?

One answer I propose to these questions is that we who confess Christ have not fully known or followed the way of Jesus. Instead, we prefer power to humility, leadership to followership, lording authority over others rather than generously sharing it. Will we dehumanize those who are more vulnerable and exploit them for personal gain? Do we prefer to hate our social and political enemies because they disagree with what we believe is right and wrong? These are not examples of following the way of our Savior. Even the phrase "servant leadership," coined by Robert K. Greenleaf in 1970,[76] has been misused by spiritual leaders to enforce a top-down leadership style that was the antithesis of the way Jesus shared authority with His disciples. The sacrificial serving of others is not compatible with the top-down leadership style of this world.

Jesus has risen above the Fall. Humans, including Christians, have descended into the curses and consequences of the Fall and refashioned them in our own image. We can choose whether to follow God's original design or live out the consequences of sin. The contrast between Jesus' life and the world's view of leadership, diversity, gender, ethnicity, power, and authority is glaring.

Are we willing to measure ourselves against His example that both redefines authority and power and lives above the Fall, in opposition to the effects of the Fall on Earth? If we do find ourselves in a position of human leadership, what does the life of Christ teach us about how to manage power and authority in those positions? Without brutal self-examination and intentionality to rise above the Fall by walking in the Spirit, we will continue to live out the consequences of the Fall and call it biblical orthodoxy.

The Extraordinary Way of Jesus

So how exactly did Jesus live out the life of the Spirit in a world ruled by the flesh of the Fall? A brief survey of the Gospels poignantly illustrates the brilliance and divinity of Jesus as He lived above the Fall and by the Spirit in a world controlled

---

76 Nouwen, Henri J. M. *In the Name of Jesus: Reflections on Christian Leadership.* Crossroad Publishers. 1992. (62–63)

by evil flesh. In the midst of a complex, polarized, and antagonistic world, Jesus lived a perfect and harmonious balance of mercy, justice, and humility. He often walked into the tension of multiple extremes. In contrast, humans often divide, choose sides, and avoid the nuanced thought demanded by complexity in favor of quick, shallow, and simplistic solutions.

If Jesus had been a mere man, He might well have come and simply criticized moral laws for how they were indiscriminately applied by the religious leaders to benefit themselves. Instead, when a woman was caught in the act of adultery, and legally could have been stoned, Jesus challenged the moral zealots to cast the first stone if they could claim to be without sin.[77] It was not enough to simply obey the commandment to not commit adultery. Jesus challenged the people to consider their internal thoughts and intentions. Lusting in one's heart for another man or woman rather than your own spouse is also considered an egregious sin.[78]

The promised Messiah could have come to Earth to criticize the Law of Moses for failing to reform His people Israel. Instead, when the Jewish religious leaders rebuked Him for disobeying the Sabbath by allowing His disciples to pluck and eat the heads of wheat in a grain field, Jesus reminded them that the Sabbath was made for humans, not humans for the Sabbath.[79] Jesus taught that it was not enough to obey a commandment like "Thou shalt not murder." Instead, abstaining from murderous thoughts and restraining the rage that dehumanizes others by calling them names like *Raca* (possibly Aramaic for empty-headed) or "You Fool" is what fulfills the spirit of the law.[80]

Jesus could have come to Earth and expressed outrage directly against gender, racial, and social class cruelty, and injustice. Instead, He built relationships with women and men that cut across these lines and was called a sinner by religious leaders because of His associations.[81] He could have revolted against government and unfair taxation or joined a particular political party. Instead, when asked about paying taxes, He invited His inquisitors to look a Roman coin and tell Him

---

77   John 8:7 (TNIV)
78   Matthew 5:28 (TNIV)
79   Mark 2:27 (TNIV)
80   Matthew 5:22 (TNIV)
81   Matthew 9:10–17 (TNIV)

whose face was reflected there, and to "give back to Caesar what is Caesar's, and to God what is God's."[82]

Jesus, a person of the Holy Trinity who was equal to His Father, could have come to Earth and rebelled against His heavenly Father's authority. Instead, Jesus,

> *"...who being in very nature God, did not consider equality with God something to be used to his own advantage; rather, he made himself nothing by taking the very nature of a servant, being made in human likeness. And being found in appearance as a human being, he humbled himself by becoming obedient to death – even death on a cross. Therefore, God exalted him to the very highest place and gave him the name that is above every, name, that at the name of Jesus every knee should bow, in heaven and on earth, and under the earth, and every tongue acknowledge that Jesus Christ is Lord to the glory of God the Father."*
>
> **(Philippians 2:6–11, TNIV)**

This humility is the way of intimacy. This is the power of mutuality in relationships.

---

82 Matthew 22:21 (TNIV)

CHAPTER 11

Transformed Friendship

> *"No longer do I call you slaves, for the slave does not know what his master is doing; but I have called you friends, for all things that I have heard from My Father I have made known to you."*
>
> **(John 15:15, NASB 1995)**

An Invitation to Humility in Friendship

Jesus, the Son of God, and rightly called Master by His students, taught a humble way of leading that was unknown in the ancient world. This was exemplified at the Lord's Supper when, just after sharing with His disciples that He was about to be betrayed, the disciples began discussing among themselves who was the greatest. In response, Jesus reminded them of the difference between the authority and power of the human world and that of the Kingdom of God:

> *"Jesus said to them, 'The kings of the Gentiles lord it over them; and those who exercise authority over them call them Benefactors. But you are not to be like that. Instead, the greatest among you should be like the youngest, and the one who rules like the one who serves.'"*
>
> **(Luke 22:25–27, TNIV)**

A human religious leader might have sharply rebuked them or even given them a lecture on the difference between pride and humility. Jesus did not criticize or condemn His disciples for exposing their ambition for power or desire to be great. Instead, He taught them the true meaning of power and greatness in the Kingdom of God. Jesus was patient with the immature parts of His students; their vulnerability was safe with Him. Jesus allowed them to be spiritually, emotionally, and socially naked and unashamed in His presence.

Still not understanding greatness in the kingdom of God, the disciples asked on still another occasion, "Who then is greatest in the kingdom of heaven? This time Jesus explained it differently. He said,

> *"Truly I tell you, unless you change and become like little children you will never enter the kingdom of heaven. Therefore whoever humbles himself like this little child is the greatest in the kingdom of heaven. And whoever welcomes a little child like this in my name welcomes me. But if anyone causes one of these little ones who believe in Me to stumble, it would be better for him to have a large millstone hung around his neck and to be drowned in the depths of the sea."*
>
> **(Matthew 18:3–6, BSB)**

Jesus was concerned about the transformation of their hearts. Even here, Jesus turned worldly power upside down by exalting children and placing the heavy millstone of responsibility on those who might abuse both their adult power and the vulnerability of a child. Despite the disciples' continued displays of human weakness, Jesus desired their friendship. Just before His arrest, He spoke to them about a dramatic change that was about to take place in His relationship with them. His words are stunning:

> *"This is My commandment, that you love one another, just as I have loved you. Greater love has no one than this, that one lay down his life for his friends. You are My friends if you do what I command you. No longer do I call you slaves, for the slave does not know what his master is doing; but I have called you friends, for all things that I have heard from My Father I have made known*

to you. You did not choose Me but I chose you, and appointed
you that you would go and bear fruit, and that your fruit would
remain, so that whatever you ask of the Father in My name He
may give to you. This I command you, that you love one another.
(John 15:12–15, NASB)

Jesus subverted human power by merging the expected words of worldly authority (the command and obedience of servant and master) with the unexpected words of friendship and mutual intimacy (shared knowledge and reciprocity), words that challenged them to follow His example and love sacrificially. Jesus exemplified the kind of confident authority that shares power to elevate intimacy in friendship. This gentle and humble attitude toward His disciples did not diminish but demonstrated Jesus' authority and power as God. They continued to love, respect, and worship Him as God.

In what is known as the High Priestly Prayer to His heavenly Father, Jesus articulated His hope to leave the post-Fall earth and return to the eternal glory of the Trinity. He desired that His disciples share in this glory and live out the New Creation by His Spirit on Earth after His death and resurrection.

"These things Jesus spoke; and lifting up His eyes to heaven, He
said, 'Father, the hour has come: glorify Your Son, that the Son
may glorify You, even as You gave Him authority over all flesh,
that to all whom You have given Him, He may give eternal life.
Now, Father, glorify Me together with Yourself, with the glory
which I had with You before the world was. The glory which You
have given Me I have given to them, that they may be one just as
We are one; I in them and You in Me, that they may be perfected
in unity, so that the world may know that You sent Me, and loved
them, even as You have loved Me.'"
(John 17:1–3,5, 22–23, NASB)

In this prayer, Jesus mentions His pre-incarnational status in the Trinity before the foundations of the world. As the Son, Jesus freely chose to submit to His heavenly

Father to fulfill the law of God on Earth, which included suffering on Earth to usher in the final law of Love. Counterintuitively, the path of submission and obedience to the Father through the grief of the cross, death, and the grave would now reverse the curse and its consequences. With this new commandment to love one another as He loved them, Jesus again overturned the authority structure of the Fall and dealt a death blow to relationships that lord authority over others and crush intimacy. The death and resurrection of Christ restored to humans the beauty of relational authority and power as it was originally intended, to reflect the generous and humble nature of our trinitarian God, a community of intimate friends united by love.

An Invitation to the Vulnerability of Friendship

The truth that the Son of God wants an intimate friendship with us as humans is quite remarkable. We often talk casually about having a personal relationship with Christ, but many of us have not encountered close intimate relationships even within our families. Our skill set may not be up to the challenge of going beyond a relationship focused on *doing* and into the deep water of vulnerable *being*. There are volumes written about relationship building and yet we humans continue to be isolated and alone, lacking the connection that brings us close to those we care about.

One of our United States Surgeon Generals, Vivek Hallegere Murthy, reported in a 2023 interview that over 50 percent of our citizens are struggling with loneliness.[83] He says that this impacts both physical and mental health in profound ways. Prolonged loneliness is akin to smoking up to 15 cigarettes a day and can increase the risk of premature death by 26 percent. It also raises the likelihood of heart disease, stroke, anxiety, depression, and dementia.[84] The next few chapters explore how mutuality and shared power impacts our capacity to experience transformed friendships and experience the intimacy that brings joy and fulfillment to our whole being.

How do we cultivate intimate friendships with God and one another? My 17-year-old friend Janet was the first person that gave me a taste of intimate

---

83   Murthy, Vivek Hallegere. "To Be a Healer." April 13, 2023. On Being with Krista Tippet

84   Osborne, Margaret. May 10, 2023. *"An 'Epidemic of Loneliness' Threatens Health of Americans, Surgeon General Says." Smithsonian Magazine.* www.smithsonianmag.com

friendship. We met in a high school Gym class, and I still remember the joy I felt as she asked me questions about who I was, what I felt, and what I thought. She wanted to know me, my history, my opinions and hurts, and she also wanted me to know her. There was reciprocity. She gave me a felt sense of safety on an emotional, spiritual, and physical level.

As mentioned before, Janet also encouraged me to form a friendship with Jesus. She taught me to listen to God speak to my innermost being through the Holy Spirit as I read my Bible. She taught me to be more aware of my thoughts, feelings, and intentions, both positive and negative. She urged me to listen to friends and adults, and even to pay attention to nature and circumstances around me, all of which could help me with discernment. As a result, I learned to share the best and worst of myself with both God and Janet yet without any condemnation, judgment, rejection, or abandonment. I experienced a deep, abiding confidence that Jesus and Janet knew me, cared for me, and desired and delighted in my presence.

This intimate friendship with Janet and Jesus was transformational because it began to heal my deep childhood wounds, provided me with vast amounts of emotional and intellectual stimulation, and eventually led me into the counseling profession, first as a client and then as a therapist. When I was 19, Janet tragically died of a heart condition at the young age of 21, shortly after I was a bride's maid in her wedding. Her brief but influential life story is yet to be written. Needless to say, I was devastated. Little did I know that her death would teach me how to grieve important losses in my life and about the critical role that the capacity to mourn plays in cultivating and maintaining intimate relationships.

Before Janet's death and by God's kind mercy, I had also begun to forge another important friendship while working at a grocery during my senior year in high school. Her name was Shannon and she became my lifelong intimate and best girlfriend. She actually delivered the news of Janet's death to me because Janet's family had called the grocery store where I worked while trying to locate me to share the tragic news. Shannon was an important comfort to me following Janet's death. Over the next few years, we spent more time together, grew close, became roommates, experienced conflict, hurt one another, healed with one another, and matured in our relationship over the next 30 years. During the early years of those three decades, I met, dated, and married my husband Keith as well. Shannon remained single and we talked about how to maintain our friendship after the wedding. We learned that our friendship need not be threatened by my marital relationship or even intimacy with other friends. By remaining open with one another and sharing our fears of loss and change, the security of our friendship, commitment to one another, and intimacy was actually strengthened.

Shannon and my husband met while we were all in college and we already deeply enjoyed one another. However, there were important new emotional and physical boundaries that could not be crossed. Keith did not share personal things with Shannon, nor did she share intimate thoughts or feelings about her life with him. Keith and I talked about what was acceptable for me to share with Shannon about our new marital relationship. I agreed to talk to him about any problem I had with him before I talked with her. She was trustworthy and would not betray our confidences. As we negotiated these important matters, Keith conveyed a great deal of understanding about her supportive role in my life and trusted that I would talk to her about him in a respectful manner, even when I was venting out my frustrations. We also talked about which of his close friends would be confidants in a comparable way, respecting our agreed upon boundaries and making adjustments when needed.

A huge factor determining the intimacy in any relationship has to do with a commitment to spend regular time together. The three of us maintained this commitment to one another even when Shannon was in graduate school out of state and when we were out of the country for three years. Just as plants and trees need regular watering and amending, so close friendships need a consistent source of nurturing. Without intentionality and commitment, neither a fruit tree nor a friendship will yield the optimum fruit, and both will become vulnerable to pests and disease without proper care and nurturing. All three of us have made this commitment to our friendship, and as a result, we have become a chosen family together. The three of us have enjoyed a close, deeply rooted, and loving friendship that spans over 40 years.

An Invitation to Discern between Love and Intimacy in Friendship

My friendship with Janet, and later with Shannon and Keith, filled me with joy and delight. We could talk long into the evening about many and varied topics and share heartfelt needs and desires without fear. I felt accepted and loved. I longed for this kind of relationship with my family members, but each time I attempted to cultivate closeness with one of them, there was hurt and disappointment on both sides. Our relationship consisted mostly of doing everyday life tasks together, but deeper conversations usually resulted in misunderstandings and arguments. Much of the conflict with my family centered around my newfound faith which increasingly became a barrier to deepening our relationship. Despite their love, care, and provisions for me, I found it difficult to talk with them on an emotional, intellectual, or spiritual level. We continued our relationship into my adulthood, but communication felt empty and superficial. When I finally understood that they did not want to engage in such conversations with me, I experienced a deep sense of inner loss. I felt disconnected from them and hurt by their lack of interest in my thoughts, feelings, beliefs, and life direction.

Although I could not name it at the time, what I had experienced with Janet, Shannon, and Keith was intimacy, and I longed to experience that with my family as well. During my own counseling, I learned that they either could not or would not engage in the kind of closeness with me that I was seeking. Since I knew Jesus wanted me to love them, I had assumed that meant that I would be close to them. Quite the opposite, our relationship felt distant and at times even adversarial. I felt shame for being unable to cultivate a deep connection with them; I experienced freedom when I realized that I was conflating love and intimacy.

I now understood that God was not asking me to be best friends or intimate with them. Jesus offered friendship to all His disciples, but only a few became intimate friends. In addition, when Jesus told His followers to love their enemies, he was not advising them to intentionally make themselves vulnerable to unsafe[85] people and to allow attack after attack.[86] In fact, on more than one occasion, Jesus slipped away from those He knew were planning to harm Him.[87] He was not encouraging His disciples to expose themselves to those who would take advantage of them or exploit intimate knowledge of their lives to hurt them. Jesus did not

---

85 For an excellent study of the characteristics of safe and unsafe people see: Dr. Henry Cloud and Dr. John Townsend. *Safe People: How to Find Relationships That Are Good for You and Avoid Those That Aren't.* Grand Rapids, Michigan: Zondervan Publishing House, 1995.

86 Matthew 5:34–35

87 John 8:59, John 10:30

seek intimacy with those who hated Him. He could love them deeply, however, and would choose when and how to die for them in order to offer the gift of salvation.

Love is a one-way command because it is possible to love others even when they do not love us in return. We can choose to be patient and kind. We can refuse to retaliate when wounded and not delight in their harm.[88] We can use our personal power to accept people for who they are rather than who we want them to be. Intimacy always involves love; but love does not always involve intimacy. Intimate friendship is not a command, but an invitation to choose mutuality. It is a two-way street where both people express a desire for cultivating a close friendship. It requires safety, sharing, and reciprocity. Through experience, both people learn that they can disclose who they really are without the constant risk of harm, rejection, or abandonment. They can tell one another what they need and do not need in the relationship. This does not mean that there will not be conflict or feelings of rejection or abandonment. It means that when there are hurt feelings, both people want to learn how to heal the wounds so that intimacy continues to grow and thrive. There is a conscious decision to stay engaged and open during conflict, lean into the relationship, and to work toward the win-win decisions of mutuality.

I have thought a great deal about how close intimate friendships form, are nurtured, and thrive over time, whether as a single person or as a couple. I have had to learn the painful lesson that it is neither possible nor advisable to be intimate in every friendship. Intimate friendships take time, energy, and commitment from both people, all of which wax and wane throughout our lifetime. Sometimes we don't have the skills to move deeper and sometimes those with whom we desire closer ties do not have the time, energy, or skills to engage with us. Many people are afraid or simply do not want to make such a commitment.

Some friendships end. I have failed at friendship. I have had friends fail me. I have invested in friends who have not been able to give back to me that for which I had hoped. I have been the friend who wasn't able to give what others wanted from me. There have been times when friendships have been fractured beyond repair. There has been painful grief. It has been necessary to learn the difference between intimacy and love because when intimacy fails, love can prevail.

---

88   1 Corinthians 13

CHAPTER 12

Transformed Intimacy

"In speaking of this desire for our own far-off country, which we find in ourselves even now, I feel a certain shyness. I am almost committing an indecency. I am trying to rip open the inconsolable secret in each one of you...our longing to be re-united with something in the universe from which we now feel cut off, to be on the inside of some door which we have always seen from the outside, is no mere neurotic fancy, but the truest index of our real situation. And to be at last summoned inside would be both glory and honour beyond all our merits and also the healing of that old ache...The whole man is to drink joy from the fountain of joy."[89]

–C.S. Lewis

Developmental Stages of Increasing Vulnerability

The joy of intimacy is worth the pain and shame of self-disclosure. To know and be known for who we are means we are willing to endure the vulnerability of potential rejection. Over the years in my counseling practice, I noticed a pattern emerging in relationships that led to increased intimacy.

---

89   Lewis, C.S. The Weight of Glory. New York, New York: HarperCollins, 1980.

As I studied the Gospels and in particular the Gospel of Matthew, I noticed a similar pattern develop between Jesus and His disciples.

At the risk of oversimplification, I want to present three developmental stages of increasing vulnerability in friendship. I admit that I don't like using the language of stages and levels because life is not that neat and tidy. But after trying numerous other ways to characterize this process, stages seemed the clearest. Although not a formula for all friendships or guaranteed success at intimacy, it is helpful to recognize some common stages and key elements that transform intimacy and distinguish close relationships from those more casual, guarded, or distant.

I have chosen to illustrate each stage with simple examples from the Gospel of Matthew and my own life to make the stages more concrete and accessible. In referencing "risk" in these relationships, I am primarily talking about the risk of being wounded on an internal emotional level. The three stages are as follows:

- Stage One: Low-Risk Friendships—Sharing Common Tasks and Interests
- Stage Two: Medium-Risk Friendships—Sharing Questions and Opinions
- Stage Three: High-Risk Relationships—Sharing Feelings and Beliefs about Ourselves and One Another

Whenever stages or levels of development are involved, we are tempted to assume that there is a highest and a lowest stage in value. In terms of friendship development, this is not always the case; such thinking can in fact put a person at risk of severe emotional injury. It is important to respect each of these three stages because of the way they allow us to discern safety, build trust, and test the capacity for mutuality and sharing power through a process of trial and error. We may attempt to skip an earlier stage that we view as superficial and a waste of time. We often want instant closeness and hope that early sharing of very personal things will fast track the relationship toward more intimacy, when instead, premature sharing often sabotages it. For example, our friend may share more personal information with us and overwhelm us with their intensity of need. On the other hand, if we share more intimate details with our friend than we anticipated, we may feel overly exposed and then avoid the person because of unexpected feelings of shame when we see them the next time. In either case, the relationship may not recover and progress to the next stage as a result of sharing too much too soon.

Another advantage of allowing ourselves to move through the earlier stages of friendship is the opportunity to identify and respond to power differentials in the relationship as they emerge. Choosing intimacy in friendship means a willingness to become more aware of the power we and others bring to a relationship and the way we and others choose to use power.

The Significance of Power Differentials

In each of the three stages, it is also important to notice the level of mutuality and any power differentials that are present. These are good questions to ask ourselves about any relationship: "To what degree do I feel that this relationship is mutual?" "Do I feel free in this relationship?" "Do we both have access to resources enjoyed within the context of the relationship?" "Am I free to extend an invitation?" "Can I decline an invitation without a threat, punishment, or fear of humiliation?"

We don't have to be the same as others for the relationship to be mutual. However, if differences—resources, position, status, or culture, for example—are used to leverage power or coerce a decision, we know that there is not only a power differential present, but there is also the potential for abuse. Without the ability to voice concerns arising from these differences to move in the direction of mutuality, there is a good chance that over time, the relationship can become hurtful, oppressive, or even abusive.

There are both subtle and more obvious power differentials. Some common power differentials in our society exist in the form of parent-child, teacher-student, employer-employee, doctor-patient, and pastor-parishioner relationships. Subtle power differentials are the most difficult to identify. People can use personality, charm, charisma, emotional intelligence, mentoring, and even skills, like the ability to listen or give good advice, to create a power differential. For example, the person who initiates a relationship is exercising their personal power to influence the formation of a relationship. Is there any pressure exerted? A person who does most of the talking, giving, or receiving may use this discrepancy as a power differential. How do we know?

It is natural and healthy for friends to differ in how much they talk and give, for example. However, if the less talkative friend cannot find the courage to ask for a turn to share, this can eventually become an obstacle to intimacy. Conversely, a person who talks little, rarely responds to bids for connection, and does not initiate a conversation, is also exercising their power by withholding. If the other friend begins to resent the lack of reciprocity, attempts to address the hurt about the lack of participation, and requests more mutuality without any change, this difference likely represents a subtle power differential that has become an obstacle that is preventing deeper connection.

There are myriad reasons that one person initiates, talks, gives, or withholds more than someone else. I am not suggesting that we are looking for symmetry or a transactional relationship. Our goal is mutual satisfaction. It is perfectly healthy in some friendships to have one friend talk very little. The key is the freedom to negotiate reciprocity when there is a desire for more or less engagement in the friendship.

Sometimes when we explore a lack of mutuality in some area of our friendships, we discover important things about ourselves that have something to do with current or past wounds. Someone who talks very little may have grown up in a home with older siblings and found it difficult to assert themselves without conflict. Finding a friend who can hear that person say that they find it difficult to get a word in edgewise in most conversations can be the beginning of healing and joy in finding more mutuality in friendship. Becoming aware and curious rather than critical about nuanced distinctions in subtle power differentials can cultivate intimacy.

We may balk at facing our own more obvious power differentials in society around wealth, access to resources, race, gender, religion, age, disability, employment, home ownership, occupation, and education. We may not consciously feel like we are better, superior, or more powerful than other people, but this does not mean that these distinctions cease to exist or impact relationships in potentially positive and negative ways. Jesus not only acknowledged these power differentials but intentionally entered into relationships with people to subvert the worldly power structures. He chose each opportunity to demonstrate how the love of God transcends power differentials that prevent others from gaining access to the life and resources that God desires to give without partiality to all humans. The Apostle James said it this way:

"My brothers, show no partiality as you hold to the faith in our Lord Jesus Christ, the Lord of Glory. For if a man wearing a gold ring and fine

clothing comes into your assembly, and a poor man in shabby clothing also comes in, and if you pay attention to the one who wears the fine clothing and say, 'You sit here in a good place,' while you say to the poor man, 'You stand over there', or 'Sit at my feet', have you not then made distinctions among yourselves and become judges with evil thoughts?

Listen my beloved brothers, has not God chosen those who are poor in the world to be rich in faith and heirs of the kingdom, which he has promised to those who love him? But you have dishonored the poor man.

Are not the rich the ones who oppress you, and drag you into court? Are they not the ones who blaspheme the honorable name by which you were called? If you really fulfill the royal law according to the Scripture, 'You shall love your neighbor as yourself,' you are doing well. But if you show partiality, you are committing sin and are convicted by the law as transgressors.

For whoever keeps the whole law but fails in one point has become accountable for all of it. If you do not commit adultery but do murder you have become a transgressor of the law.

So speak and so act as those who are to be judged under the law of liberty. For judgment is without mercy to one who has shown no mercy. Mercy triumphs over judgment."

(James 2:1–13, ESV)

Behaviors that show partiality to one group over another is not limited to the poor and the rich. In churches, a great many programs and resources can be directed to children, families, and married couples. Not all churches have a Sunday School class or program that meet the needs of singles. Even in the literature, there are not many books written about Jesus as a single man who enjoyed the intimacy of friendship with both single and married men and women.

There are many more books written about Christian marriage, and yet Jesus lived, died, and was resurrected as a single man. Marriage is not the pinnacle of human intimacy. There are many single women and men in our churches and communities who long for intimate friendship and can be satisfied through intimacy with Christ and a few trusted friends. Conflating intimacy with sex is extremely limiting. Loneliness is not overcome through sexual relations. Even within marriages and committed relationships, partners may not experience a deep sense of security, belonging, and connection. It is important to support and encourage single adults, who make up approximately 31 percent of the American population, with their efforts to cultivate intimacy in friendships.

The Gospels of Matthew, Mark, Luke, and John illustrate a process over three years in which Jesus developed a friendship with His disciples. Christ chose and loved all of His disciples, yet there were some disciples in particular with whom He was more intimate. There are multiple passages describing the intimate friendship Jesus enjoyed with Mary, Martha, and Lazarus. In John 11:5 ESV, we read, "Now Jesus loved Martha, and her sister, and Lazarus."

Using a power-laden phrase from our Western culture, we often refer to Peter, James, and John as Jesus' "inner circle." Were they some spiritual elite among the 12 disciples? Did they have more inherently loveable traits than the others? When John refers to himself as the beloved disciple in the Gospel he wrote, was he boasting? Or did the three of them discover the art of intimate friendship that was equally available to the other disciples as well?

As I examined the relationship between Jesus and His disciples in the Gospel of Matthew in particular, I noticed how the relationships progressed from a fairly superficial stage, centered around common tasks with all the disciples, to the intimate sharing of vulnerability and feelings about one another with just a few of the disciples. As we observe this example of friendship development, be sure to notice the power differentials present during each of the stages. Jesus was the master of humility and the sharing of power in relationships without compromising His deity or authority. In each stage, I will illustrate this process first with an example from the Gospel of Matthew and then an example from my friendship with Shannon, whom I introduced to you earlier in my chapter on Transformed Friendship.

Stage One: Low-Risk Friendships—Sharing Common Tasks and Interests

Low-risk friendships help us become comfortable with one another and build the kind of trust we need to risk vulnerability in more intimate friendships. When we look at the life of the disciples and Jesus in Chapters 4–9 in the Gospel of

Matthew, we see that Jesus initiated the relationship. He saw Simon and Andrew fishing and asked them to follow Him so He could make them fishers of men. He called the others where they were living and working. The disciples followed Him, listened to His teaching, observed His miracles, and shared in the common tasks and interests of Jesus' ministry of good news. This first stage of interaction is a time of noticing things about one another's personalities and our own internal thoughts and feelings without risking sharing them. The power differential included Jesus initiating the relationship and inviting the men to follow Him as a leader and to learn from Him as a teacher.

When my friend Shannon and I first met, we were both working in a grocery store. I initiated a personal relationship when I invited her to go with me to a work-related party. Our Stage One relationship was based mainly on what we did together: working, skiing, and talking about our common interests. We both noticed that our personalities were very different, and some things bothered us about one another, but we did not risk sharing those things. The power differential was that I initiated a more personal relationship.

Stage Two: Medium-Risk Friendships—Sharing Thoughts, Questions, and Opinions

In Stage Two, the disciples continue to follow Jesus and proclaim the good news from town to town. In Chapters 10–16 of the Gospel of Matthew, we see a major shift in the power differential as Jesus shares His power and authority and empowers the disciples to go out two by two without Him to do the work of preaching, healing, and casting out demons (Matthew 10–11). "Jesus summoned His twelve disciples and gave them authority over unclean spirits, to cast them out, and to heal every kind of disease and every kind of sickness" (Matthew 10:1, NASB). They go out and come back with stories of both success and failure. Mutuality and trust continue to grow between them.

When we share power with others, we also entrust them with more responsibility. As students and partners, the disciples noticed that Jesus did not shame or humiliate them for their lack of understanding, fear, or unbelief, but demonstrated His willingness to know them, respond to them, care for them rather than condemn them, and provide for their needs. It is safe for them to risk more honesty in the relationship with Him, and they began to question Jesus privately about the meaning of the parables that they do not understand (Matthew 13:10). He explained the parables in more detail with His disciples than with the crowds, indicating a more intimate relationship with them.

Jesus is still the teacher, and they are still the students, but their vulnerability is valued by Jesus, who invited them to be more honest about their thoughts and opinions. In one case, just before being invited into a Stage Three, high-risk relationship with Jesus, we see the disciples are unwilling to admit their questions and confusion directly to Him. Instead, they discuss their thoughts privately among themselves. Knowing what they are thinking, Jesus interrupts this indirect communication (typical of low- and medium-risk relationships) and challenges them to speak directly to Him (Matthew 16:7). This is important because intimate friendship requires sharing the vulnerability of our true thoughts and feelings directly with one another. Jesus is preparing them for even more mutuality and an even higher level of risk in their relationship to soon to come. Choosing to risk direct communication with someone increases the potential for both mutuality and intimacy, whereas choosing to talk about others creates barriers and distance.

When Shannon and I ventured into stage two territory, I was 17 and she was 21 years old. This itself represented a power differential. We were getting to know each other better by doing activities together outside of work. I risked telling her that my family disapproved of my newfound faith and had forbidden me to spend time with my friend Janet, who had led me to Christ. Shannon surprised me when she told me that her grandparents were Christians and I could talk about God all I wanted with her, as long as I understood she was not interested in becoming a Christian. Over time, she asked more and more questions; I shared my faith with her and was delighted when she decided to become a follower of Christ.

This change in our relationship created a new power differential. Despite being younger, I was happy to take on the teacher role, which was very familiar to me; my friend Janet had discipled me, and now I had the opportunity to do the same with Shannon. Janet had been trained by a Christian group called the Navigators, which emphasized teacher-student discipleship relationships. Shannon was smart, honest, and insightful. She quickly grew out of our student-teacher oriented relationship. Her willingness to take the risk of asking me to be a friend rather than a teacher represented another shift in the power differential, but this time toward mutuality.

For example, Shannon noticed that most of my relationships were rather one way, with me in the position of strength or giving. She saw through my façade and took the risk of asking me questions and giving me her opinions. She wanted a best friend, not a teacher. I tried to tell her I didn't have best friends but loved everyone the same. She called me out on this and wanted to know why I couldn't have a best friend. She wanted more mutuality and more intimacy. I stood at a crossroads. I could deny her observations, enter into a power struggle, and attempt to keep my role as "teacher," or I could admit that I needed and wanted a best friend too. This was a tremendous opportunity for both of us, and little did we know at that time that we were embarking on a friendship journey of deep joys and sorrows that would grow us up in Christ and in the lessons of intimacy for the rest of our lives. We are indeed still learning and growing.

Stage Three: High-Risk Friendships—Sharing Feelings and Beliefs about Ourselves and One Another

As the time for Jesus to suffer and die approaches, we observe in the Gospel accounts that He begins to be more vulnerable with them and invites them to be vulnerable with Him. First He asks His disciples a Stage Two question, followed by a pivotal Stage Three question. The less risky question is posed to the disciples as, "Who do people say that I am?" More than a few disciples offer a Stage Two answer about what others are saying about Jesus. "Some say you are John the Baptist, others say Elijah."[90]

The next question is a pivotal, Stage Three, high-risk invitation into mutual vulnerability: "But what about you? Who do you say that I am?" (Matthew 16:15, NIV). As far as we can tell in the text, only Peter takes the vulnerable risk of declaring that he believes that Jesus is the Messiah, the Son of the Living God. Jesus reciprocates with praise and prophecy revealing to Peter that He will build His church upon the rock of Peter's solid confession.

---

90   Matthew 16:13–16

Now notice the shift toward even more mutuality with the vulnerable sharing of inner thoughts and feelings by both Jesus and Peter. Jesus exposes His own vulnerability and risks rejection as He shares with His disciples who He really is as a suffering servant and savior. He is not the political leader they hoped for but will soon be delivered up by the Jewish religious leaders and Roman government officials to be crucified.

Peter responds to this disclosure transparently and boldly. He confronts Jesus directly, signaling a shift in the power differential on his side from being primarily a student to being more of a peer and wanting more say in what happens to Jesus. Peter actually takes Jesus aside to rebuke Him:

> *"'God forbid it, Lord! This shall never happen to You.' But He turned and said to Peter, 'Get behind Me Satan! You are a stumbling block to Me; for you are not setting your mind on God's interests, but man's.'"*
> **(Matthew 16:22–23, NASB 1995)**

What we need to see here is that Peter is exposing both his best and his worst to Jesus in response to Jesus exposing His vulnerability to the disciples. Though certainly not pretty or pleasurable, Peter's disclosure invites mutuality and reciprocity. Jesus and Peter talk about their own relationship and how they perceive one another. Developing intimacy is messy at times. Far from rejecting Peter for his folly, only six days later Jesus still includes Peter in the invitation with James and John to go with Him to the Mount of Transfiguration. Jesus further exposes His vulnerability, not only the worst of His suffering but also the best of His glorification:

> *"He was transfigured before them; and His face shone like the sun, and His garments became as white as light. And as they were coming down from the mountain, Jesus commanded them, saying, 'Tell the vision to no one until the Son of Man has risen from the dead.'"*
> **(Matthew 17:7–9, NASB 1995)**

Jesus honors rather than shames or humiliates us for such vulnerability and integrity of emotion and truth in our innermost being. Jesus expressed the vulnerability of needing their confidentiality about this exposure. He requests they keep the experience private until He has risen from the dead. The ability to keep a confidence can make or break intimacy. In the final chapters of the Gospel of Matthew (18–28), we continue to see examples of high-risk, direct communication between Jesus and His disciples. There are invitations to intimacy, mutuality, and the sharing of power so characteristic of the person of Jesus Christ. In the Gospel of John, we learn even more details that reveal the ultimate shift in the power differential between Jesus and His disciples when He says, "No longer do I call you servants, for a servant does not understand what his master is doing. But I have called you friends, because everything I have learned from My Father I have made known to you" (John 15:15, NASB 1995).

Shannon and I were able to work through the several shifts of power leading toward Stage Three vulnerability in our relationship. One of the high-risk conflicts in our friendship was when Shannon and I were living together as roommates. I was now 18 and she was 22. After several months of living with her, I found myself angry and irritated with her on a daily basis. She let her toilet develop a gross, black, moldy ring inside the bowl because she didn't clean it regularly. She didn't make her bed before she left in the morning. She didn't like displays of emotions and saw them as a weakness or manipulative ploy to gain sympathy. When I would get emotional or teary eyed during a conversation about something that was bothering me, she would become defensive and say, "Oh yeah, turn on the tears."

I still can remember getting on my knees beside my bed with my Bible open and crying out to God. I complained to Him about all her faults and many other things I thought ought to change in her life. In between my tears and fault-finding, I read Philippians 4:2–14 and the word *harmony* seemed to jump off the page. Since I sing and love music, God began to impress upon me that I needed to live a song of harmony with Shannon. We had different notes and I was busy trying to make her sing my note when God was needing me to just sing my own note and tune up to hers. I was so busy trying to prove that her note was wrong that I wasn't even singing the song anymore. What this meant on a practical level was that I could clean my toilet and she could, without my criticism, let her toilet gather mold. It seems like a silly thing, but my critical spirit and blaming attitude could have easily spread to other areas of our relationship, crushing any emerging mutual intimacy.

This encounter with my Lord in God's Word revolutionized my relationship with Shannon. As sisters in Christ, we were singing the same song, but we were singing very different notes. We began to see that it was okay to have and express different opinions and to even debate topics to clarify the notes in our chord. Discussion does not equal division. A different opinion does not equal divisiveness. God loves our diversity. God is not teaching uniformity when He urges us to walk in unity. The very nature of our triune God teaches us how to live diverse and yet united lives.

After this, Shannon and I were both willing to risk sharing our feelings and faults more readily. I was able to express how hurt I was when she mocked my tears. She apologized and became tender toward me instead of calloused when I took the risk of sharing my hurts. She expressed how much it hurt to be criticized for her style of housecleaning. I apologized and accepted that her way was not wrong just because I found it distasteful. We negotiated and found mutually acceptable solutions. We worked on ourselves. We found joy in accepting one another.

Over the next many years, we continued to reveal the best and the worst of ourselves to one another. We both met with therapists to discover and heal from wounds that were underneath our hurtful behavior toward one another. There were two times when we wounded one another in such painful ways that we did not know if our friendship would survive. During the painful time of waiting on God and one another for healing, we continued to love one another even if we could not be close. We walked the path through the valley of the shadow of loss multiple times for multiple disappointments.

Today there is a bedrock of trust in our friendship with Jesus and one another and confidence that God can lead us into intimacy through conflicts. We don't like the pain of conflict, but we no longer fear that it will tear us apart because we both believe it is an opportunity for increased intimacy. It is worth working for and worth enduring. We are enjoying the fruit of over 45 years of friendship. It is sweet. It is joyful. It is comforting and fulfilling. We are not alone.

I truly believe that if we as sisters and brothers in Christ can be found trustworthy of one another's personal and interpersonal pain and minister to one another in ever-increasing stages of mutual intimacy, that we will banish overwhelming loneliness and experience a revival of joy, fulfilled souls, and relationships. Jesus said, "If you keep my commandments, you will abide in My love; just as I have kept My Father's commandments and abide in His love. These things I have spoken to you so that My joy may be in you, and that your joy may be made full" (John 15:10–11, NASB 1995). Jesus was not advocating for us to become outstanding Pharisees and follow every rule and regulation of the Mosaic Law. Jesus was commanding us to put love in relationship with God and others above all else. This kind of love, joy, and intimacy in Christ revolutionizes society and glorifies the only King worthy of our submission. As we reveal ourselves to Him, obey His command to love one another, and accept His invitation into more intimacy, He will disclose more of Himself to us and make His joy in us full and overflowing. This is the prize of choosing intimacy (John 14:21, NASB 1995).

CHAPTER 13

Transformed Grief

"Grief is like a long valley, a winding valley where any bend may reveal a totally new landscape...Sometimes the surprise is the opposite one; you are presented with exactly the same sort of country you thought you had left behind miles ago. This is when you wonder whether the valley isn't a circular trench."[91]

— C.S. Lewis

It may seem counterintuitive to end chapters about the delight of transformed relationships and intimacy only to begin a chapter on grief—yet sorrow is closely related to joy. The writer of Hebrews captures the tension between joy and grief in this passage, "fixing our eyes on Jesus, the author and perfecter of our faith, who for the joy set before him, endured the cross, despising the shame, and has sat down at the right hand of the throne of God" (12:2). The joy of reconciliation and redeeming intimacy with God, His children, and all of Creation inspired Jesus to make a choice to endure the pain and despise the shame of the cross.

What does intimacy, mutuality, and the sharing of power have to do with loss? The answer to this question is deeply personal. Loss puts us in touch with

---

91   Lewis, C.S. A Grief Observed. New York: HarperCollins Publishers, 1996 (60).

our helplessness and powerlessness to change our circumstances. In a sense, we negotiate with ourselves, the persons or things involved, and with God in order to cope with imminent or real loss. We say to ourselves and God that we want things to be different. We repeatedly ask and even argue with God about why there is no other way out of the dilemma we are facing. In the end, we must decide to acknowledge the loss of control and grieve or deny its reality and continue our efforts to control or change the situation. The last days and hours of a human life can still be full of intimate moments despite the heartbreak of impending loss. It is tragic to watch loved ones in the last hours of their lives still unable to accept the reality of their deaths and therefore unable to say goodbye to their loved ones in meaningful ways. This too, however, is the power of personal choice.

Jesus modeled how to walk through the valley of the shadow of death by preparing for His own suffering on the cross and death. He shared this openly with His disciples on many occasions. He spent time in prayer with His Father and expressed grief in the Garden of Gethsemane. In Mark 14:34 (NASB 1995), Jesus said, *"My soul is deeply grieved, to the point of death;"* Though Jesus was one with the Father, in his humanity he was not above wanting another way out. He asked His Father three times if there was any other way to reconcile the world to God. In the end, Jesus said, *"Not my will but yours be done."*

I am convinced that this process released both power and comfort for enduring His suffering, shame, and rejection. He now was the one who was blessed and comforted through His willingness to mourn. Still, the decision to let go and grieve did not insulate Him from the pain of grief nor from crying out the painful words, "My God, my God. Why have You forsaken me?" (Matthew 27:46, NASB 1995). As we move through this chapter, we will see that in the initial stages, the healing pain of grief feels much the same as the injurious pain of avoiding grief.

Trying to find a way out of pain is human. If Jesus could ask His heavenly Father three times for a way out of the coming pain of enduring the cross, with the sins of the world laid upon Him, surely we can ask the Father 3000 times for another way out. God is big enough to handle every emotion we bring to Him, even if we blame Him or express anger, rage, fear, doubt, depression, or guilt. There eventually comes a time, however, when we face a crisis of decision. Our grief will not be resolved by continuing to blame God, others, or ourselves.

Pain relievers, whether ancient or modern, are not long-term solutions. The ancient wisdom of the Preacher insists,

> *"It is better to go to a house of mourning than to go to a house of feasting because that is the end of every man, and the living takes it to heart. Sorrow is better than laughter, for when a face is sad a heart may be happy. The mind of the wise is in the house of mourning, while the mind of fools is in the house of pleasure."*
> **(Ecclesiastes 7:2–4, NASB 1995)**

The only way out of the valley of the shadow of death is walking through it with our Savior. God has given us the power of choice. The way we choose to cope with loss will determine the quality of our physical and mental health as well the depth of intimacy in our relationships with God and one another. Our desire to avoid pain, though understandable, becomes a highway to hard-heartedness. Scripture teaches us how to grieve and mourn loss so that our hearts stay tender and receptive to love after loss. Ezekiel 36:26 promises us that God can remove a heart of stone and replace it with a heart of flesh, tender to both healing and harm. Our Lord and Shepherd bids us to walk through the valley of the shadow of death, not over it, under it, or around it. He promises to walk with us through the valley, to guide us and comfort us on the journey.

Jesus said, "Blessed are those who mourn, for they shall be comforted."[92] There is no comfort if we refuse to walk through the process of grief and mourning. As a therapist, I can say with a great deal of confidence that the inability to grieve tremendous loss and disappointments in life is a source of great pain in the body of Christ and humankind in general. Refusing to grieve is found underneath trauma, abuse, and addictions of all kinds; it shows up in the compulsion to hoard, to overachieve, and overwork but can also underlie addiction, depression, anxiety, panic disorders, attachment problems, and personality disorders. Grief and loss that remain unresolved can show up in physical ailments that shorten our own life spans and significantly decrease the quality of our shortened

---

92   Matthew 5:4 (NASB 1995)

lives. So, what is grief and how do we walk that path so we get to a place of healing and comfort?

Grief and Mourning

This brief summary is intended to provide some definitions and tools to begin exploring the importance of grief as it relates to maintaining openness to intimacy in the wake of disappointment. The power of choice is key to both cultivating intimacy and maintaining it through inevitable losses and the necessary grief and mourning that heals our hearts. Even in the grimmest circumstances imaginable, humans have God-ordained authority and power to choose how they will respond to their losses.

There is a difference between the words "grieving" and "mourning"–though they are essentially two sides of the same coin. Grieving involves the hurt or pain experienced in the wide range of internal thoughts, feelings, and physical sensations we experience with loss of any kind. Mourning is the external expression of the hurt or pain through talking, wailing, weeping, shaking, losing appetite, trouble sleeping, and a host of other psychological and physiological symptoms associated with the pain of loss.

A fascinating article by developmental psychologist Deborah L. Davis tells us that our brain actually redraws its neural map when we grieve. It turns out that the brain is hardwired to keep track of our most important relationships along three dimensions referred to as here, now, and close. Davis calls this a "powerful, implicit sense that they are 'everlasting.'" We have a neural map for close relationships that contains detailed information about this person, the relationship, and the life we have lived together. This neural map is used to predict and make sense of what happens between us and this person.

Predictable knowledge about the people we love is soothing, comforting, and reassuring and one of the reasons we fantasize and write songs about long-term relationships that we hope will last forever. When someone we love dies or leaves, our brain has to begin the arduous task of overwriting a neural network that matches the present reality despite a strong and stable neural network that has stored memories to the contrary. This is why when a loved one leaves or dies, we may feel, smell, see, or hear them. Our brain is still holding on to the here, now, and close, and interprets common sensations, sights, and sounds associated with them as sure signs of their continued presence. "This struggle explains some of the more bewildering and crazy-making aspects of grieving."[93] The closer and longer the relationship, the more time and repetitions of thought, feeling, and experience is needed to recreate a stable and more realistic neural network. This is part of why grief is so mentally exhausting.

There is also extreme and complicated grief that is mixed with trauma, death, torture, and many other forms of loss. For example, Nazi concentration camp survivors, Viktor Frankl and Edith Eger, both experienced unspeakable horrors that faced them with loss upon loss and trauma after trauma for years.[94] The power over life and death seemed exclusively in the hands of their captors, yet they speak of another kind of power in their books, *Man's Search for Meaning* and *The Choice*, respectively. Their daily reality demonstrated surprising power over life and death held exclusively in their own minds as captives. Eger and Frankl both illustrated the power of their choice by the way they lived in the midst of chronic deprivation and danger. They chose generosity over greed, care, and concern over a blatant disregard for the lives of others. This was not an easy choice for them. They struggled with feelings and thoughts that could have turned them against themselves and others. They watched with horror as fellow inmates identified with their captors and used favors to inflict even more abuse on other captives. Still others gave up on living and planned ways to kill themselves.

The suffering experienced by these survivors of the Holocaust did not end after they were released. The power of choice continued. Edith, a Hungarian, and Viktor, an Austrian, did not know one another while interred at Auschwitz. Following the war, both practiced psychotherapy and taught that the most powerful path to healing involved personal choice. They chose to acknowledge loss by facing the reality of trauma and grief. Despite their pain and suffering, they found meaning and a path toward healing and wholeness. Others attempted to heal by avoiding memories of the experience, turning to substance abuse to numb the pain, or allowing the legitimate anger of grief to project itself onto others as blame and

---

93 Davis, Deborah L. "As You Grieve, Your Brain Redraws Its Neural Map: Neuroscience Offers Useful, Comforting Insights on Grieving a Beloved." PsychologyToday.com. Posted March 29, 2023.
94 Frankl, Viktor E. *Man's Search for Meaning.* Beacon Press: Boston, Massachusetts, 2006.

sabotage important relationships. For Edith, it would take years of practice as a psychologist before she was able to process certain elements of the grief and loss.[95]

There are myriad examples of important losses that do not involve death but whose pain requires a grieving process. Grief occurs with changes in our lives—even good changes such as when an adult child goes to college or gets married. Success and the gaining of notoriety carries with it a host of potential losses including a loss of privacy. The emotions of grief also surface when we move, make a job change, get demoted at work, or experience a divorce. Unfulfilled desires and expectations are often neglected areas of grief in our lives and eventually become barriers to cultivating intimate relationships with both God and others.

Some significant disappointments within relationships begin with our earliest relationships with primary caregivers, whether biologically related or not. We may have been hurt by foster parents, adoptive parents, biological mothers, fathers, siblings, extended relatives, neighbors, or friends. Perhaps we have experienced disappointment in friendships we once thought would endure. Friendships that once nourished our souls suddenly ended or simply faded into the distance, the hurt only surfacing with a memory or chance meeting with that person in a grocery store or theater lobby.

Our husbands, wives, partners, children, as well as community leaders, employers, educators, and pastors can disappoint us and hurt us more than we thought possible. Many devoted believers in Christ have experienced deep wounding within their churches by church members or church leaders. Equally significant, we may find ourselves suffering because we have greatly disappointed someone else, whether intending or not, and we are unable to restore the relationship regardless of our attempts at reconciliation. Whatever the circumstance surrounding our pain and sorrow, we can take comfort in knowing that we are not alone.

I have always believed Scripture to be the foundation of psychological healing and wellness. Still, I admit I was rather stunned by the nuanced emotion and depth of the Hebrew language. Our one rather pallid word "grief" is translated from 44 distinct, emotionally accurate, and highly descriptive Hebrew words. Let's take a look at a table I compiled during a simple word study of "grief" using the *Strong's Exhaustive Concordance*. It is important to know that going to God with our pain

---

95   Eger, Dr. Edith, with Weigand, Esme Schwall. *The Choice: Embrace the Impossible*. Scribner: New York, New York, 2017.

cultivates our relationship with God. We are often ashamed of expressing negative emotions like fear, anxiety, or rage that expose our vulnerability during times of intense grief and loss. Understanding that these emotions do not disappoint God and are not evidence of a lack of faith is important. Sadly, many people experiencing deep grief and loss are given empty cliches and platitudes such as, "It was God's will," or, "Time heals everything," which leave us far from comforted. We need validation that our pain is real and serious. The Hebrew language does this for us brilliantly.

The 44 Hebrew Words for Grief

Webster defines grief as "a deep and prolonged state of mental anguish over loss." Each time that the English word "grief" is used in the Old Testament, one of these following 44 Hebrew words corresponds to the single word for "grief" in English. Here are the English translations of the Hebrew words, reading from left to right, as documented by *Strong's Exhaustive Concordance.*

Adversity	Affliction	Anguish	Anxiety
Bitterness	Bothered	Broken to Pieces	Cruel
Cut Down	Detestable	Disgusted	Inflamed
Faint-hearted	Grief	Heaviness	Indignant
Languish	Malady	Pain	Provoked to Anger
Rage	Rubbed Raw	Sad	Self-Loathing
Shaking	Sickness	Slothful	Sorrow
Sorry	Sour Tasting	Spite	Spoiled
Suffering	Tired	Toil	Trembling
Troubled	Twisted	Vexed	Weak
Weary	Worn Out	Wrath	Writhed into a Fetal Position

As you can see, the Hebrew language captures subtleties and nuances of the emotional and physical symptoms of grief and mourning. Even the word "slothful" captures the guilt many people feel in response to the lack of motivation they experience related to physical and mental exhaustion. Dr. Eric Lindemann, in his now classic article on the symptoms and management of acute grief, described feelings of shock, depression, panic, guilt, and anger. He noticed physical symptoms of grief and described predictable, distressing bodily sensations occurring in waves and lasting from 20 minutes to one hour. This distress might include a feeling of tightness in the throat, choking, shortness of breath, a need for sighing, an empty feeling in the abdomen and a lack of muscular power.[96] Sometimes we experience the presence of a lost loved one, imagine we have seen them, recognize their scent nearby, or hear their voice in the middle of the night. This can be unnerving, and some people feel they are going crazy. Lynn Caine, the author of *Widow*, described her experience of "the crazies" and quotes actress Helen Hayes as saying, "For two years (after my husband died) I was as crazy as you can be and still be at large. I didn't have any really normal minutes during those two years. It wasn't just grief. It was total confusion. I was nutty. How did I come out of it? I don't know, because I didn't know I was in it."[97]

Because of the pain and complexity of grief, some of us no longer want to risk loving again. Intimacy doesn't seem worth the pain of loss that may be encountered. We stop trying to get close to people and build a wall around our hearts. We have resigned ourselves to being alone or we tell ourselves we don't need to get close to anyone except the Lord. We reassure ourselves that the pain isn't as bad as it used to be because we simply don't get our hopes up anymore. We allow our hearts to cease from hoping. We become numb. We use social media, drugs, alcohol, sex, overeating, overworking, and a host of other unhealthy habits to bury the pounding ache outside our consciousness.

It is not wrong to feel the pain of loss and disappointment. It is not wrong to want the pain to stop. The reality is that it is impossible to completely stop the pain of disappointment—unless we resort to destructive artificial means. Even then, it is a temporary numbing that creates an exponential number of new problems. So, what is the alternative? We can learn to manage pain that leads to healing. There is a way to tolerate distress. Working through the grief of loss and disappointment can lead to an increased capacity to enjoy even deeper intimacy with Christ and others. The poet David Whyte, in his book *Consolations,* said it this way:

---

96 Lindemann, Eric. "Symptomatology and Management of Acute Grief." *American Journal of Psychiatry*, September, 1944.

97 Neils, Robert. "How People Grieve." Human Resource Development Specialist, Cooperative Extension Service, Montana State University.

"Disappointment is a friend to transformation, a call to both accuracy and generosity in the assessment of our self and others, a test of sincerity and a catalyst of resilience. disappointment is just the initial meeting with the frontier of an evolving life, an invitation to reality, which we expected to be one particular way and turns out to be another, often something more difficult, more overwhelming and strangely, in the end, more rewarding."[98]

The Gift of Pain

If we are to experience comfort and healing, we must first challenge our notions about the purpose of pain in our lives. In Western culture we do all we can to eradicate pain. Ironically, it is our obsession with obliterating pain that has decreased our capacity to endure the healthy discomfort needed for healing and growth. Avoidance of pain has led to addictions, overdoses, suicides, and increases in physical and mental suffering.

I remember the first bone I broke in my body. I jumped off my horse and landed on my feet instead of tucking and rolling. That was a poor choice. I didn't know at the time, but I had broken the talus bone, which is right at the ankle joint. The pain was so bad that I crawled out of the arena on my hands and knees. It turned out that, because I did not put any weight on the ankle, I had a better than average chance of recovering some use of my ankle without surgery. The orthopedic surgeon told me that surgery would permanently fuse the joint in my ankle. With the fusion I would have less pain but at the cost of limited flexibility. I opted for following the doctor's instructions for a long recovery period. He assured me that regardless of whether or not I had the surgery, I would likely never walk or run again without pain.

Recovery without surgery meant I could put absolutely no weight on that ankle for eight weeks. When I was able to finally get into the support boot and put some weight on my ankle, it was excruciatingly painful. Based on the pain level, I was convinced I was doing it a great deal of damage. When I spoke to my doctor, he assured me that this time the pain was not injurious but healing. I was

---

98 Whyte, David. *Consolations: The Solace, Nourishment, and Underlying Meaning of Everyday Words.* Langley, Washington: Many Rivers Press, 2015. (75)

to be respectful of the pain and not overdo my activity, but I was also to endure it for the purpose of healing.

This is a rich metaphor for healing the human soul. Healing from the pain of grief and loss involves challenging our belief system that our pain is always an enemy to be defeated or avoided. Dr. Paul Brand was an orthopedic surgeon who worked and lived among lepers in India. Leprosy was once thought of by physicians as a flesh-eating disease. He discovered, however, that leprosy actually disables the body's ability to feel pain. As a result, when persons with leprosy injure themselves, they do not feel the pain and do not take corrective action to deal with wounds. This leads to more infection and eventually the disease spreads to the bone, which can result in amputation and even death. The doctors and missionaries working in the area where his family served in India often wondered why children would show up to their clinics with missing fingers and toes. Eventually, they realized that the children were unable to feel mice and rats gnawing at them while they slept.

One of my favorite quotations from his book, *Pain: The Gift Nobody Wants*, is that "pain is not the enemy, but the loyal scout announcing the enemy…once regarded as the enemy, not a warning signal, pain loses its power to instruct. Silencing pain without considering its message is like disconnecting a ringing fire alarm to avoid receiving bad news."[99] I often tell my clients that emotional pain is to the soul what physical pain is to the body. It is an important alarm worthy of proper investigation. We don't want our emotions to control our decisions, but we absolutely need to allow all our emotions, both the negative and the positive, to inform us.

The Gift of Hope

If you dare to hope, you will deal with disappointment. Solomon, hailed as the wisest king who ever lived, said, "Hope deferred makes the heart sick, but desire fulfilled is a tree of life" (Proverbs 13:12, NASB 1995). For believers in Christ, grief and loss are never the end of the story. True hope has an eternal perspective. Hope sees beyond what is momentary and believes there is value in delaying short-term gratification for long-term benefits. Hope remains with Christ, who holds our lives in His hands. He knows the joyous end of our stories. Resurrection

---

99   Brand, Paul W., and Yancey, Philip. *Pain: The Gift Nobody Wants*. New York: HarperCollins Publishers, 1993. (187–188)

came for Christ despite the pain, suffering, and abandonment, and as a result, we gain the hope of eternal life and the resurrection of our mortal bodies.

Can we hold on to the hope of resurrection and new life in the midst of pain and suffering and the deeply gut-wrenching disappointments of life? I like what Job said in the midst of his great disappointment with God: "For there is hope for a tree, when it is cut down, that it will sprout again, and its shoots will not fail. Though its roots grow old in the ground, and its stump dies in the dry soil, at the scent of water it will flourish and put forth springs like a plant" (Job 14:7-9; NASB, 1995). In the New Testament, the Apostle Paul addresses his own despair while maintaining the hope of God's ability to raise the dead and the help of praying believers. Paul writes openly of deep emotion:

> *"For we do not want you to be unaware, brethren, of our affliction which came to us in Asia, that we were burdened excessively, beyond our strength, so that we despaired even of life; indeed, we had the sentence of death within ourselves so that we would not trust in ourselves, but in God who raises the dead; who delivered us from so great a peril of death, and will deliver us, He on whom we have set our hope. And He will yet deliver us, you also joining in helping us through your prayers, so that thanks may be given by many persons on our behalf for the favor bestowed on us through the prayers of many."*
> **(2 Corinthians 1:8–11, NASB, 1995)**

One of the many Hebrew words for hope literally means a binding cord used for attaching or securing something together. I immediately imagined myself in a shipwreck on an open sea. I find a piece of wood from the broken ship, and I use rope to tie myself on that wood to keep me afloat on seas I have no control over. To endure the storm of emotion on a treacherous sea called disappointment, we attach ourselves to Jesus Christ—our Deliverer—who will be with us until our feet find solid land to walk on once again.

There is much in life over which we have little or no control, but we do have control over how we choose to manage our thoughts, feelings, and behaviors toward disappointment. We can't control exactly how long the voyage through disappointment and grief will take, but we can learn from other mariners who have braved the open sea. We cannot control the winds, but we can become experts at the skills that navigate the ship safely during the worst of the storms.

Many of us have never made it through disappointment to renewed hope. We have not yet endured through conflict to experience resolution or through grief to find the joy of increased intimacy. What the Lord has for us may not be what we expected, but it will be well worth the journey through the valley of the shadow of death: "But just as it is written, 'Things which eye has not seen and ear has not heard, and which have not entered the heart of man, all that God has prepared for those who love him'" (1 Corinthians 2:9, NASB 1995).

The Gift of Walking through the Valley of the Shadow of Death and Loss

"The best way out is always through."[100]
– Robert Frost

Over the years, I have thought about how to illustrate the process of healing from losses of all kinds. In order to keep our hearts tender toward cultivating deep connection and intimacy, we must face this valley of the shadow. What follows is a descriptive map through the treacherous terrain of loss. I want to give credit to one of my talented clients who created a graphic to illustrate what she believed I was teaching her in our counseling sessions. She and a hospice social worker I met in college inspired the visual aid.

The map is circular and shows two main paths. Notice that the hurt and pain of loss is experienced whether or not we choose to grieve and that at times we vacillate between the two. This is natural. Yet at some point we face a crisis of decision. There is a fundamental difference between the pain that heals, *grief*, and the pain that injures, *blame*. Whether we blame ourselves, others, or something else for the loss, blame becomes a refusal to take responsibility for using our personal power to

---

100 Frost, Robert. North of Boston. Originally published in the United States, 1917. Public Domain. 2021. (43)

The Grief Map

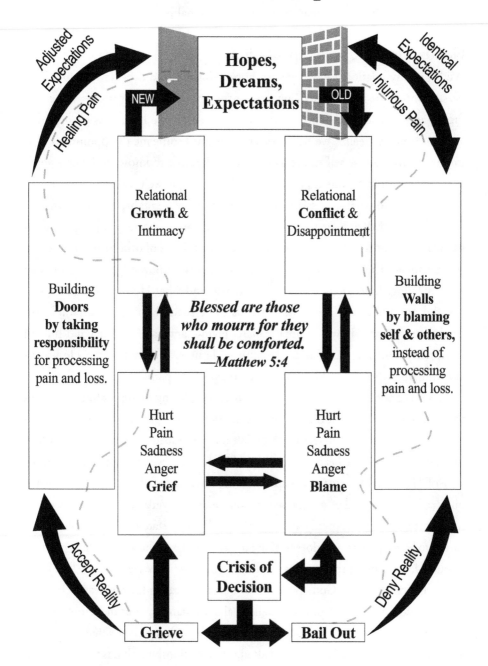

grieve, heal, and recover. As a result, we may no longer welcome the joy of mutual intimacy in the future but may even use our personal power to prevent it.

Hopes, Dreams, and Expectations

We begin any relational journey with hopes, dreams, and expectations for closeness, companionship, mutual joy, and intimacy. It is not wrong to hope and dream and even expect good things from the people we love. It is curious that at times we don't realize we have expectations until someone disappoints us. It is important to practice self-awareness and take the time to know, and when possible, to communicate, our expectations with the people we love.

Contrary to what Christians have sometimes been taught, it is not selfish to have wants and desires or to express them. Selfishness means grasping for what we need or want without regard for the needs and wants of others. It is not selfish to care for and nourish ourselves. Self-care and self-knowledge are essential to healthy living. Jesus knew exactly who He was and what He needed and wanted and did not allow even His closest friends to persuade Him to be any different. At the same time, He was compassionate, giving, and sacrificial beyond human comprehension. He was able to do both without ever denying who He was or allowing others to define His personality, purpose, or path.

As we consider where we are in the process of grieving disappointments, I want to point out an important distinction and caution with regard to women, men, and children caught in harmful relationships. We must be outside of abusive relationships in order to truly do the healing work of grief. Otherwise, we are living in the chronic state of "fight, flight, freeze or collapse." We are not able to use good judgment when our cerebral cortex takes a back seat to the brain's amygdala, which keeps us on high alert both physiologically and psychologically. This state helps us survive but is meant to be temporary and does nothing to heal trauma in the aftermath. A practical resource for exploring this process is a book called *The Developing Mind*, by Daniel J. Siegel. Grief is one of God's paths to comfort and healing for the heart. Our map through grief and loss may provide intellectual understanding, but these tools assume we are in a safe place for the work of healing. I often tell my clients that because we are wounded in relationship, we must also heal in relationship. That is the reason that a counseling relationship is more than simply learning intellectual knowledge. This goes against our self-help culture that wants to believe it is possible to heal ourselves. We need Christ and His beautiful body, including the physicians of heart, mind, soul, and body. If we are not emotionally or physically safe, we must exercise the dignity of self-care and get professional help to remove ourselves from unhealthy relationships.

Relational Conflict and Disappointment

In any healthy relationship, a time will come when we experience conflict and disappointment. Although we may initially enjoy the differences we discover about one another, eventually differences can feel wrong and offensive. Instead of "opposites attracting" we experience "opposites detracting." Diversity in culture, personality, anger management, work ethic, communication, family history, and a host of other things can create intense conflict. It is not uncommon to become critical of ourselves and others as conflict brings out the worst in us. When unresolved, conflict, chronic disappointment, and disillusionment often lead to discouragement and despair.

Hurt, Pain, and Avoiding the Emotions of Grief and Loss

During times of conflict and disappointment, we must resist the temptation to act out, medicate, dismiss, minimize, rebuke, or spiritualize away the pain of our negative emotions. Surprisingly, emotions like fear, anxiety, jealousy, depression, anger, and rage can move us forward along the path toward healing. Our instincts are to avoid, deny, or suppress the pain. However, when we try to keep our negative emotions out of awareness because they are uncomfortable, we cannot be informed by them. Remember, emotional pain is to the soul what physical pain is to the body. If we keep emotions out of awareness because they are uncomfortable, we cannot learn from the important information they have for us. We can ask important questions like, "What is the legitimate need underneath this strong, negative emotion?" and, "How can I support myself without taking my negative emotions out on others or simply internalizing them?" Remember when God asked Cain why he was angry (Genesis 4:6)? How might have the story of Cain and Abel changed had Cain thoughtfully answered that question and dealt directly with God about what he was feeling?

A first step in dealing with disappointment then, is to take full responsibility for both our expectations and the wide range of emotions that follow when we experience disappointment and loss. A startling 40 percent of the Psalms are of lament in which the writer cries out to God with the intense human emotions of grief. These ancient songs chronicle the joys and sorrows of God's people. There is a good reason the Psalms were often sung, and that King Saul found relief through the music of David. According to researchers at McGill University, "evidence for the beneficial effects of music on reward, motivation, pleasure, stress, arousal, immunity, and social affiliation is mounting."[101]

Denying Reality, Building Walls, and Injurious Pain

When we see no resolution in sight, we are in danger of building defensive walls to safeguard our heart. At first, we may doubt our feelings and instincts that something in the relationship is wrong. We may consciously dismiss and deny the clues around us that indicate a problem. Later, when the pain urges us to admit the conflict, we may still choose to deny the need to address the problem, feeling trapped and not seeing any way out. We may initially blame ourselves or the person who has disappointed us without addressing the conflict directly with the person involved.

In Western culture, we Christians can also tend to spiritualize emotions away with trite truths such as ("I just need to pray and trust God") or intellectualize them ("Love is not a feeling; it is an act of the will"). Though containing some elements of truth, such comments do not help others to process the immense pain we feel. We can at times encourage those who are grieving to stay busy. Yet overworking, over involvement with ministry, and an inability to rest or enjoy solitude can be indicators that we are avoiding painful emotions. This is often the reason people struggle to prayerfully listen as well as talk to God, which requires the practice of quieting ourselves before Him and allowing all manner of thoughts, feelings, and desires to surface. In her book *Interior Castles*, St. Teresa of Avila referred to these as inner reptiles which must be confronted within ourselves if we are to achieve intimacy with God.[102]

When at last we do have the courage to openly address the conflict within ourselves and with others, there is an opportunity to find mutually satisfying

---

101 Chandra, Mona Lisa and Levitin, Daniel J. "The Neurochemistry of Music." Department of Psychology, McGill University, Montreal, Quebec, QC H3A 1B1, Canada. *Trends in Cognitive Sciences.* April 2013. Vol.17 No.4 ISSN 1364–6613.

102 Teresa of Avila. *Interior Castles.* Translated by E. Allison Peers. New York, New York: Doubleday, 1989.

agreements. If this fails and the hurt continues, we may still not be ready to admit the looming loss but instead again return to our original expectations of the person or situation despite evidence that those expectations are unrealistic. We again try to change ourselves, the person, or the situation. This kind of pain and unresolved conflict can go on for decades if we refuse to identify and adjust our expectations.

Women and men who live in failing relationships often learn to close their hearts to their partners to protect themselves from what has now become chronic hurt. The longer we allow our spouses to harm us without seeking help and healing, the more damage is done to the hearts, minds, and even the bodies of both partners. Feelings of shame and a fear of failing God and others often keep us in harmful relationships when in fact seeking treatment outside the home may be the first step toward saving a marriage.

For example, we would not prevent a partner from going into the hospital for a needed physical treatment or view the necessary separation in the hospital or rehabilitation facility as abandonment or divorce. Yet those suffering from emotional and psychological wounds are often denied treatment—which in such cases may require physical separation from the home or family—on what is believed to be biblical grounds.

This kind of pain intensifies our level of stress, which eventually manifests itself not only as depression, anxiety, and anger, but also as a host of physical symptoms from high blood pressure to irritable bowel syndrome. Staying in hurtful relationships may allow us to avoid the way of grief for a time, but not without damaging consequences to our relationships with God and others. Separation and divorce can happen while still married and living together. Both marriage and divorce are much more than a paper certificate.

It is important to reach out for professional help when we are in chronic pain in a relationship. There are many different ways to approach such situations, but we are rarely in a position to do so without wise counsel. In any case, we will need to face existing and potential losses. What drives the pain and creates massive walls against our healing is the discrepancy between what we have hoped for and what reality presents to us. Our goal is to reduce the discrepancy. Simple resignation, which determines not to care anymore, does not move us forward. We can, however, reduce the discrepancy between our expectations and reality, when we choose to acknowledge the painful loss, grieve, and adjust our expectations accordingly.

The intense pain of loss becomes a genuine cry to God to give us the grace to tread the path of grief fraught with the unknown and unexpected. The time needed to complete this process is as varied as each unique human being; there is no perfect timeline. The Lord is our Shepherd and will not forsake or abandon us in the valley of the shadow of loss. This is an opportunity for more intimacy with Jesus and others when we are willing to lean into Him for help, healing, and endurance.

The Crisis of Decision: Grieve or Bail Out

The crisis of decision around grief is rarely a clear-cut, obvious moment in time. We can go back and forth for years between grieving a loss and bailing out of the pain of loss. The decision to grieve may be a moment when we realize we simply have nothing left to give or recognize that we are stuck in an unproductive pattern. The longer we wait to grieve, however, the more difficult it is to stay tenderhearted and open to the people who have wounded us. It is difficult to gather the strength to work on a relationship when our physical strength and inner resources have been depleted by denying reality.

Hurt, Pain, and Choosing to Feel the Emotions of Grief and Loss

Whether we choose to grieve or continue bailing out of the grief, the pain feels much the same at the beginning. The conflict, feelings of hurt, pain, and anguish devastate us. The anger, rage, depression, anxiety, and panic at times immobilize us; the related physical symptoms of a headache, racing heart, nausea, back pain, fatigue, loss or increase of appetite, insomnia, and gastro-intestinal problems may surprise us and add further distress. Instead of feeling grief emotions, some people somaticize their feelings and focus on physical sensations and ailments. Anxiety about anxiety becomes a vicious cycle. Without oversimplifying complex mental health treatment, I can attest to having seen a surprising number of people heal from chronic anxiety disorders once the underlying loss issues have been recognized and addressed.

As shown in the Grief Map, where arrows move back and forth between healing pain and injurious pain, the boxes on either side are very similar with one exception. Note that the healthy alternative to blaming is grieving. Grieving is saying goodbye and releasing any perceived control over the loss, whether a loved one, a treasured possession, job, health, position, or dream. How deeply we experience the sorrow of saying goodbye, and how long it takes, is unique for each person. Eventually we finish our goodbyes and move on with our lives, though we might still feel the pangs of sorrow from time to time. When we are unable to move on, grief may be complicated by an accumulation of underlying additional losses and trauma, which will require the help of an experienced therapist to facilitate continued healing.

Accepting Reality, Building Doors, and Healing Pain

As we begin to accept reality, we also take increased responsibility for ourselves within the context of the relationship. We see our own part in continuing the hurt that has characterized our interactions. This is different from self-blame. Personal responsibility for our own healing is a powerful way to build doors that open us up again for relationships.

If we remember back to the beginning of the Post-Fall Era, we saw how fundamental the reaction of hiding and blaming is to our human nature stained by the knowledge of good and evil. Adam blamed Eve and God, and Eve blamed the Serpent. Chronic blame does not move us toward accepting reality or help us build doors of access to healing in the relationship. This does not mean that we excuse others from taking responsibility for their part in wounding us. It does mean however, that we acknowledge that others cannot heal us. The most miserable people I have counseled are those who refuse to grieve losses, or who see themselves as the chronic victims of others. They perpetuate their pain by not exercising the power of personal responsibility with the choices available to them.

God took responsibility for the power and freedom He gave to Adam and Eve. He knew His part in the relationship, which included giving the freedom of choice to humans and allowing the curses and consequences of knowing evil to befall His beloved Creation. Personal responsibility means that we see our part in a situation. Sometimes this means allowing others to experience the pain of our choice as well as their own. A refusal to set healthy boundaries in a relationship will keep us stuck in an unhealthy cycle of wounding, building walls that keep out healing, growth, and intimacy. Boundaries are doors that can both open and close when needed for ensuring our well-being and safety.

Taking responsibility for our part in painful relationships doesn't necessarily mean we are at fault for wrongdoing. A woman who is beaten or raped, or a child who is physically and sexually abused is in no way at fault. Yet victims (even children) often look back with regret and report things they wish they had done to escape or steps they might have taken to participate in their own rescue. It is tempting to try to convince them that they are wrong about this. We know they could not have prevented the abuse. The emotional reality for the victim is that our intellectual explanation does not heal this wound. Yet to thrive, victims often need to emotionally grieve their powerlessness and self-perceived failure to act before they can reclaim their personal power to stop blaming themselves.

Let me give another example to help clarify this. Let us consider a child who wishes a parent dead in the heat of an argument. Later that day, the child learns that the parent died in a car accident and is convinced the accident is their fault. In my experience, there is no way to intellectually convince that child (or adult) that he or she is not responsible. This is often a visceral response unconnected to logical thinking. What we can do however is to enter into their world of responsibility and listen deeply to all the feelings of self-incrimination. For some in this situation, the child can only begin the grief process by being allowed to confront the loss of not being able to take back those words. This becomes the doorway to grieving the actual loss of the parent's death. This is the time when the reassuring words that they are not at fault for the death can be more readily heard and accepted as truth.

In the case of disappointment about what someone is like, there is great healing and freedom when we begin to build a relationship with them based on the reality of who they are rather than on who we would like them to be. It is not wrong to want them to be different or to work with them to make changes that are mutually agreeable and satisfying. However, when they cannot or will not make changes, we still have the power to grieve. Doors to a new kind of relationship are created by our acceptance of reality and our capacity to feel deep grief (including anger) for the loss rather than continuing to try to change or blame ourselves and them. This is often a time when the possibility of forgiveness begins to emerge, not just as a spiritual responsibility, but as a genuine emotional need.

We want and need to be free of the heavy burden of anger and a desire for revenge. Forgiveness, however, is completely different from reconciliation. Forgiveness, like love, can operate in one direction. I can forgive those who have not forgiven me. Reconciliation, like intimacy, is two-way and requires reciprocity. Reconciliation occurs when one or both parties admit and take responsibility for any wrongs, willingly earn future trust, and respectfully negotiate mutually agreeable ways of treating one another in the future.

Relational Growth and Potential for Intimacy

The reward for enduring the healing pain of grief is personal and relational growth. Increased intimacy with God is available throughout this process but in particular when our Lord reveals joy and desire fulfilled in some unexpected way that may have nothing to do with the loss we have just grieved. In some cases, walking this path may result in resolved conflicts that have the surprising effect of drawing two people closer to one another emotionally. This provides confidence for the next time conflict arises. The threat of losing a relationship is not quite as frightening once you have successfully worked out a mutually satisfying solution to a problem. Trust is built that the relationship can endure a future conflict and be resolved in a way that cultivates rather than crushes intimacy.

Adjusted Hopes, Dreams, and Expectations

The expectations we brought to the relationship initially have now been tested in the fire of truth and reality. We have adjusted our expectations and made them more realistic, so the pain found in the discrepancy between our hopes and reality has lessened. Conflict may still be present at times, but now we believe that we can find our way through the grief that comes with disappointment and loss. We do not welcome it, but we have more understanding of its purposes and the benefits of working it through. We know some of the skills and discipline needed to journey through the valley of the shadow. We are open to learning new skills. We recognize the quagmire of emotion and seek to be informed but not controlled by them. We see how chronic blaming reinjures ourselves and prolongs the healing process. We know the difference between hurting pain and healing pain and are willing to tolerate the one and get help for the other. We get excited about new hopes and dreams as God leads us, and we know there is a path that leads to life, love, and greater intimacy with God and others. We are more at peace with ourselves because we practice personal responsibility and the power of choice.

The Gift of a Disciplined Love

The process I have just outlined is a rigorous discipline of heart, mind, soul, and strength. We see evidence of this in the life of Christ, particularly in the Garden of Gethsemane (Matthew 26:36–56). There could be no resurrection for our Savior without His willingness to be deeply grieved, suffer, and die a humiliating death on the cross. Likewise, there is no victorious love for God and others without a journey through the valley of the shadow of death—even if it is the death to our dearest desires. Our God demonstrated love to us in that while we were yet sinners, Christ died for us (Romans 5:8). We too will be asked to love others while they are yet sinners like ourselves and remember our Savior's sacrifice.

In the next chapter, we will take the Map of Grief into the home of my friend Jay and learn about a conflict between him, his parents, and his older brother, Jared. It took regular and extraordinary discipline for these family members to learn how to love one another. They were at great odds with one another and yet through the power of personal choice, they found the courage and discipline to exercise love, despite having to walk through the valley of the shadow of loss.

CHAPTER 14

Transformed Lives

"You have heard that it was said, 'You shall love your neighbor
and hate your enemy.' But I say to you, love your enemies and
pray for those who persecute you, so that you may be sons of your
Father who is in heaven; for He causes His sun to rise on the evil
and the good, and sends rain on the righteous and the unrighteous.
For if you love those who love you, what reward do you have?"
(Matthew 5:43–46a, NASB 1995)

The Way out of the Culture War

Many families are living in a state of war with family members because of cultural, political, theological, or moral differences. I meet so many people in my office, at church, or in my community who tell me of their pain related to family members who have become like enemies. The same Savior who told us to love our enemies also said that "a man's enemies will be the members of his household" (Matthew 10:36, NASB, 1995).

We live every day in the tension of life and death, truth and lies, love and hate, law and grace, and justice and mercy, to name a few. It is in Christ and the power of His Holy Spirit that we experience the resolution of these seeming opposites. It is in the crucible of our differences that the Holy Spirit forges a Christlike character capable of loving others when it is easier to hate them. We must be willing to have Christ transform our own lives if we want to see the lives of others transformed. I am challenged to put these principles into practice every day and want to share a story I have witnessed that has included both grief and hope for love in the midst of painful disappointment and loss.

Taking the Grief Map to Jay's House

Hopes, Dreams, and Expectations

Remember Janet, the young high school girl who introduced me to Jesus? I would like to introduce you to her family, especially her younger brother, Jay. Janet also had an older brother, Jared. They grew up in a devout Christian family with a loving mother and father. All three siblings attended Bible college and their parents had high hopes of their children continuing to follow Jesus and serve in vocational church ministry. Jared was married and in the ministry, and Jay was a gifted musician studying to be a music minister. I have already shared the sad reality that my friend Janet died very young at the age of 21. Her younger brother Jay and I had a special bond in the early days of my conversion to Christ, especially after he lost his only sister and I lost my dearest friend.

I did not know that Jay had a secret. He hoped that his mom, dad, and brother would graciously accept the important news that he was about to share with them. He had struggled with his sexuality growing up and had tried to talk to people at the church where he grew up, but with little success. Throughout his young adult life, he tried to make sense of his conflicting thoughts, feelings, beliefs, and the teachings about homosexuality in his family and church. He had been through horrendous trauma as part of the reparative sexuality movement. He suffered a great deal from the pressure exerted upon him to be someone he was not and still maintain his own sense of personal integrity.

Relational Conflict and Disappointment

When Jay finally came out about his homosexuality to his family, they all felt deep devastation, hurt, anger, guilt, fear, and sadness. Both Jay and his family experienced a profound sense of loss and grief. It was difficult to express the level of pain and disappointment they all experienced as they were forced to enter a new relational reality. The issues at stake were existential for everyone involved. As they grappled with the people they dearly loved, the conflict intensified, difficult and hurtful words were exchanged, and conversations more often than not became arguments that escalated and found no resolution. There was the threat of complete rejection and separation by Jay's family and church leaders. There were moments of blaming self and others for the disappointment, loss, and hurt. Bible bullets were fired in both directions and everyone was being shot and bloodied in the theological fight.

Hurt, Pain, and Avoiding the Emotions of Grief and Loss

Over the next few years, when Jay and his family saw each other, they still felt stuck in a vicious cycle of pain, hurt, anger, and frustration. Each time they tried to talk, they were determined to change one another's perspective. In some ways, this tug of war was a way of avoiding deep emotional pain and loss in their relationships. It was easier for his brother, mom, and dad to blame Jay, society, or even themselves for the change in the relationship. They could more easily spiritualize or intellectualize away the pain than face this profound loss. It was easier for Jay to blame rigid religious doctrines, or his parents for their ignorance and hurtful beliefs, than to go through the pain that would lead him to acknowledge his profound permanent loss.

Denying Reality, Building Walls, and Injurious Pain

There was a continued and basic denial of reality. Jay was a homosexual man who was at peace with himself and had chosen to be honest with them because he dearly loved them. His mom, dad, and brother were at peace with their strong belief that homosexual sex was a sin. They kept debating the Bible with him, hoping he would change. Jay kept coming home to them and hoping he would experience their understanding and acceptance. This was a time when the relationship was most at risk. It would be easy to stay in the pain of this conflict with irreconcilable beliefs and just walk away. This is the place where many families facing a similar dilemma become fractured and do not find a way back to one another. This is the place where understanding the difference between love and intimacy can make a difference. This is the place where taking responsibility for grieving loss in the relationship can carve a path for relational healing without compromising personal integrity.

The Crisis of Decision: Grieve or Bail Out

A decision to grieve does not mean that Jay will no longer hope that his mom, dad, and brother will come to have more love, understanding, and compassion for him as a gay man. Going through the grieving process does not prevent his parents from praying for him to return to the beliefs about God and sexuality that they hold so dear. What it does mean is that both are prepared to accept the reality of what has been expressed in the present. It was at this point that Jay and his family stood at a crisis of decision. How long would they continue in this pattern of injurious pain? Would they acknowledge that this was a true loss in the relationship that needed to be grieved?

Hurt, Pain, and Choosing to Feel the Emotions of Grief and Loss

The difference between the hurt and pain of loss that heals and the hurt and pain that continues to injure is a choice to actually feel and not block the emotions of loss. Although there are many emotions associated with grief, as we have already discussed, it is the willingness to experience these emotions deeply and face the reality of the loss that heals us. Jay and each of his family members must make this decision and go through the grieving process.

Accepting Reality, Building Doors, and Healing Pain

When I called to talk to Jay about his story and ask for his permission to share it with you, I was reminded that he and his parents made this decision differently and at different times in the relationship. It took Jay five years of going back and forth and in and out of injurious pain before he realized that his parents were simply not capable of loving him in this area of his life the way he had hoped. From his perspective, it was not wrong for him to want this nor was it unreasonable. But it was unrealistic to expect that he could change their minds or that they would change his mind. During these five years, there was the proverbial walking on eggshells and tiptoeing around the topic of his being a gay man. He had received his doctorate in Sexology and was a professional practicing therapist, but this part of his life could not be shared. These kinds of joys and successes were not celebrated with his parents without igniting the old fire of hurt and anger around his sexual orientation.

Jay finally realized that it was going to be up to him to stop the fruitless conflict and take responsibility for accepting his family members as they were, even if they could not accept him. It was painful for him as a son to be the one to love them, despite their absolute disapproval of him and any future partners he might like to invite to their home. This, however, is exactly what he did in order to put the relationship above the debate and loving them above agreement on the issues. How did he do this? He finally came to them and told them he was placing a moratorium on the subject of homosexuality and the Bible. He would take a break from the discussions. It was not a taboo subject, but simply a subject that created too much injury. The topic, though important to all of them, would take a backseat to their relationships as parent-adult child and siblings. This would limit the level of closeness he had previously enjoyed, but it would also allow him to stay in a relationship with them without escalating injury.

Jay deeply grieved the loss of openness he had experienced with his family up to this point. The relationship felt superficial and stiff. He shared with his mom and dad that he had gotten to the point at which he was not wanting to visit or attend family holidays anymore. His family realized how much the chronic debate was hurting him and agreed that the topic of conflict had overtaken their relationship. They all agreed to the conditions of a cease-fire, and there was more peace. Over the next 10 years, Jay would continue to come home and build a relationship with his mom, dad, and brother based on who they were rather than who he wanted them to be. Without compromising their beliefs about homosexuality, his family also demonstrated a capacity to accept and love Jay for who he was rather than for who they wanted him to be.

Relational Growth and Potential for Intimacy

Interpersonal truth is the foundation of intimate knowing, caring, desiring, and delighting in one another's presence. When there is less blaming, less hiding, and more acceptance of one another, there is a freedom to mature. Though extremely painful to everyone involved, the willingness to listen to each other's honest thoughts, feelings, and beliefs became a foundation for healing and future growth. Both Jay and his parents grew to understand that they could hold on to their own valued beliefs and still love one another. They used their personal power of choice to stop demanding understanding and agreement on issues. They began to see that accepting one another meant learning the skill of tolerating the tension between their antithetical beliefs when they were together. They each needed to learn to take responsibility for managing their own outrage, anger, hurt, and sadness in the relationship privately. Each had to learn how to exercise self-control so that love, joy, peace, patience, kindness, goodness, faithfulness, and gentleness could characterize interaction with one another.

Adjusted Hopes, Dreams, and Expectations

Jay is not sure when, over the next 10 years, that his mom, dad, and brother made the decision to grieve the loss of their son and brother as they had hoped he would be, or whether or not the process was in any way conscious. But they did begin to talk about conferences they were attending on the topic of homosexuality in the Church. This signaled a new beginning for the family in the process of talking together again about Jay's being gay without expecting him to change, and without the extreme and virulent emotions.

Jay remembers his mom talking to him about something she had heard while attending a conference. She asked him if he thought it was her fault that he was gay. At that time there was quite a lot of literature asserting that parents were responsible for the homosexuality of their children. Jay absolutely disagreed with that view and explained more about his beliefs and the research to the contrary. He felt heard by his mom and that felt very good. She valued his opinion, and they were able to talk openly on the topic without it escalating into blame or an argument.

I remember one of my visits to Jay's parents' home. His father told me that he had confronted a church member who was condemning homosexuals and uttering painful slurs after the service they had just attended. His father turned to the church member and said, "I don't appreciate the way you are talking about my son right now. I'd rather you'd pray for him." This led to more conversation and some education in this man's life and within the church about homosexuality as seen through Jay's eyes and through his Christian father's eyes. I was moved and grateful for these changes.

These may seem like trivial things and not much of a return after 15 years of hard emotional and relational work by Jay and his family. Not everyone in a comparable situation chooses to do this or learns how to do it. For each of them, however, the relationship they have today, nearly 30 years later, is more than worth the effort it took to get there. Jay valued relationship with his family enough to endure the pain of grieving. He found a way to adjust his expectations about the kind of love and closeness he would receive from his parents and brother when it came to this important and existential aspect of his life. He was able to set boundaries that allowed for healing and self-care. His mom, dad, and brother valued their relationship with Jay enough to grieve the loss of the son and brother they had hoped for without changing their beliefs that homosexuality was wrong. Both Jay and his family showed compassion toward one another without compromise. Their love for one another has now opened the door for God's story to unfold in unexpected ways.

CHAPTER 15

Transformed Human Authority

"Shepherd the flock of God among you, exercising oversight not
under compulsion, but voluntarily, according to the will of God; and
not for sordid gain, but with eagerness; not yet as lording it over those
allotted to your charge, but proving to be examples to the flock."

(1 Peter 5:2–3, NASB 1995)

Choosing the Way of Jesus

We have just spent the last four chapters digging deeply into the soil of intimacy and its close relative, grief. You may be wondering what these two topics have to do with transforming human authority. Both intimacy and grief require us to exercise authority over ourselves and take responsibility for choosing the way of Christ in our relationships. Both require us to respect the choices of others even when we disagree with them. The Apostle Peter reminds us that those who are entrusted with the oversight of others are to shepherd in the way of Jesus rather than simply import the top-down way of the world.

Human authority is transformed by Christ when we serve one another by finding mutually satisfying solutions to conflict rather than by using our power to insist on our own way. Although the world's human authority may allow us and others to exercise authority in controlling or punitive ways, we are to choose mutuality whenever it is within our power to do so.

Honoring Human Authority without Legitimizing Abuse

As I have already said elsewhere, we need human law to help keep order. We obey governing authorities in that spirit. When believers teach that obeying Caesar is the same as obeying God, they are perpetuating the lie that humans and governments have used for millennia to gain and abuse their power over people for personal or political gain. It bears repeating that our first obligation is to obey God, not humans, whether the human is a king, pope, pastor, teacher, military leader, employer, slave holder, parent, or husband. As soon as we say that obeying those in human authority is the same as obeying God, we have moved from honoring those in authority to idolatry (Acts 5:29).

Let us not forget that we will be tempted to grasp worldly and religious power. Satan tempted Jesus in the wilderness with this very promise. Matthew 4:8–11 (NASB 1995) says,

> *"Again, the devil took Him to a very high mountain and showed Him all the kingdoms of the world and their glory; and he said to Him, 'All these things I will give You, if You fall down and worship me.' Then Jesus said to him, 'Go, Satan!' For it is written, 'You shall worship the Lord Your God and Serve Him only.' Then the devil left Him; and behold, angels came and began to minister to Him."*

Christ alone deserves our submission, obedience, and worship above all human authority. Regardless of how much we respect, honor, and obey our human leaders, they are never to be equated with the leadership of Christ. Much abuse of power has been perpetrated against the most vulnerable using this kind of argument.

I have made the claim that our sinful human nature and our penchant for power over others account for much of the innate power struggle among human beings, whether Christians or not. However, it is no mistake that Ephesians 6 ends its discussion about mutual submission to one another as believers by telling us to put on the full armor of God to equip us against the schemes of the devil. We must take seriously the spiritual enemies that fight against the Spirit of God in believers every moment of every day. Distorting God's Word is the oldest scheme of the devil.

I have argued that the lens of the curses and consequences of the Fall continue to distort our view of Scripture and God's highest intentions today for power relations among believers and all humans. Without the capacity to see God's original design and highest intention for sharing His authority with humans rather than lording it over us, we will not see how our misuse of authority and power sabotages intimacy in all relationships, even in our relationship to God.

Acknowledging Human Vulnerability to Power

As believers, we can go before the throne of God daily and ask the Holy Spirit to expose in us any lust after power over others and, in particular, personal desires that masquerade as biblical authority. We are invited to choose and enjoy the sacred intimacy God designed to satisfy the human heart and reflect the equality, distinct persons, and unity of our triune God. This is only possible by consciously and intentionally cooperating with the Holy Spirit to put to death daily our own lust of the eyes, lust of the flesh, and boastful pride of life.[103]

Living out Love in a Land of Slavery

There is perhaps no better place in the New Testament that exemplifies the delicate balance between life in a post-Fall world of human authority and life in the New Creation world under the authority of Christ than in Paul's short letter to Philemon. It helps us recognize the tightrope walk between our New Creation identity of freedom and our post-Fall reality of slavery. The principles that governed Paul's plea to this first century Roman slave-owner for the slave Onesimus can also be applied to Paul's appeal to first-century husbands for a Christlike love for their wives.

Paul writes first of his authority as a human leader to command Philemon to do what is right and to regard Onesimus as a brother in Christ. Though the text does not say this explicitly, Paul may have been urging Philemon to release him completely from the bondage of slavery. Paul says in his own words,

"Therefore, although in Christ I could be bold and order you to do what you

---

103 1 John 2:16

ought to do, yet I prefer to appeal to you on the basis of love. It is as none other than Paul—an old man and now also a prisoner of Christ Jesus—that I appeal to you for my son Onesimus, who became my son while I was in chains. Formerly he was useless to you, but now he has become useful both to you and to me.

I am sending him—who is my very heart—back to you. I would have liked to keep him with me so that he could take your place in helping me while I am in chains for the gospel. But I did not want to do anything without your consent, so that any favor you do would not seem forced but would be voluntary. Perhaps the reason he was separated from you for a little while was that you might have him back forever—no longer as a slave, but better than a slave, as a dear brother. He is very dear to me but even dearer to you, both as a fellow man and as a brother in the Lord.

So, if you consider me a partner, welcome him as you would welcome me. If he has done you any wrong or owes you anything, charge it to me."

(Philemon 1:8–18, TNIV)

Paul, respectful of Philemon's authority as a slaveholder in the Roman culture of the day, does not stop there. He appeals to Philemon on the basis of love—the New Creation Way –and urges Philemon to see his slave Onesimus as "in Christ"—a brother in the Lord. Paul urges this slaveholder to live up to the highest intention of the gospel: freedom. Yet Paul restrains his own ability to exert human power as a leader and apostle by demanding obedience. Instead, he appeals to Philemon as both a brother and partner. Paul takes personal responsibility to pay for any losses due to the disobedience of Philemon's runaway slave during the time he was with Paul. Paul returns Onesimus to Philemon, despite his own desire to have the company of Onesimus while in prison. This encounter offers a poignant portrait of what true New Testament Christian love looks like in a fallen world that often takes advantage of authority over others. It demonstrates that, although spiritual or worldly leaders may have a right to assert and even enforce their authority according to the laws of the world, Jesus has given us an even higher calling, the New Creation way.

Freedom for Slaves but Not for Wives?

History shows that in the 18th and 19th centuries, many Christian men in England

and later in America began to oppose slavery on biblical grounds and lobbied for laws that would free slaves,—yet were still opposed to laws that would grant married women the right to be viewed as their own persons. In England, slavery was abolished in 1807, whereas new legislation countering coverture laws were not in place until the Married Women's Property Act of 1882. The system of *feme covert*, or Coverture laws developed in the Middle Ages, was institutionalized as common law in Britain, and was brought to America by British colonists.

Coverture laws ensured that women were deprived of a personal and separate identity, the ability to make their own decisions, own property, or even have legal custody of their own children—all on the biblical grounds that husband and wife were considered "one flesh." The principle of coverture was described in William Blackstone's *Commentaries* in the late 18th century:

> *"By marriage, the husband and wife are one person in law: that is, the very being or legal existence of the woman is suspended during the marriage, or at least is incorporated and consolidated into that of the husband: under whose wing, protection, and cover, she performs everything; and is therefore called in our law-French a feme-covert...under the protection and influence of her husband, her baron, or lord; and her condition during her marriage is called her coverture...For this reason, a man cannot grant anything to his wife, or enter into covenant with her: for the grant would be to suppose her separate existence; and to covenant with her, would be only to covenant with himself: and therefore it is also generally true, that all compacts made between husband and wife, when single, are voided by the intermarriage...Further, a 'married woman' or 'feme covert' was a dependent, like an underage child or a slave, and could not own property in her own name or control her own earnings, except under very specific circumstances. When a husband died, his wife could not be the guardian to their underage children."*[104]

---

104 Blackstone, William. *Commentaries on the Laws of England*, Vol, 1, 1765 (442-445), and OLL, "The Women of Seneca Falls and William Blackstone," OLL, Accessed July 11, 2023. https://oll.libertyfund.org/quote/the-women-of-seneca-falls-and-william-blackstone

Grievously, laws that would grant women the right to own property and vote, and that would decriminalize her ability to make decisions without her husband's consent, were seen by many men as opposed to the biblical pattern. Rather than freeing women from the similar societal bondage that oppressed slaves, women were not set free to enjoy their New Creation identities. These husbands did not interpret Paul's statements about mutual submission and sacrificial love as having anything to do with the distinct personhood of their wives as reflected in the creation of humankind. They did not see that projecting the top-down leadership structure of the world onto the words of Paul about husbands being the head of their wives was actually the antithesis of Christ's sacrificial love for his Bride and worked directly against mutuality inherent to intimacy.

In Matthew 23:10–12, Jesus warns, "Do not be called leaders; for One is your Leader, that is, Christ. But the greatest of you shall be your servant. Whoever exalts himself shall be humbled, and whoever humbles himself shall be exalted" (NASB 1995). This does not mean that leadership is wrong or that there are not legitimate lines of authority to be respected and obeyed in our world. What it does mean, however, is that our sinful, fleshly nature is vulnerable to worldly abuse of power and that we must diligently guard against enforcing our will upon other human beings.

Paul's letter to Philemon therefore gives us wisdom and a lens through which to view human lines of authority. God's Pre-Fall and New Creation intention for shared power and control does not negate the need for biblical authority in relationships any more than Christ fulfilling the Law abolished it. They both serve a role and purpose. However, if we do not understand God's highest intention, we will default to post-Fall authority structures, and ignore, misunderstand, misuse, or even abuse the authority of God that is taught throughout the Scriptures. When men and women do not champion the freedom and equality of a woman's inheritance in Christ, intimacy is crushed. The power of mutuality in relationships is diminished and we become slaves to the degradation of the Fall.

CHAPTER 16

Transformed Marriage—Part 1

"Modern Western readers immediately focus on (and often bristle at) the word 'submit,' because for us it touches the controversial issue of gender roles. But to start arguing about that is a mistake that will be fatal to any true grasp of Paul's introductory point. He is declaring that everything he is about to say about marriage assumes that the parties are being filled with God's Spirit. Only if you have learned to serve others by the power of the Holy Spirit will you have the power to face the challenges of marriage."[105]

—Timothy Keller

Judging from how many books, seminars, sermons, and retreats have been created to address the words of Paul to husbands and wives in Ephesians 5, I can say with confidence that this chapter addresses one of the thorniest passages of Scripture for couples and especially for wives. Many of us do not notice how Paul emphasizes mutual submission in Ephesians 5:21 as the overarching and guiding principle of all Christian interaction. Although readers often get overly focused on the husband-and-wife relationship, Paul goes on to give practical advice that applies to parenting and slavery as well. Paul was not advocating for slavery, nor for treating women and children as property as they were considered in first-century Ephesus.

---

105 Keller, Timothy, with Keller, Kathy. The Meaning of Marriage: Facing the Complexities of Commitment with the Wisdom of God. New York, NY: Penguin Books: 2011. (47–48)

Let us take some time for a rather lengthy but important contextual review of this often-debated passage of Ephesians 5 and continue reading some of Chapter 6 for clues about how to develop New Creation Era mutuality and intimacy in marriage.

> *"[15]Be very careful, then, how you live—not as unwise but as wise, [16] making the most of every opportunity, because the days are evil. [17] Therefore do not be foolish, but understand what the Lord's will is.[18]Do not get drunk on wine, which leads to debauchery. Instead, be filled with the Spirit, [19]speaking to one another with psalms, hymns and songs from the Sprit. Sing and make music from your heart to the Lord; [20]always giving thanks to God the Father for everything, in the name of our Lord Jesus Christ.*
>
> *[21]Submit to one another out of reverence for Christ.[106]*
>
> *[22]Wives, submit yourselves to your own husbands, as you do to the Lord. [23]For the husband is the head of the wife as Christ is the head of the church, his body, of which he is the Savior. [24] Now as the church submits to Christ, so also wives should submit to their husbands in everything.*
>
> *[25]Husbands, love your wives, just as Christ also loved the church and gave himself up for her, [26]to make her holy, cleansing her by the washing with water through the word, [27]and to present her to himself as a radiant church, without stain or wrinkle or any other blemish, but holy and blameless. [28]In this same way, husbands ought to love their wives as their own bodies. He who loves his wife loves himself. [29]After all, people have never hated their own bodies, but they feed and care for them, just as Christ does the church—[30]for we are members of his body. [31]For this reason a man will leave his father and mother and be united to his wife, and the two will become one flesh.*

---

106 Personal Communication. Philip B. Payne. September 6, 2021. "There is no paragraph break here in Paul's letter. Payne, Bible, 112 more accurately translates it: "submitting to one another out of reverence for Christ, wives to your own husbands, as to the Lord, because man is the source of the woman as also Christ is the source of the church, he the savior of the body."

³²This is a profound mystery--but I am talking about Christ and the church. ³³However, each one of you also must love his own wife as he loves himself, and the wife must respect her husband.

⁶:¹Children, obey your parents in the Lord, for this is right. ²'Honor your father and mother'-- which is the first commandment with a promise—, ³so that it may go well with you and that you may enjoy long life on the earth.

⁴Fathers, do not exasperate your children; Instead bring them up in the training and instruction of the Lord.

⁵Slaves, be obedient to your earthly masters with respect and fear, and with sincerity of heart just as you would obey Christ. ⁶Obey them not only to win their favor when their eye is on you, but as slaves of Christ, doing the will of God from your heart. ⁷Serve wholeheartedly, as if you were serving the Lord, not people, ⁸because you know that the Lord will reward each one of you for whatever good you do, whether you are slave or free.

⁹And masters, treat your slaves in the same way. Do not threaten them, since you know that he who is both their Master and yours is in heaven, and there is not favoritism with him." ¹⁰Finally, be strong in the Lord and in his mighty power."

(Ephesians 5:15–6:10, TNIV)

The Way of Christ in Marriage

These words, "Wives, submit yourselves to your own husbands, as you do to the Lord" (Ephesians 5:22, TNIV), often strike fear in the hearts of women, particularly those who have been abused by authoritarian men throughout their lives. Married women in particular wrestle with gnawing and unanswered questions about equality and the exercising of authority by men and women. The backlash to the feminist movement by some Christians has not given much room for women and men to sort out what they believe without fear of being shamed into silence or labeled unorthodox. Many believers suffer and some even choose to walk away from their faith in Christ to resolve this tension and their own cognitive and emotional dissonance.

Thoughtful Christian women and men are asking important questions about how to understand and apply a biblical perspective to power and gender relations. The men who want to share power and leadership with their wives and ministry partners wonder how to do so without neglecting their God-given leadership responsibilities. Wives long for involvement with final decision-making yet do not want to neglect the biblical command to respect and obey their husbands and church leaders. These believers need and deserve safe places to ask questions and struggle with Scripture for the purpose of developing a strong, mature, and biblical faith.

Believers who submit to the lordship of Jesus Christ in their lives and marriages need not be frightened or overwhelmed by the words of the Apostle Paul. Only when we impose the burden of a worldly, top-down hierarchy onto the living Bride of Christ do we find bondage and abuse of power instead of mutual friendship and love.

It was and is therefore a mistake to think that Paul's command for slaves to obey their masters legitimized slavery. It was and is equally a mistake to think that Paul's command for wives to submit to their husbands legitimized the practice of men having authority to rule over their wives as do worldly leaders. Any command of Paul's must be viewed through the lens of the New Creation and the New Commandment of Christ to love one another as He loved them. Jesus turned the authority of this world upside down and reversed the curse.

So how are we to reconcile these seemingly mutually exclusive commands to love, submit, lead, and share authority and power as Christ did? This Ephesians 5 passage begins with the admonition to be wise, to not be drunk with wine, to be filled with the Spirit, to sing joyfully, and give thanks to God. Grammatically, the sentence in verse 18 begins with a conjugated verb, "Don't be drunk with wine"… and continues with "but be filled with the Spirit." Every verb after that to verse 21 is a participle dependent on verse 18 reading: be filled with the Spirit (by) singing…, (by) giving thanks…,(by) submitting to one another,…" The wisdom of Spirit-filled living is the prerequisite for the mutuality that characterizes the New Creation era.

Mutual Submission

Greek scholars note that in the original text, the verb "submit" (*hypotassō*) is not present in verse 22 ("wives *submit* to your husbands"). It is in verse 21, where it is a command to all believers, regardless of gender. The problem is isolating verse

22 from its literary context, as if verse 21 did not include husbands submitting to wives, instructions which are further clarified and defined in 5:25–33. It is difficult to overemphasize the importance of distorting this grammatical fact. The Greek text literally reads, "wives to their own husbands," which clearly reaches back for the verbal participle *hupotassomenoi*, "submit" of verse 21.

The point of this whole passage, from 5:21–6:9 is that all of our relationships are to be governed by a Spirit–filled type of mutual submission, which is very different from worldly submission. Other than the statement to respect their husbands, there is no specific elaboration in this passage for wives on the meaning of submission. There could be little confusion, considering that wives, children, and slaves were legally bound to place themselves under husbands, parents, and masters under Roman law. There were harsh consequences for disobedience. Husbands, fathers, and slave-owners, on the other hand, would have considered the idea of mutual submission not only unthinkably foreign, but weak and degrading.

It is therefore not surprising that Paul goes on to give an extended theological explanation of "love" as defined by submission (Christ's submissive self-sacrifice on the cross). This is also the reason that Paul argues that mistreating your wife is essentially mistreating yourself. Both fathers and masters were asked to treat those under their authority not as Roman Law would allow but according to the law of love in Christ. Indeed, even some of the most conservative evangelical pastors[107] and theologians agree that the bulk of Paul's statements in Ephesians 5 addresses men and the sacrificial and loving way that husbands are to care for their wives. Why, then, do some of these same pastors and theologians add so much explanation that sets up an authority structure that encourages husbands to be leaders of their wives?

One answer is that we have not given adequate credibility to the robust theme of mutuality present in this passage from beginning to end. Paul continues to give examples of how to submit to one another in a way that is mutual, even within the harsh structures of an authoritarian culture. Notice that Paul not only tells the

---

107 MacArthur, John. "Ephesians 5:25-33, Husbands, Love Your Wives" (February 26, 2012). https://www.gty.org/library/sermons-library/80-383/husbands-love-your-wives and Piper, John. "Husbands Who Love Like Christ and the Women who Submit to Them" (June 11, 1989). https://www.desiringgod.org/messages/husbands-who-love-like-christ-and-the-wives-who-submit-to-them, and Keller, Tim. *The Meaning of Marriage* (New York: Penguin Books) 2011, (192–217)

party with less power to obey, but also challenges the one who has more power in the relationship to obey the higher law of love in submission to Christ. He tells children to obey their parents, but he also tells the father not to provoke the child to anger. He tells the slave to obey the master, but he charges the master to not treat the slave unjustly and to remember that the slave owner also has a master in Heaven. Although our monocular, post-Fall vision often obscures it, Paul is bringing the complexity and responsibility of binocular mutual submission into primary focus through each of these examples. In other words, each believer was to find a way to submit to existing authority structures but in ways that would most exemplify the law of love. Let us never assume for a moment that the existing first-century structures of marriage, family, and slavery legitimized a top-down approach by Paul's words or metaphors.

Paul most certainly did not endorse such cultural and legal structures any more than we now endorse such practices in some Middle Eastern countries that believe in capital punishment for women caught in adultery or that forbid girls to attend school on the basis of their gender. If you talk to missionaries in Middle Eastern countries today, they will tell you that they cannot simply encourage new women believers to exercise their freedom and equality in Christ to defy their husbands and government laws. Some women believers may indeed be led to civil and domestic disobedience in order to challenge these structures. They may even risk imprisonment and death to promote the cause of freedom for women in their country. Missionaries, however, will likely tell most believing wives, husbands, and children some of the same things about submission and obedience that Paul was saying to believers in Ephesus to avoid becoming targets of severe persecution and to further the gospel of Christ.[108]

Cultural Codes of Conduct

Those who traditionally hold to a post-Fall perspective of leadership will tend to read biblical passages dealing with human authority as a call for unquestioned obedience to a top-down hierarchy and leadership structure. This is defended on biblical grounds, particularly the verses that make up what are often referred

---

108 Keener, Craig S. *Paul, Women, & Wives: Marriage and Women's Ministry in the Letters of Paul.* Peabody, Massachusetts: Hendrickson Publishers, Inc. 1992. (146)

to as the house codes or *Haustafeln*[109] in the New Testament letters by Peter and Paul. But comparable house codes for women, children, and slaves were already in place in Aristotle's time and were based on the belief that men were superior to women. Peter and Paul were not legitimizing the wholesale use of these house codes as God's highest intention for believers, nor were they encouraging women and children to be treated as legal property.

In another discussion about human authority, Paul addresses Jewish traditions and customs, such as the practice of head coverings. He even uses a hierarchy of God over man and man over woman in 1 Corinthians 11:3. Yet a contextual reading of this passage shows that Paul is not legitimizing a top-down approach but acknowledging that it is a part of the tradition he delivered to the Corinthians about head coverings. We must look to the whole cultural context of this passage for clues about gender relations, rather than proof texting in order to support a theology of top-down leadership. Paul writes, "However, in the Lord, neither is woman independent of man, nor is man independent of woman. For as woman originates from the man, so also the man has his birth through the woman; and all things originate from God. Judge for yourselves: is it proper for a woman to pray to God with her head uncovered?" (1 Corinthians 11:11–13, NASB 1995)[110] Even here, there is the intimacy of mutuality, interdependence, reciprocity, and the freedom to judge for themselves.

---

109 *Haustafeln* (literally "house blackboard" in German). The household codes can also be interpreted as a list of household rules which might have been posted on a sign or blackboard for all to see. School children write on *Tafeln* (blackboards) at school. The *Haustafeln* assumed a unilateral command for wives, children, and slaves to submit to husbands, parents, and masters respectively and referred to in the Epistles of Paul and Peter as *Haustafeln* in German.

110 Paul frequently gave his opinion on matters of tradition (1 Corinthians 7:10, 25), but was careful to acknowledge they were not to be seen as commands of the Lord. This certainly does not mean they were not trustworthy statements but if he was careful to acknowledge the distinction, so must we be careful to acknowledge it.

CHAPTER 17

Transformed Marriage—Part 2

"Human beings have deep needs both for closeness and for independence. We need unity with others, and we need space for ourselves. Thwart either of these needs and we create misery beyond belief."[111]

—Gay Hendricks, Ph.D., and Kathlyn Hendricks, Ph.D.

Leaving for Cleaving

Adam and Eve were not two halves that made a whole. Your wife or husband is not your other half any more than the Father, Son, or Holy Spirit is the other's better third. Instead, the one whole person of the Father multiplied by the one whole person of the Son multiplied by the one whole person of the Holy Spirit equals our One triune God. As has been discussed at length throughout this book, we were created separate and equal in order to display the beauty of unity in diversity.

We have seen that God's original design for marriage was corrupted by the knowledge of good and evil, and later restored men and women to their former beauty as new creations in Christ. As believers, wives and husbands have the joy of cultivating the kind of mutual intimacy and connection God imagined when He

---

111 Hendricks, Gay, Ph.D., and Hendricks, Kathlyn, Ph.D. Conscious Loving: The Journey to Co-Commitment. New York: Bantam Books, 1992

said that a man shall leave his father and mother and be joined to his wife. In order to become one flesh, there is a separation from mother and father that must occur. Although the passage in Genesis does not explicitly state the need for the wife to do the same, it is certainly implied. It would be impossible for oneness to occur were the wife or husband to remain attached to or dependent on a mother or father. The capacity of both partners to leave their parents and cleave to one another is essential for marital intimacy in the Pre-Fall, Post-Fall, and New Creation Eras.

The essential and healthy process of leaving involves the grieving process discussed at length in Chapter 14. A couple must become free emotionally, spiritually, socially, and financially to make their own decisions about places to live, ways to worship, and their choice of careers. Surprisingly, leaving for cleaving is by nature a path through the valley of the shadow of loss. The vast and varied emotions of grief present an opportunity for personal responsibility and growth but can also expose a miry pit filled with avoidance and blame. Rather than working through the conflicts inherent to a healthy separation from families of origin, we can fall into chronic power struggles that often signal a refusal to let go and grieve.

Separating becomes infinitely more difficult for couples who depend on parents for meeting some of their basic needs, whether financial, emotional, or relational—and who fear severe consequences should they choose a path that meets with parental disapproval. It is equally difficult for a husband or wife to leave his or her parents if one or both of them are still dependent on an adult child (and consequently now on the new couple) to meet critical needs. In both cases, fear of loss becomes an obstacle to the priority of a couple learning to become one.

Leaving for cleaving does not mean that married couples cannot work and live with their extended family members. The question that will determine the health of such close involvement will be whether or not the couple's autonomy remains intact when differences between the needs and desires of the couple and extended family members emerge. Seemingly innocuous decisions, such as where the couple will spend holidays, can disrupt long-held family traditions. Suddenly a choice will be made that exposes family alliances. If the couple's loyalty to one another has not yet been tested, these decisions will either put the heart of each spouse at ease or create anxiety about who really is the priority in the marriage. As long as the couple has divided allegiances, marital intimacy will suffer.

The ideal scenario is one in which healthy families can negotiate win-win solutions to situations that impact extended family members, such as when the wife or husband is part owner of a family business. The integrity of the couple as a separate and independent body from the extended family is often tested in the crucible of conflicting and overlapping needs and desires. As both a therapist and a wife, I have seen how fundamental and foundational this first and continuing marital task of becoming united through leaving and cleaving is to laying a firm and safe foundation for cultivating a strong and intimate marriage.

Cultures and individual families differ greatly in the amount of connectedness that is both needed, expected, or wanted. In addition to allegiances, the capacity and skills for sharing power with family members is also exposed during the leaving and cleaving process. Blended families have unique challenges in this regard because they have children from other marriages that will also be grieving during this process. Co-parenting can be even more difficult if there is still acute pain and unresolved conflict from the previous relationships. The need to plan ahead to serve the best interests of the children and reduce conflict can require legal and psychotherapeutic intervention. In each of these cases, leaving and cleaving represents a tremendous loss for both parents and children. The inability to acknowledge and grieve such significant losses can become an equally tremendous barrier to the stability of the family and the intimacy of the couple.

Cleaving for Connection

The skills required for building deep connections and intimate friendship discussed at length in Chapters 3,12, and 13 also create a stable foundation for building intimacy in marriage. When we have a common faith and share similar interests, we can continue to develop intimacy for a lifetime by staying interested, curious, and engaged with our spouse. We can also continue to talk and learn from one another, work through conflict, grieve disappointments, and accept one another for who we are rather than who we would like each other to be. Throughout this book, we have seen that a willingness to be self-aware and reflect on the ways our history has impacted our development, makes the difference between staying stuck in destructive patterns or growing in our capacity to bond with God and others.

In their book *How We Love*, Milan and Kay Yerkovich outline how our early bonding and attachment experiences (or lack thereof) can determine how we love. They introduce "The Comfort Circle" as a tool in which couples can 1) seek awareness of feelings and underlying needs, 2) engage with feelings and acknowledge needs openly, 3) explore the speaker's thoughts and feelings—listening, validating, and concluding with, "What do you need?" and 4) resolve needs verbally and with touch, seeking how and when needs may be met in the future." They note that "completing the circle should bring relief—an increase in trust and feelings of connectedness. If hurtful action or inaction is experienced at any point in the circle, you should begin again."[112]

It is not uncommon for a close friendship and marriage to become an opportunity to heal both partners from early attachment wounds. God can use both our strengths and weaknesses to expose the best and the worst of ourselves to one another for the purpose of growth and healing. If both partners are willing to work hard on these areas without turning against each other in the process, we may learn from the stories of our "Old Testament" past so that we do not continue to repeat a history of disconnection and loneliness.

How do we cultivate a spiritual partnership when one partner is not a believer in Christ or is of a different faith? Even among Christians, opposing theological views can strain or fracture a relationship, despite both being children of God. It is a comfort to know that even in such cases, our Lord is still our spiritual partner and will give us the grace, courage, and power of the Holy Spirit to love our spouse in the absence of the spiritual closeness for which we long. We will need to travel that path of grief and loss discussed in Chapter 14 regularly in order to keep our heart tender toward our spouse when we are not experiencing what we hoped for in the relationship.

Spiritual friendships are particularly important in such cases and give us the strength to nurture connection in areas where it would otherwise not be possible. We must be careful, however, not to allow other relationships or service in the Church to interfere with and become a substitute for developing a solid marital relationship. We can still nurture intimacy with our unbelieving spouse by continuing to take

---

112 Yerkovich, Milan and Kay. *How We Love: A Revolutionary Approach to Deeper Connections in Marriage.* Colorado Springs, Colorado: Waterbrook Press, 2006. (197)

time to get to know them, by learning how to care for them in ways that are meaningful to them, and by communicating a desire and delight to be in their presence.

Regardless of whether or not we have a spiritually compatible partner, we will need the power of the Holy Spirit and an openness and curiosity about what is going on inside of us to both discern a proper response to our negative feelings and to overcome the habits of the flesh. The Apostle Paul speaks of a spiritual battle that wages within believers in Christ. The old sinful nature is at war with our new creation nature. He says it this way:

> *"You, my brothers and sisters, were called to be free. But do not use your freedom to indulge the sinful nature; rather, serve one another humbly in love. For the entire law is fulfilled in keeping this one command: 'Love your neighbor as yourself.' If you keep on biting and devouring each other, watch out or you will be destroyed by each other.*
>
> *So I say, walk by the Spirit, and you will not gratify the desires of the sinful nature. For the sinful nature desires what is contrary to the Spirit, and the Spirit what is contrary to the sinful nature. They are in conflict with each other, so that you are not to do whatever you want. But if you are led by the Spirit, you are not under the law.*
>
> *The acts of the sinful nature are obvious: sexual immorality, impurity and debauchery; idolatry and witchcraft; hatred, discord, jealousy, fits of rage, selfish ambition, dissensions, factions and envy; drunkenness, orgies, and the like. I warn you, as I did before, that those who live like this will not inherit the kingdom of God.*
>
> *But the fruit of the Spirit is love, joy, peace, patience, kindness, goodness, faithfulness, gentleness and self-control. Against such things there is no law. Those who belong to Christ Jesus have crucified the sinful nature with its passions and desires. Since we live by the Spirit, let us keep in step with the Spirit. Let us not become conceited, provoking and envying each other."*
>
> **(Galatians 5:13–26, TNIV)**

A Spirit-filled, Christ-centered marriage means that both husband and wife are free to live into God's highest intention for them as individuals and as a couple. The hard work of marriage is discovering how to produce the fruit of the Spirit in every practical aspect of the marriage relationship. In marriage and family life (as well as with roommates and fellow employees), the Spirit seeks a solution that honors the "we" of mutuality, integrates diversity, and enhances unity. If the flesh (or sinful nature) is in control when we are making decisions, we will live out the Fall and the deeds of the flesh.

Creating for Partnership

In a transformed marriage, husbands and wives are creative partners who thrive on encouraging the development of one another. The creativity of partners is crushed when attempts are made by either wife or husband to define who the spouse will be and how she or he will exercise her or his unique personality, life experiences, gifts, and talents. Indeed, something powerful happens when the partners do not compete but collaborate and help one another grow to their full potential in Christ to the glory of God. In the transformed marriage, women and men are called by God to exercise power and authority in Christ for the purpose of intimacy, oneness, and creativity. A first-century example of creative partnership in marriage is that of Priscilla and Aquilla. Both wife and husband labored alongside Paul as a team in tentmaking, taught new converts like Apollos in the faith, and spread the gospel (Acts 18:2–3, 26).

In 1 Corinthians 9:24–27, Paul compares our efforts and need for discipline in the Christian life with preparation for the Greek Olympic games. Team sports involve the development of skills similar to those needed in friendships, marriage, and within our work together as the Body of Christ. Daniel James Brown wrote brilliantly about the necessity of mutuality and equality in the success of a rowing team of nine Americans who prepared, competed, and won gold in the 1936 Berlin Olympics. In his book, *The Boys in the Boat*, Brown writes,

> "Crew races are not won by clones. They are won by crews, and great crews are carefully balanced blends of both physical abilities and personality types. In physical terms, for instance, one rower's arms

might be longer than another's, but the latter might have a stronger back than the former. Neither is necessarily a better or more valuable oarsman than the other; both the long arms and the strong back are assets to the boat. But if they are to row well together, each of these oarsmen must adjust to the needs and capabilities of the other. Each must be prepared to compromise something in the way of optimizing his stroke for the overall benefit of the boat—the shorter-armed man reaching a little farther, the longer-armed man foreshortening his reach just a bit—so that both men's oars remain parallel and both blades enter and exit the water precisely the same moment. This highly refined coordination and cooperation must be multiplied out across eight individuals of varying statures and physiques to make the most of each individual's strengths. Only in this way can the capabilities that come with diversity—lighter, more technical rowers in the bow and stronger, heavier pullers in the middle of the boat, for instance–be turned to advantage rather than disadvantage. [113]

Our equality in Christ, our diversity as individuals, and our commitment to mutuality in marriage foster the "We" of creative partnerships. All too often friendships, work relationships, ministry teams, and marriages degrade into power struggles about who will lead and who will follow, rather than joining together carefully to assess the unique blend of qualities present in the relationships. The strengths, weaknesses, gifts, talents, needs, and desires combine under the leadership of the Holy Spirit to move partnerships forward. Together they experience the joy and even ecstasy of accomplishing something together that could never be accomplished alone.

Strong women with loud voices are often told that they must work on having "a gentle and quiet spirit,"[114] which is the only acceptable Christian demeanor for a woman. They suddenly feel embarrassed about their extroverted personality, refrain from asserting themselves, or view their leadership capabilities negatively. Likewise, men who are soft-spoken, prefer to be in the background, and do not

---

113 Brown, Daniel James. *The Boys in the Boat*. New York: Penguin Books, 2013. (179)
114 1 Peter 3:4

take a direct approach to leadership are often told they are not stepping up to their God-given responsibility to lead their wife and family. As we saw in the life of Stan earlier in this book, these stereotypes crush the spirit of the individual as well as the intimacy of a couple. It is possible to have a gentle and quiet spirit with an introverted or extroverted personality.

Creative partnerships that yield the joy of intimacy require the kind of respect for differences and commitment to training that athletes invest in developing their skills individually and as a team. Another rich metaphor is thinking about marriage and even the Body of Christ as a complicated musical score being written, played, and sung together with our Creator, the only capable Conductor. With parts in this magnificent chorus and symphony, a husband and wife each practice and discover their unique giftedness. Will they sing and play? Will one play while the other sings? Will both sing or both play at times? All must learn the notes that correspond to their instrument and part, even if one partner's notes are completely different from his or her spouse's. The wife must remain firmly on her own note while the husband remains securely on his. The conductor will help them learn to tune up to one another. They learn to sing and play while watching the conductor for cues about how to unify with the rest of the chorus and symphony in the body of Christ.

The beauty of music consists not of a single monotone note, but of the multiple layers of notes sung and played harmoniously and confidently together in submission to one another. If you have ever become proficient at playing an instrument or singing with others, you understand the amount of commitment and daily practice that is required to play beautiful music with other musicians. Likewise, the development and maintenance of mutuality and equality within marriage is a lifelong but worthwhile and satisfying practice that frequently requires improvisation.

Musical improvisation, according to Jeremy S. Begbie, respects the uniqueness of the circumstances of the occasions for marital improvisation. Begbie calls this the "occasional constraint."[115] In some ways, the uniqueness of a husband or wife within the marriage is also felt as a constraint. Unique and different can

---

115 Begbie, Jeremy S. *Theology, Music and Time*. New York: Cambridge University Press, 2000. (204–207)

feel wrong. Yet, when viewed as the opportunity to let the Holy Spirit create something new and unexpected from the playing off of one another's differences, improvisation can become exhilarating.

Post-Fall thinking will use the occasion to create a power struggle and demand a response rather than honoring the uniqueness of both partners and asking the Spirit to bring harmony to the situation. When I think of couples invited into mutual submission, the head and body both leading and following in reciprocal and creative ways, improvising according to the giftedness of one another and the inspiration of the Holy Spirit, I get a glimpse of a divine and well-coordinated marital symphony and chorus.

When we find ourselves in conflict with anyone, it is important for each person to take the time to ask themselves questions about how they feel, what they want, and what they may need. As Christians, we are particularly vulnerable to not knowing what we are wanting and needing because we have been taught to completely deny ourselves and think only of the other person. This is another typical distortion of biblical truth and has created an epidemic of what is now referred to in the recovery world as codependency. According to *Psychology Today*, codependency is "a dysfunctional relationship dynamic where one person assumes the role of the 'giver,' sacrificing their own needs and well-being for the sake of the other, 'the taker.'"[116]

Just as we need a nuanced and contextualized interpretation of Scripture related to authority and submission, we also need a nuanced and contextualized understanding of Scripture related to giving and sacrifice. Chronic giving and sacrificial behavior of one person that enables the damaging and hurtful behavior of others can strip both the giver and the receiver of their God-given identity in Christ. Jesus was very clear on who He was, what He wanted, what He would and would not do, and when—He would do things. He had no problem telling people "no," even when He risked offending them, such as when Peter tried to protect Him from the suffering and death He was foretelling. Jesus rebuked him. Self-nourishment is not the same as selfishness.

Marital experts Gay and Kathlyn Henricks tell us that inequality is the hallmark of codependency. Mutuality is not an option because both people have not

---

116 Psychology Today Staff. "Codependency." *Psychology Today*, 2023/ https://www. psychologytoday.com/us/basics/codependency

yet learned how to take full responsibility for themselves, as they are invested in making one person the victim and the other person the perpetrator. This is just another form of the blame game begun in the Garden. The Hendriks' recommend a co-committed relationship in which,

> *"...two or more people support each other in being whole, complete individuals. The commitment is to going all the way, to letting the relationship be the catalyst for the individuals to express their full potential and creativity. In a co-committed relationship between two people, each takes 100 percent responsibility for his or her life and for the result each creates. There are no victims in co-committed relationships. In fact, victimhood is impossible when both people are willing to acknowledge that they are the cause of what happens to them. There is little conflict because neither person plays the accusatory, victim role."*[117]

There is much wasted energy in power struggles attempting to establish who is at fault. When each spouse realizes that they are 100 percent responsible for their own well-being in the relationship, an important shift in focus can begin. This does not mean they are responsible for the behavior of their partner. Both partners realize they are not trapped and can make choices to change the circumstances under their own control. We cannot change or control others. We can ask for a change, but when they cannot or will not change, we alone have a God-given duty and responsibility to support and protect ourselves. We may need to take steps to heal our own wounds if our partner cannot or will not help to bind them up. When we take this personal power seriously, we will be surprised at how the destructive energy being depleted in continued power struggles can then be invested in healthy problem solving and creative decision-making.

---

117 Hendricks, Gay, Ph.D., and Hendricks, Kathlyn, Ph.D. *Conscious Loving: The Journey to Co-Commitment.* New York: Bantam Books, 1992. (11–12)

CHAPTER 18

Transformed Sexual Relations

"The passion, the sexual element, was there: and sexual harmony like sexual playfulness was an important dimension of our love. But it wasn't itself the whole thing; and we knew that to make it the whole or even the most important element was to court disaster. Those who see love as only sex or mainly sex do not, quite simply, know what love is."[118]

—**Sheldon Vanauken**

Mutuality, not Sex on Demand

Sexual intimacy is the natural outgrowth of a commitment to mutuality. Like the branch that stays connected to a vine, the fruit of knowing one another deeply comes from abiding or staying close in healthy ways. Mutuality and interconnectedness are at the core of Paul's metaphor of Christ and the Church and husband and wife in Ephesians 5 discussed in Chapter 17.

Instead of inspiring God's highest intention for the mutual satisfaction of both women and men in marriage, the language of head and body has frequently been misused to create a vast male hegemony over sexual relations. Religious beliefs about

---

118 Vanauken, Sheldon. A Severe Mercy. New York, New York: Harper and Row Publishers, 1977. (43)

a woman's sexual duty to perform on demand and cultural taboos against the use of birth control together resulted in copious births in the life of a woman, depleting her of resources and leaving her dependent upon men and families who at times abused both the woman and her children. In some cultures, women have been mutilated with a clitoridectomy in order to ensure that women could not enjoy sexual relations.[119] Among many other reasons, this was thought to be a way to ensure fidelity.

In 1 Corinthians 7:4 (TNIV), Paul says, "The wife does not have authority over her own body, but yields it to her husband," but then he immediately follows up with this reciprocal statement: "In the same way, the husband does not have authority over his own body, but yields it to his wife." It is easy to focus on the idea that the wife or husband's body belongs to their partner, particularly if you want sexual power over your spouse. But here we see the magnificent theme of shared authority and mutuality without the loss of personhood. Mutuality does not mean that your body no longer belongs to you as a wife or a husband. A woman and a man must still take responsibility for the health and well-being of their own bodies. This passage is about shared intimacy and the power of mutuality in the sexual relationship as believers.

For example, if a wife or husband is awakened in the middle of the night being touched in a sexual way and is not interested in lovemaking, they have the responsibility to be honest and decline the advances. The partner making the advance is as responsible for respecting a lack of interest as much as rejoicing when the interest is mutual. If this is a frequent source of frustration, it is important that this couple begin a process of negotiation around how to come up with a win-win solution. Paul emphasizes mutual consent in the next verse with, "Do not deprive each other except perhaps by mutual consent and for a time, so that you may devote yourselves to prayer. Then come together again so that Satan will not tempt you because of your lack of self-control. I say this as a concession, not as a command" (1 Corinthians 7:5–6, TNIV).

In a culture where it was legal for a man to treat a woman as his own property, the statement by Paul that the husband's body does not belong to him alone but

119 Unicef for Every Child. "What is female genital mutilation? Everything you need to know about FGM and What UNICEF is doing to stop it." Accessed July 11, 2023. https://www.unicef.org/stories/what-you-need-know-about-female-genital-mutilation

also to his wife would have been shocking. The idea of mutual consent would have been revolutionary. Even today, Christian marriages are plagued by an inability to negotiate mutually satisfying sexual relations where power is shared without guilt or shame. It is heartbreaking that women are repeatedly raped in their marriages by husbands who insist that sex on demand is their right as leaders of their homes, without regard to a wife's wishes. In my counseling practice, I have frequently heard the above passage used not for ensuring mutuality, but to make women responsible for meeting the sexual needs of their husbands without regard to their own needs. A group of pastor's wives once shared with me the belief that to say no to a sexual advance in marriage would tempt their husbands to sexual sin and that they as wives would be at fault for depriving them.

Although it can be argued that men have predominantly been the perpetrators of the sexual abuse of females, women have also abused their power over both males and females. I have counseled women who have abused their power over children by cloaking sexual abuse under the guise of daily nurturing activities such as bathing, changing diapers, and other domestic activities. Women have withheld sex from their partners to punish them for not giving them what they wanted in the relationship. They have offered and given sex in a *quid pro quo* to ensure desired outcomes for centuries. This reality in no way minimizes the disproportionate abuse of women by men, but reminds us that abuse is not primarily a gender issue but a human sin and power issue. Neither should it eclipse the ordinary yet exceptional men of every generation, including Joseph of Nazareth (Matthew 1:19, TNIV), who have loved their betrothed and wives sacrificially. These men chose to put the needs of women above their own interests, even when the culture and religious laws were in their favor, and they could have easily used their power to shame and punish women in order to protect themselves, their interests, and reputations.

Engaging in the Hard Work of Negotiation

With the binocular vision of our new creation identity, we cultivate the practice of sharing power generously with one another in every area of our lives. In reality, humans often prefer extreme roles to wrestling with one another to cultivate and grow mutually satisfying relationships. Engaging in the hard work of relational conflict requires all involved to develop the skills to face conflict head-on in order to genuinely share authority in Christ as a New Creation couple. It is a sad reality that many Christian books and seminars on marriage spend as much or more time defining the roles of husband and wife and proving who is the leader and follower than on teaching the relational skills that foster mutual submission and develop intimacy.

When a woman willingly submits to her husband as the Church does to Christ, she does not surrender her personhood and freedom, nor her responsibility to lovingly challenge a husband who attempts to lord his authority over her in the marital relationship. There are times when she must obey Christ rather than her husband. Every believer must be prepared to put obedience to Christ above every other allegiance. Prayer and discernment require reliance upon the Holy Spirit to make wise choices that honor God and exemplify the life of Christ on Earth. God's highest intention is that couples freely follow Him and one another.

Like the beauty of three-dimensional vision, when the brain organizes two unique images for a complete picture rather than the distorted image of one eye dominating the other, the Pre-Fall and Post-Fall realities are brought into proper focus by the finished work of Jesus Christ. Authority and power, redefined by Jesus, and exercised equally by women and men, bring into focus the true beauty of God's holiness in marriage. However, if couples are to share in the power of the post-resurrection transformation marriage that Christ suffered and died to effect in all believers, it will only be accomplished with great intentionality and the supernatural power of the Holy Spirit. All intimacy, including sexual intimacy is enhanced by the capacity to communicate honestly about one's desires, needs, and wants.

Linking Verbal Intercourse with Sexual Intercourse

I am continually sobered by the number of couples struggling with how to have a healthy sexual relationship. Whether a Christian couple or not, the men and women who come to my office with pain around sexual intimacy inevitably struggle with how to share power that leads to mutual enjoyment. The first thing I learned from these couples is that they do not actually talk about what they desire in a sexual relationship. In our culture, there is often an unspoken rule that good sex does not require much talking. You have heard the quip, "If I have to tell him, there is something wrong." Yet it is this lack of communication in any area of a relationship that undermines a mutually negotiated and satisfying sexual relationship.[120] It was not uncommon for women to disclose to me for the first time that they had not yet experienced climax during sex, despite being married for decades. Women often struggle with painful sex, called Vaginismus, and must find new ways to nurture a sexual relationship without intercourse. Men with erectile dysfunction will sometimes avoid sexual intercourse completely rather than share this struggle with their wives.

It turns out that asking directly for what you are wanting and needing in a relationship is extremely vulnerable. Each partner must risk asking for something important to them that might be refused. Many of us have trouble with both saying and accepting no because of how vulnerable it makes us feel. Depending on our past experiences, we may associate both rejection and abandonment with the word "no." If sharing a need has later resulted in someone taking advantage of the information and using it to exploit, punish, or humiliate a spouse during a fight, it is unlikely that such a risk will be taken again without some significant repair work.

Andrea and Anthony

Andrea and Anthony were communicating about sex but only about their differences in desire for frequency. That was the stage upon which their struggle was played out week after week, year after year. The fighting about how often to have sex had actually begun on their honeymoon. Andrea was surprised that Anthony was not interested in having sex more often while they were in Hawaii. After the first night of lovemaking, Anthony seemed content to return to the hotel room from the beach and watch Netflix. He avoided Andrea's invitations to spend time together talking and snuggling. Andrea showed her disappointment by withdrawing and waiting for him to initiate. Anthony did not initiate sex again until after

---

120 A great resource for couples wanting conversation starters is the Gottman Card Deck. You can download the application or go to their website and order at gottmanconnect.com.

they were home from their honeymoon for a month. Exasperated, Andrea asked her husband why he wasn't interested in sex as often as he seemed to be before they got married.

Anthony loved the Lord and his wife. He felt guilty for the change in his interest in sex. He was secretly unsatisfied with their sexual relationship but did not want to hurt her feelings. Each time they did have sex, she seemed unwilling to do the things that he found most arousing. He didn't tell her this verbally, but tried non-verbally to coax her into positions that were most satisfying for him. In contrast, Andrea enjoyed their time together immensely and did not realize that he was asking non-verbally for something different from what they were doing. She actually felt increasingly attracted to Anthony as time went on and thought both of them enjoyed their times of intimacy together. She simply could not understand the lack of frequency and began to wonder if he really still loved her or was perhaps involved with another woman. All these thoughts and feelings were internalized and left unexpressed.

Eventually, the disappointment and hurt they both felt escalated into blame, anger, bitterness, and resignation. Andrea began to accuse Anthony of not loving her and quoted 1 Corinthians 7:3–5 about how he was depriving her and not doing his duty as a husband. Anthony's guilt about his lack of desire for her intensified. He resigned himself to finding other ways to satisfy his sexual needs, which included using pornography as he had before they were married. Andrea found herself emotionally involved with a co-worker and was having fantasies about sex with him. When the fantasy became more of a real possibility, Andrea was shocked and frightened by her thoughts and desires. It was at this point that she reached out to make the appointment for marital therapy.

This couple ultimately realized that they both feared rejection if they were emotionally honest with themselves and one another about their sexual needs and desires. Anthony was hiding a pornography addiction that he thought would go away when he got married. He hoped that once he was able to morally have sex without any guilt, that he would stop the behavior. His deep sense of shame kept him from verbalizing some of the sexual positions he wanted to try out with his wife. He also did not realize how the pornography might impact his sexual desires and even his ability to have an erection.[121] This had become another barrier to his desire for sexual intimacy that he was finally able to share openly during counseling.

Anthony expected anger from Andrea when he disclosed his struggles and desires. He was surprised at her openness to him once she knew more about what he was wanting to experiment with during their lovemaking. He was relieved that she did not shame him for his past pornography use. He also listened quietly when she expressed her fears that he would continue the pattern. She felt hurt and betrayed and repulsed by the objectification of women on the porn sites he frequented. This was an important issue for both of them that needed to be addressed more thoroughly in their therapy. She also expressed certain boundaries that she did not want to cross and was relieved to hear that Anthony would respect her by not asking her to do things that she found uncomfortable.

When it came to frequency, they would also need to negotiate something that was respectful of both of their needs. Although Andrea wanted sexual intimacy several times a week, Anthony was not able to honestly agree to that. He did agree to a weekly date night when he would not use Netflix as a way to relax in the evening which usually immobilized him for the rest of the night. He agreed to be more responsive to her gestures and invitations for emotional and physical closeness.

Andrea was also willing to come clean about the emotional affair she had begun at work. She too was ashamed of her behavior and both Anthony and Andrea gave each other time to process the hurt and anger they felt toward each other for these betrayals. She also apologized for her tendency to use Scripture to try to get her own way. This was a subtle misuse of power in the relationship. Anthony agreed to verbalize his hurt and be honest about any trouble with getting an erection rather than withholding sex, another subtle misuse of his personal power. When disappointed, she agreed to come to him without arming herself with Bible verses. Trust would need to be rebuilt between them. This would take

---

121 Park, Bryan W., Wilson, Gary, Berger, Jonathan, Christman, Matthew, Reina, Bryn, Bishop, Frank, Klam, Warren P., and Doan, Andrew P. "Is Internet Pornography Causing Sexual Dysfunctions: A Review with Clinical Reports." National Library of Medicine: National Center for Biotechnology Information, August 6, 2016. https://www.ncbi.nlm.nih.gov/pmc/articles/PMC5039517/

time and a commitment from both of them to communicate more quickly, frequently and openly.

There is no greater joy than being invited to share, layer upon layer, who we really are spiritually, emotionally, intellectually, socially, physically, and sexually. Have you ever chosen to share a secret about yourself with someone and experienced the freedom of finally coming out of hiding? At times, like with Andrea and Anthony, there is much pain as we reveal a deep truth about ourselves. Even with people whom we have known to be safe and trustworthy, there may indeed at first be some rejection, especially if that secret is a hurtful one to the very one to whom it is being revealed. But ultimately, hiding is much more damaging. Finding the courage to endure the "spiritual surgery" of coming into the light, as my late friend Janet always put it, yields even deeper healing, joy, and intimacy. The truth does set us free.

There are special treasures available as we change, and new truths about our heart, mind, souls, and bodies emerge as we age. Though frightening, we can choose to see aging and limitations as new opportunities for revealing ourselves to God and one another. Just as someone who has lost their sight develops a heightened sensitivity to hearing and touch, so can our physical and emotional limitations heighten our spiritual senses and communication. We can still pursue different kinds of satisfying intimacy after pregnancy, while busy working and raising children, or when our partner is ill or becomes disabled. This is not done alone in isolation but in cooperation with our Lord, our partner and when needed, with qualified mentors and professionals.

CHAPTER 19

Transformed Choices

"The killer of love is creeping separateness...
Taking love for granted, especially after marriage.
Ceasing to do things together...'We' turning into 'I.'"[122]
—**Sheldon Vanauken**

The Power of Choosing the "We Principle"

The last four chapters have addressed couples, but transformed authority principles impact singles as well as married adults. Some of the most satisfying decisions made by roommates, friends, and even employees and employers are win-win decisions made together according to the "We Principle" of "Let Us" (Genesis 1:26), rather than the "me principle" of "Let me."

Choosing the way of Christ in relationships, however, is only possible when all parties work hard at mutuality. There is no "one-size-fits-all" design for singles or couples. Each person has the freedom to develop and agree upon a style of decision-making that is most effective for them. Ultimately, there is nothing wrong with a decision-making style that allows the husband (or wife) to make the final decisions about certain areas in the marriage, providing the other spouse truly has

---

122 Vanauken, Sheldon. A Severe Mercy. New York, New York: Harper and Row Publishers, 1977. (37)

the freedom to give such consent. This also means there is the shared freedom to renegotiate agreements based upon prevailing circumstances, situations, or a change of mind.

Although modern women often have education and work experience when they enter into marriage, they still may experience the impact of a power imbalance between husband and wife. There can be feelings of insecurity and inferiority when it comes to asking for access to resources and decision-making. Sometimes the husband or wife who works outside the home insists on having more decision-making power because their work is generating income for the family. This can become a grievous blow to intimacy in marriage unless a mutually agreed solution can be forged. When a man or woman is given the message that the work they do in the home is valued less than the work of the partner with a salary, then mutuality and equality in the relationship has been compromised and intimacy will suffer.

Delegating tasks in marriage or in business partnerships come with some risks. We must not assume that delegation means relinquishing all responsibility, control, and oversight in any area of decision-making. I have seen wives who have no knowledge of their financial status until their husbands die and then are stunned by the level of debt the family has accrued. A parent who has delegated child discipline to the other parent may discover bruises on a child's body after disciplinary action. The delegating parent is not out of line by privately asking questions, registering concerns, and later taking unilateral action to protect the children if needed. It is advisable to stay involved in all affairs that are delegated. If a partner refuses to allow involvement or access to resources, there has been a significant breach in trust and mutuality. If either is denied or conflict escalates with further investigation, professional legal intervention will be required to safely explore what has happened and once again find a mutually satisfying solution.

When we married, Keith believed that God's call for him to love me as Christ loved the Church was to honor me as a co-heir of Christ without a worldly style of leadership in the home. He believed that loving me as Christ loved the Church was to treat me as a friend who has mutuality in final decision-making power. This meant that we would endeavor to wait rather than go forward with a big decision until both of us were in agreement. If one of us submitted to the other due to an impasse and both were not completely in agreement, it was understood that the one in submission would freely take responsibility for the decision to submit. It was understood that the spouse was not under compulsion and would not harbor resentments that would result in later accusations such as, "I only agreed because it was what *you* wanted." We agreed that regardless of the outcome, we both took full responsibility for that course of action. Finding the way of "We" is not simply the passive compliance or acquiescence of a partner but a prayerful, working hard to hear and understand one another.

Keith also understood that Christlike love involved serving me by taking on household tasks that our culture—and some churches—often relegate to women alone. He shared in housework, changed dirty diapers, and took responsibility for childrearing so I could pursue becoming a professional psychotherapist. I served him by sharing equal responsibility for work often relegated to men, including earning part of our household income, mowing the lawn, and caring for home repairs. We did not choose these tasks to simply defy sexual stereotypes. Our goal as a couple was to incorporate our unique and diverse personalities, gifts, talents, feelings, thoughts, ideas, and opinions into our marriage, parenting, and ministry decision-making. It was our choice to wait and pray for God to make us united on a decision if there was no agreement. It still astonishes both of us to see the way God creatively transforms our individual "me" into a united "we," that is both the joy and delight of our existence, and a true reflection of the nature of our Triune God.

After nearly four decades of marriage, I understand that there are absolutely times when a couple hits an impasse and cannot seem to find a mutually agreed-upon decision. We too have had fierce arguments and long discussions, with days and sometimes months, of unresolved conflict. We too spent much time in personal prayer, counseling with mentors and professional therapists, and returning to one another time and time again to have the difficult conversations. But our commitment in Christ was to find creative "we ways" that reflected the best interests of our Lord and one another in both humility and love. This is done supernaturally by the power of the Holy Spirit and requires a dying to our natural inclination to demand our own way or disregard the needs and desires of others. There are, however, times when we both have made decisions outside of this "we" pattern. The hurt and pain that accompanied those times of unilateral decisions have demanded our attention and we have worked hard to heal and not become bitter and resentful so we could return to a place of peaceful harmony instead of tumultuous discord.

There is great joy and peace when both husband and wife take time to listen to what God has put on their individual hearts about their personal as well as corporate goals. As each of them hones the skill of listening to the Holy Spirit, and to one another, they also cultivate the skill of asking Christ to show them the way of "We."

Ron and Melissa

Ron and Melissa served together at their church for over 10 years. They were both in their thirties with two children under five. They enjoyed being involved in short-term mission projects at home and abroad. After a short-term mission trip to Uganda with the Men's Ministry at their church, Ron came home deeply moved by his experience. He shared his love for the people and asked his wife to begin praying about accompanying him to Uganda in an upcoming trip with their Missions pastor. She also had a heart for missions and eagerly went with him when the time arrived. Their children stayed with Melissa's parents during their two-week journey.

During the trip, Ron became convinced that God was calling them as a couple into long-term missions. He shared this conviction with Melissa, who was surprised at the urgency in his voice. She told him she had not yet heard from the Lord about becoming a long-term missionary. Ron insisted as the spiritual leader that Melissa simply follow him into the mission field. She wanted more time to think and pray.

Ron and Melissa entered into a power struggle about the decision to go into missions. Ron was hurt and angry that his wife would not submit to this calling and his leadership. Melissa was hurt and angry that he expected her to leave everything without careful consideration of her needs, the needs of their children and her aging parents, and their financial obligations. Ron insisted that Melissa was not trusting the Lord to provide, and Melissa insisted that he was not acting in loving consideration for his family. The two now stood at a crossroads. This conflict could either become an opportunity for intimacy with God and one another or drive them apart. It was an opportunity for both to submit to the authority of Christ rather than engaging in a power struggle over which spouse was in charge. Would they believe that God was working in and through them both to come to a win-win "We" decision? Would they take the opportunity to get to know one another better through inviting one another to share their underlying hopes, fears, and concerns?

Many couples who become trapped in such a struggle do not recognize that it is rooted in a post-Fall perspective. Over time, this decision-making strategy drains the marriage of joy and intimacy. Yet, choosing to leave the power struggle can literally feel like a dying to self; a crucifixion of sorts, but not in a literal, masochistic, or even self-injurious way. Like the athlete who trains for a game, we must imagine the pain of practice that leads to the possibility of the prize. When we die to the demand of our own way, the Spirit lives to invite us into mutually beneficial solutions to our dilemmas.

In the case of Melissa and Ron, the conflict continued to escalate into a spiritualized version of the blame game. Ironically, since they both believed their way was God's will, they continued attempts to persuade, argue, coerce, and even shame one another into submission. The truth is that they both may have heard the Lord's voice for themselves, but they had not yet discovered His will for them as a couple. This would require the belief that God could bring a creative solution that incorporated the concerns of both partners; it also would mean giving up attempts to change and control one another.

The Spirit-filled alternative to this power struggle is a willingness of both to work toward a "We" decision, something the triune God excels at in the Spirit. Both spouses will likely have to give up something individually in order to gain something in common. This often takes time, especially is one or both partners are convinced that they are right and the other is wrong. Ron felt an urgency that made him irritable and impatient. He even called Melissa names and threw things during their arguments. Melissa felt the weight of Ron's pressure and gave him the silent treatment, being resentful of his attempts to shame her for not agreeing with him. Her fleshly style of coping with the disagreement and anger was not to attack him but to passively withdraw. The end result was the same, however: profound alienation from one another.

Freedom in Christ means we can patiently wait on God and one another as we struggle to find a new way. Melissa may need to risk open conflict instead of retreating into silence, where anger can turn to bitterness and resentment. Ron may need to take frequent breaks during their conversations before his anger escalates but also come back and resume the conversation when he has calmed down. This means finishing the conversation could take days or even weeks instead of hours, depending on the intensity of emotion.

As long as we are wrestling with God and one another (as opposed to blaming and attacking), we are in close proximity. As Ron and Melissa leave the blaming and shaming behind, they can begin to listen attentively to the honest hopes and fears of one another without defensiveness. Ron surrenders to Christ his desire to go as soon as possible to Uganda and Melissa surrenders to Christ her concerns about all the details related to leaving their home and family. They submit to one another by making Christ Lord of this decision and trust that they can come to a win-win decision that both can wholeheartedly support. Ron is relieved to hear Melissa say that she really has a heart to go to Uganda as a missionary family. Melissa is relieved to hear that Ron will no longer push her to make a decision to move within the year. Both will work on perceived obstacles and wait to see how God will sort out their concerns and the challenges ahead.

In the end, Ron and Melissa were in awe of the way God met their needs as individuals and as a couple so that, when they did finally leave for Uganda, both were completely at peace and ready to face together whatever hardship might confront them. There will be no need for future accusations that Ron forced Melissa to go or that Melissa prevented Ron from fulfilling God's will. Mutuality requires that both partners take full responsibility for their decisions as individuals and as a couple; mere acquiescence is not mutual submission.

But what about cases of impasse where there is no meeting of the minds? In such cases, one couple I know has given the mutual gift of veto power. They work hard to find a compromise and creative win-win decision but in its absence, either spouse can veto the final decision. Rather than feeling that this is acquiescence or resignation, they have decided that it is a way of honoring the "we" in their marriage. Ironically, with the freedom of a powerful veto voice, that spouse has space to continue to pray and in some cases, God may even move that spouse toward a new win-win proposition or even a complete change of heart. Looking back on years of marriage, the husband of this couple said, "More often than not, eventually the veto vote seemed to be the wise choice. Regardless of decision-making strategies and styles, the most important factor in cultivating rather than crushing intimacy is learning how to convey to one another that we want genuine mutuality and that we have one another's best interests at heart."

An Unexpected Gift

Keith and I had only been married 18 months when he demonstrated the most excellent way of love. He gave me a practical example of what it looks like when a husband believes that Christ is the head of the marriage, and he is to imitate that Christlike love, not by lording his authority over his wife, but by seeking and serving her best interests as well as his own in the marriage. Without either of us being conscious of it, Keith demonstrated all the elements of what I call the "new creation marriage" to me in a most extraordinary way.

I received a letter from the International Studies Department of our university, informing me that I had qualified to apply for a Fulbright Scholarship during graduate school. We were both studying German and Psychology when we met in 1982 and both of us hoped to study abroad, even before we met. We were also considering going into overseas missions. I will never forget Keith saying to me, "You should apply for that!" The pastor of the church we attended at that time agreed and saw this as a "tent-making" missionary opportunity, not unlike the mission work Paul did while supporting himself by making tents (Acts 18:1–3). We would not have to raise support as traditional missionaries, but would be supported by the scholarship and commissioned by our church. I was thrilled when my application was accepted. Keith was elated, proud, and also refreshingly honest when he said, "I admit I am jealous, but God can absolutely lead through you, my wife." He was 25 years old when he said those profound words to me. Together we decided to embark on this journey, although he did not know what he would do while in Germany as he was midway through his teaching credential program in English. As young marrieds in our early twenties, we had no idea what a tremendous gift the Lord was about to give both of us as we trusted Him for our best interests, both as individuals and as a couple.

Back at college, we shared the good news with our college German professor, Herr Hoffmann, who was thrilled for us. When Keith lamented not being able to finish his teaching credential program during our absence, we learned that this same professor had just been granted a fellowship in a nearby German city and knew of an American Base where Keith might do his student teaching. Excited, Keith approached his college dean, who promptly dismissed the idea because a California teaching credential required supervision by a California credentialed master teacher. Disappointed and then dumbfounded, we learned that Herr Hoffmann was a former California credentialed master teacher in Keith's English program. He offered to travel by train weekly while in Germany to provide supervision for Keith, should the dean agree to his offer. Much prayer, God's grace, and the kindness of the college staff allowed Keith to become the only teacher in the history of our college up to that time to do part of his student teaching outside of California. We were in awe.

This example became the foundation of our style of decision-making in marriage. We learned that God cared greatly for the best interests of both husband and wife. Instead of becoming competitive in our relationship, Keith and I continued to share power in our relationship generously. At the end of that wonderful year, we were challenged once again to apply this style of decision-making in our marriage.

The Fulbright Commission offered me a second year grant to begin doctoral research, but this time, when Keith spoke with the dean about doing his last semester of student teaching in Germany, he declined saying the third semester had to be completed in a California school. Before accepting the grant extension, we boldly approached the Fulbright Commission and requested a six-month delayed start. I needed to return in order to finish my second year clinical internship and master's degree and Keith needed to complete his teacher training. Concerned that I would not return to complete my research, the commission declined my delay request and said I should stay in Germany while Keith returned home to complete his training.

Keith was vehemently against this proposal, and though I protested, his example of loving generosity caused me to plead with God for a creative way that was mutually advantageous and would not involve physical separation. I met in person with the commission and expressed our concerns regarding our separation and tried to allay their concerns that I would not return to finish the research project. To our astonishment, not only did the Fulbright Commission allow me to delay my grant start date and return with Keith, but during our six months in California fulfilling our graduation requirements, Keith applied for and received his own Fulbright Fellowship as a teaching assistant in a German gymnasium. I was thrilled to see how our Lord honored my husband with this extraordinary gift that not only fulfilled the desire of his heart, but set the course of his career, teaching German as well as English in high school.

I only wish that we could both say that, after 40 years of marriage, we no longer grieve one another or the Holy Spirit. Instead, I must admit that my husband and I still hurt one another when our flesh rather than the Spirit of God triumphs in our marriage. We do get caught up in power struggles at times, despite all that we know and have experienced with our Lord and one another. In reality, such times continue to humble us and draw our souls back to Christ and one another for the grace we so desperately need. We are caught between the Post-Fall Era, with our carnal nature battling our New Creation Era nature, and the day coming when Jesus returns to make all things new. Let us press on to have our joy made full by following Christ in learning daily how to love one another as Christ loves us.

Conclusion of Part III

In Part III, we have covered much ground in our survey of the New Creation life modeled by our extraordinary Savior. Jesus felled the Fall's curses and consequences and ushered in the New Creation Era by sharing his authority with all believers, regardless of gender, age, race, religion, or social class. Far from legitimizing the abusive Roman power that governed social and domestic order in the first century, Jesus turned all worldly power structures upside down. Without relinquishing his power and position as God, Jesus transformed the expected top-down relationships of teacher-student and master-slave into the unexpected mutuality of friendship.

We learned the difference between love and intimacy and how Jesus invited His disciples to risk the vulnerability of disclosing the best and worst of themselves to Him. Rather than shaming or rejecting them, He was gentle with their weaknesses. He honored their vulnerability by disclosing more of Himself to them in a reciprocal way, which deepened their love for one another.

We also learned that grief has a surprising role to play in our transformation as new creations in Christ. Mutual intimacy is cultivated by a willingness to acknowledge painful losses and let go of unrealistic expectations in relationships. Jesus grieved deeply in the Garden of Gethsemane and released the hope of God granting Him another way to redeem the world. We learned some practical tools for navigating the treacherous and changing landscape of grief, including ways to recognize the difference between healing pain and injurious pain.

In the New Creation Era, we looked closely at how authority and social structures of the day were transformed by the power of Spirit-led believers in social institutions like marriage, parenting, and slavery. New Testament writers respected Roman laws but also subverted them with the law of love in Christ. Wives and children were no longer property to be owned and dominated, but precious believers in Christ to be sacrificially loved and tenderly cared for. Christian slave owners like Philemon were urged to treat their slaves, who were believers and Christian brothers, with love, forgiveness, and grace—and even free them, if possible. This promoted the attitude of Christ in sharing power and authority without partiality. Transformed marriage and sexual relations reflect the beauty and mutuality of unity and diversity without lording power over one another according to the Fall.

Finally, we saw the creativity of the "We Principle" in action. Intimacy is cultivated when we share power with one another, and is crushed when we lord authority over others. Jesus shared both authority and the power of the Holy Spirit with us to provide a deep, abiding confidence that He knows us, cares for us, and desires and delights in our presence.

We now look forward to the Second Coming of Christ. Orthodox Christians believe that the soil of our decaying human bodies and even the natural world still await their final redemption in the New Heaven and Earth Era. I believe we humans intuitively know that we and this marvelous world that God made are good and worth the blood of Christ shed to redeem us. Humans, male and female, are indeed very good. But we also intuitively know that there is something very wrong within us and our world. Indeed, all of Creation groans for the new heavens and earth that will return all of life to God's highest intention and even beyond that which was described in the pre-Fall Garden.[123]

But let us not be mistaken. Christ came to Earth to bring transformation to human beings so that we could continue His mission on this earth today through the Spirit until His second coming. Christ's desire for mutuality and shared authority with His Bride and Body has the power to transform our hearts, human relationships, and society with love, against which there is no law. There is a reason Christ taught us to pray, "Your kingdom come, Your will be done, on earth as it is in heaven."[124] Jesus and the early Church rocked the ancient world with God's Kingdom values of sacrificial love and service to "the least of these" in society. The reversals of human authority that Christ modeled on Earth inspired and empowered His disciples then and continue to inspire and empower us today to leave the pre-Fall definitions and exercises of power, and instead live into the New Creation Era, which is to be a foretaste of the feast to come.

Our hope for the New Heaven and Earth Era does not mean that we do not fight for social justice today. On the contrary, our efforts to abolish slavery, end the abuse of women and children, and bring humane and just treatment to all humans—especially the vulnerable poor—are a reflection of Christ's work on this earth. We must work hard to tenderly care for the elderly, the homeless, the disabled, those with unwanted pregnancies and their unborn children, and single parents with children, to name just a few. Walking in the Spirit of Christ means the kind and fair treatment of those without homes, those who have arrived as illegal immigrants, as well as the convicted prisoners in our midst with God's love. Jesus began His public ministry by declaring that He fulfilled the prophetic scripture of Isaiah 61:

> *"And He came to Nazareth, where He had been brought up; and*
> *as was His custom, He entered the synagogue on the Sabbath and*
> *stood up to read. And the book of the prophet Isaiah was handed*

---

123 Wright, N.T. *Surprised by Hope: Rethinking Heaven, the Resurrection, and the Mission of the Church.* New York: Harper One, 2008.

124 The Lord's Prayer

to Him. And He opened the book and found the place where it was *written, '**The Spirit of the Lord is upon Me because He anointed** **Me to preach the gospel to the poor. He has sent Me to proclaim** **release to the captives and recovery of sight to the blind. To set** **free those who are downtrodden. To proclaim the favorable** **year of the Lord.'** And He closed the book and gave it back to* *the attendant and sat down; and the eyes of all in the synagogue* *were fixed upon Him. And He began to say to them. 'Today this* *Scripture has been fulfilled in your hearing.'"*

(Luke 4:16–21, NLT, emphasis added)

This Son, Jesus the Messiah, Immanuel, God with us, was on the earth, bringing His Father's Kingdom to this good, though cursed, soil, transforming it and preparing it for the perfect soil to come. The mutual intimacy lost in the Fall is restored to God's highest intention for humans through the finished work of our Savior. As new creatures in Christ, we are invited to continue the work of our Lord on Earth until Jesus returns to make all things new, removing or replacing every remnant of the post-Fall world. Our old sinful nature and dying human flesh, the kingdoms of this world, and the forces of the devil have already been defeated by Christ and will soon have no sway in the story of our final era, the New Heaven and Earth Era. Maranatha.

PART IV:

Perfected Soil In The New Heaven And Earth Era

"Then I saw a new heaven and a new earth; for the first heaven and the first earth passed away, and there is no longer any sea. And I saw the holy city, new Jerusalem, coming down out of heaven from God, made ready as a bride adorned for her husband."
(Revelation 21:1–2, NASB 1995)

CHAPTER 20

The Perfected New Creation

"And I heard a loud voice from the throne, saying, 'Behold, the tabernacle of God is among men, and He will dwell among them, and they shall be His people, and God Himself will be among them, and He will wipe away every tear from their eyes; and there will no longer be any death; there will no longer be any mourning, or crying, or pain; the first things have passed away. And He who sits on the throne said, 'Behold, I am making all things new.'"

(Revelation 21:3–5a, NASB 1995)

"Then he showed me a river of the water of life, clear as crystal, coming from the throne of God and of the Lamb, in the middle of its street. On either side of the river was the tree of life, bearing twelve kinds of fruit, yielding its fruit every month; and the leaves of the tree were for the healing of the nations. There will no longer be any curse; and the throne of God and of the Lamb will be in it, and His bond-servants will serve Him; they will see His face and His name will be on their foreheads. And there will no longer be any night; and they will not have need of the light of a lamp nor

the light of the sun, because the Lord God will illumine them; and they will reign forever and ever."

(Revelation 22:1–4, NASB 1995)

"For behold, I create new heavens and a new earth; And the former things will not be remembered or come to mind. But be glad and rejoice forever in what I create; For behold, I create Jerusalem for rejoicing and her people for gladness; I will also rejoice in Jerusalem and be glad in My people; and there will no longer be heard in her the voice of weeping and the sound of crying."

(Isaiah 65:17–19, NASB 1995)

A new heaven. A new earth. A perfect and incorruptible soil. No serpent. No curse. No consequences. No contaminants or possible corruption by sin. No soil amending. This is an earth that brings forth the assurance of life and delight where there once was the threat of death and dread. In the New Heaven and Earth Era, there is no exhausting labor or vulnerability to decay. There will no longer be toxic weeds, thorns, or thistles in the garden. There will never again be weather that destroys life, ultraviolet rays that cause cancer, predators that ravage prey animals, creatures that bite and devour, insects that sting and consume, or earthborn pathogens that carry disease and death associated with evil.

Perfected Authority of Body and Soul

"Behold, I tell you a mystery; we will not all sleep, but we will all be changed, in a moment, in the twinkling of an eye, at the last trumpet; for the trumpet will sound and the dead will be raised imperishable, and we will be changed.

For this perishable must put on the imperishable and this mortal must put on immortality. But when this perishable will have put on the imperishable, and this mortal will have put on immortality, then will come about the saying that is written, 'Death is swallowed up in victory.'

'O death, where is your victory? O death, where is your sting?' The sting of death is sin, and the power of sin is in the law; but thanks be to God who gives us the victory through our Lord Jesus Christ."

(1 Corinthians 15:51–57, NASB 1995)

"All flesh is not the same flesh, but there is one flesh of men, and another flesh of beasts, and another flesh of birds, and another of fish. There are also heavenly bodies and earthly bodies, but the glory of the heavenly is one, and the glory of the earthly is another. There is one glory of the sun, and another glory of the moon, and another glory of the stars; for star differs from star in glory. So also is the resurrection of the dead. It is sown a perishable body, it is raised an imperishable body ..."

(1 Corinthians 15:39–42, NASB 1995)

"...I am the resurrection and the life; he who believes in Me will live even if he dies, and everyone who lives and believes in Me will never die..."

(John 11:25–26, NASB 1995)

It is fascinating that the New Testament compares entrance into the New Heaven and Earth Era to the painful process of childbirth. For Christians, death is the birth canal through which we are born into our new and eternal life; the portal into a completely new reality.

"For we know that the whole creation groans and suffers the pains of childbirth together until now. And not only this, but also we ourselves, having the first fruits of the Spirit, even we ourselves

*groan within ourselves, waiting eagerly for our adoption as sons,
the redemption of our body."*

(Romans 8:22–23, NASB 1995)

Our resurrected body is a perfected body. Yet it is difficult to know exactly what our lives will be like in these new bodies as we enter into this new heaven and earth. Jesus had a resurrected body that could appear and disappear at will and was not always recognized immediately upon being seen by His followers. He walked, talked, and even ate with His disciples (John 21:12–15). In Revelation 19:7–10, we learn about the Marriage Supper of the Lamb. Scripture offers clues, but in fact much remains a mystery.

A perfected soul means no humans hiding from the light of God's brilliance. There is no shame about being exposed for who we are. No blaming or attacking or defending. No competition for authority, power, attention, or resources. There is no separation or distance from God, ourselves, one another, or Creation. There is no woundedness, no crying or pain or mourning. The struggle between flesh and spirit has ended. Each person has chosen the beauty of God's authority. Each has chosen intimacy and the fruit of the Spirit over alienation and the fruit of the flesh. Having once had the freedom to choose the knowledge of both good and evil, humans of the New Heaven and Earth confidently choose life and use their freedom to obey God's law of love eternally.

In this last chapter of *Choosing Intimacy*, I find myself on sacred ground as I face the challenge of sharing thoughts regarding some of the most difficult passages of prophetic Scripture as they relate to the topic of this book. I acknowledge both the mystery and limitations inherent to theology and eschatology but I would be remiss not to pose questions and present thoughts as they relate to intimacy.

In the New Heaven and Earth Era, God's highest intention for humanity and all of Creation is reborn into an intimate relationship with God in Christ. Imagine male and female humans from every tribe, tongue, and nation creatively and joyfully working together without sin, selfishness, or struggle. They delight in the chorus of harmonious voices together with a symphony of musical instruments. Together, they move in cooperation with their holy and triune God to beautifully multiply, bless, and build this new universe. There are abundant resources without scarcity or poverty. Creation shares without reservation. Similarities and differences combine like flawless DNA to create a more unique, resilient, and sustainable life for all of eternity.

In this new heaven and earth, every man, woman, tribe, and nation will become united as the Bride of Christ, without losing agency or personhood. We will exist as one, uniquely created, completely united and submitted to God in Christ. Jesus is the only true sacrificial Husband who treats His Bride (the Church—all believers in Christ) with the dignity of being a co-heir who co-leads with Him. This does not make her equal to God nor does she aspire to usurp God's sovereign authority. She is satisfied as His resplendent Bride and joyfully accepts His invitation to marriage. She is no longer vulnerable to temptation, nor does she question, doubt, or fear the supreme authority of God or submission to Him. Instead, she now sees Him as the only One beautiful authority in the universe capable of wielding supreme power and sharing it for the purpose of generous loving, giving, growing, and the blessing of all Creation. He gives her the freedom to choose intimacy and she rejoices to do so.

Perfected Design of the New Heaven and New Earth

"But now Christ has been raised from the dead, the first fruits of those who are asleep. For since by a man came death, by a man also came the resurrection of the dead. For as in Adam all die, so also in Christ all shall be made alive. But each in his own order: Christ the first fruits, after that those who are Christ's at His coming, then comes the end, when He delivers up the kingdom to the God and Father when He has abolished all rule and all authority and power. For He must reign until He has put all His enemies under His feet. The last enemy that will be abolished is death. For He has put all things in subjection under his feet. But when He says, All things are put in subjection, it is evident that He is excepted who put all things in subjection to Him. When all things are subjected to Him, then the Son Himself also will be

subjected to the One who subjected all things to Him, so that God may be all in all."

(1 Corinthians 15:20–28, NASB 1995)

"For if by the transgression of the one, death reigned through the one, much more those who receive the abundance of grace and of the gift of righteousness will reign in life through the One Jesus Christ."

(Romans 5:17, NASB 1995)

"It is a trustworthy statement: For if we died with him, we will also live with him; if we endure, we will also reign with Him."

(2 Timothy 2:11–12, NASB 1995)

"Grace be unto you, and peace, from Him who is, and who was, and who is to come; and from the seven Spirits who are before his throne, and from Jesus Christ, the faithful witness, the firstborn of the dead, and the ruler of kings of the earth. To Him that loves us, and released us from our sins by His blood, and He has made us to be a kingdom, priests to His God and Father—to Him be the glory and the dominion forever and ever. Amen."

(Revelation 1:4b–6, NASB 1995)

"Behold, I stand at the door and knock; if anyone hears My voice and opens the door, I will come in to him, and will dine with him and he with Me. He who overcomes, I will grant him to sit down with Me on My throne, as I also overcame and sat down with My Father on His Throne."

(Revelation 3:20–21, NASB 1995)

Prophets like Isaiah declared the coming of the new heaven and new earth. Not only will the earth enjoy pristine soil, but a New Heaven and Earth Era ushers in an animal kingdom where there will be neither predator nor prey: "The wolf and the lamb will graze together, and the lion will eat straw like the ox; and dust will be the serpent's food. They will do no evil or harm in all My holy mountain, says the Lord" (Isaiah 65:25, NASB 1995).

The city and country will co-exist in mutually nourishing ways as seen in the vision of a river of water flowing from the throne of God in the midst of a city street nourishing the tree of life with healing in its leaves. The tree has spread to both sides of the street, bearing 12 kinds of fruit, yielding its fruit every month. Even the seasons have changed in the New Heaven and Earth. Apparently, we will not need to wait for a cycle of 12 months for trees to complete their fruit-bearing season. The leaves of these trees heal the nations once at war with one another. In the New Heaven and Earth, all the swords have been transformed into implements of harvest for the benefit of all.

In the New Heaven and Earth, all corrupt human authority has been destroyed by Christ and replaced once again with the beauty and generous sharing of God's authority and power. It seems that the subjection of Jesus to His Father's will is the final act of human submission on Earth when He hands over the Kingdom to His Father, that "God may be all in all" (1 Corinthians 15:28). God the Father has answered God the Son's high priestly prayer:

"I do not ask on behalf of these alone, but for those also who believe in Me through their word; that they may all be one; even as You, Father, are in Me and I in You, that they also may be in Us, so that the world may believe that you sent me. The glory which You have given Me I have given to them, that they may be one just as We are one; I in them and You in Me that they may be perfected in unity so that the world may know that You sent Me and loved them, even as You have loved Me. Father, I desire that they also whom You have given Me, be with Me where I am so that they may see My glory which You have given Me for You loved Me before the foundation of the world."
(John 17:20–24, NASB 1995)

Another change in the New Heaven and Earth is that God actually dwells among humans where He can be seen. God is not veiled, distant, separated, or removed from humans. There is no tabernacle or temple in the City of Jerusalem because God *is* that Temple (Revelation 21:22, NASB 1995): "And I saw no temple in it, for the Lord God the Almighty and the Lamb are its temple." There will even be a change in the heavenly constellations. The purpose of the sun and moon in the Old World will be replaced by the light of God's presence: "And the city has no need of the sun or of the moon to shine upon it for the glory of God has illuminated it and its lamp is the Lamb" (Revelation 21:23, NASB 1995). The lamp as Lamb of God indicates that though transformed and new, this world does not hide from or forget the price He paid for redemption. Truth will not tarnish joy.

It is significant that nations will still have distinctions and there will be kings of the earth. This is consistent with the other New Testament writings (1 Peter 2:9) that declare that all believers become co-heirs with Christ (Romans 8:17; Revelation 5:9). In the New Heaven and Earth, the inhabitants have chosen the Lamb of God and life on His terms. The gates of Jerusalem are never closed, in direct contrast to the gates of Eden, which were closed to Adam and Eve to keep them from eating of the Tree of Life:

> *"And in the daytime (for there will be no night there) its gates will never be closed; and they will bring the glory and honor of the nations into it; and nothing unclean and no one who practices abomination and lying, will ever come into it, but only those whose names are written in the Lamb's book of life."*
> **(Revelation 21:25–27, NASB 1995)**

Not only is God dwelling among humans, but humans are reigning as kings and priests in this New Heaven and Earth with God in Christ. There is no need for anxiety about discrimination based on gender, race, or socio-economic status, for in Christ we are one. There is no need to fret about whether a king or priest is male or female. Whatever rewards distinguish us as individuals in this new era will be considered fair and just by all. There will be no concern about double standards or false scales of measurement. There is a completely different kind of gendered language in the New Heaven and Earth and it will be a language of inclusion, not exclusion. Together we will all be singing our unique notes in harmony to a new song:

> *"Worthy are You to take the book and break its seals; for You were slain, and purchased for God with your blood those from every tribe and tongue and people and nation. You have made them to be a kingdom and priests to serve our God; and they will reign upon the earth."*
>
> **(Revelation 5:9–10, NASB 1995)**

In the New Heaven and Earth Era, God graciously shares His power and authority. His sharing does not diminish His divinity or make Creation His equal. There will still be power and authority in this new era, but they will be united in love and service and worship. The beautiful authority of God and our joyful submission to Him further beautifies all of Creation. This is the intimacy that displays the power of mutuality in relationship to God and one another.

Perfected Marriage

> *"Let us rejoice and be glad and give the glory to Him, for the marriage of the Lamb has come and His wife has made herself ready. It was given to her to clothe herself in fine linen, bright and clean; for the fine linen is the righteous acts of the saints. Then he said to me, 'Write, Blessed are those who are invited to the marriage supper of the Lamb.' And he said to me, 'These are true words of God.'"*
>
> **(Revelation 19:7–9, NASB 1995)**

> *"The Spirit and the bride say, 'Come.' And let the one who hears say, 'Come.' And let the one who is thirsty come; let the one who wishes take the water of life without cost."*
>
> **(Revelation 22:17, NASB 1995)**

"For Zion's sake I will not keep silent, And for Jerusalem's sake I will not be quiet, Until her righteousness goes forth like brightness, and her salvation like a torch that is burning. The nations shall see your righteousness and all kings your glory, And you will be called by a new name Which the mouth of the Lord will designate. You will also be a crown of beauty in the hand of the Lord, And a royal diadem in the hand of your God. It will no longer be said to you, 'Forsaken,' Nor to your land will it any longer be said, 'Desolate,' But you will be called 'My delight is in her,' and your land, 'Married,' for the Lord delights in you, and your land shall be married. For as a young man marries a virgin, so your sons marry you, and as the bridegroom rejoices over the bride, so your God will rejoice over you."

(Isaiah 62:1–5, NASB 1995)

The language of marriage, like the language of authority and power, is transformed in the era of the new heavens and earth. The marriage that we associate with the post-Fall world has died. Scripture gives us numerous and even mixed metaphors when talking about the Marriage of the Lamb and the Wife who has made herself ready for the wedding. The new Jerusalem is even referred to as the Bride adorned for her Bridegroom (Revelation 21:2). Yet, all of Creation builds upon the ability of humankind, male and female, to become one and mirror the intimacy, unity, diversity, and generativity of their Creator. The biblical themes and metaphors of wedding and feast, bride and bridegroom, husband and wife, are all central to marriage from Genesis to Revelation.

Jesus, when discussing the theology of resurrection and the afterlife with the religious leaders of His day, made the comment that humans would not be marrying or being given in marriage in the Kingdom of God as they had done while on Earth. Yet the Marriage Feast and the reunion of Bridegroom and Bride is greatly anticipated by Christ and His Church throughout the New Testament. Surely marriage on Earth is meant to be just a shadow of a greater reality of marriage between Christ as Bridegroom and the Church as Bride in the new earth to come. As Paul says, this is a profound mystery (Ephesians 5:32, NIV).

How far can this metaphor be stretched in application to gender in the New Heaven and Earth Era? While there are widely varying interpretations (and speculations) regarding the New Heavens and the New Earth, there does appear to be general consensus on some things. Orthodox theologians agree that individuals in the New Heaven and Earth will have resurrected bodies that will remain unique to our personhood, gender, and race. We will recognize one another and retain characteristics of our unique selves. We will not be individually married or given in marriage as was done previously in the pre- and post-Fall world. Biblical scholars also agree that all believers, past, present, and future are corporately called the Church and are represented in the New Testament as the Bride of Christ. She will know and be known by Christ and know and be known as the Bride with a clarity and intimacy beyond our present comprehension. She waits longingly for His return.

However, what is glaringly and grievously absent from literature on this topic is the transformational shift in power from men ruling over women in the post-Fall world to men and women ruling together with Christ as a female Bride in the new era. Certainly to make too much of the Bridegroom and Bride metaphor in the New Heaven and Earth Era is as problematic as making too much of the Head and Body metaphor in the New Creation Era. But giving too little attention is also problematic, especially in light of the way our Lord interacts with His Bride and her exalted status. This is revolutionary for understanding the power of mutuality in our most intimate relationships with God and one another. It is significant, and holds vital meaning for the most sacred of mutual intimacy.

Why is there so little emphasis on this and in some cases no mention of this?[125] The dearth of attention given to this topic is troublesome. Perhaps the answer lies in the following questions. What might happen if the evangelical community were to take seriously the example of Christ's desire to co-rule and share power with His Bride, the Church? How do we justify continuing in the post-Fall tradition of men ruling over women and justifying it as "biblical author-

---

125 Wright, N.T. *Surprised by Hope: Rethinking Heaven, the Resurrection, and the Mission of the Church.* New York, New York: Harper One, 2008 and Gorman, Michael J. *Reading Revelation Responsibly—Uncivil Worship and Witness: Following the Lamb into the New Creation.* Eugene, Oregon: Cascade Books, 2011.

ity"? How would those now in power feel about the collapse of top-down and male-dominated homes, churches, schools, and seminaries? What would happen if men brought the biblical and inclusive attitude of Christ into every encounter with women in every sphere of society and culture? Would men and women be willing to learn how to share power? Or are the curses and consequences of sin so entrenched within us and our institutions that even our Savior's example and His indwelling Holy Spirit cannot persuade us to follow Him in sharing power and authority for the sake of love? The New Heaven and New Earth Era will upend and reverse all the consequences of the Fall, including gender discrimination, oppression, abuse, and exclusion.

All believers, regardless of race or gender, become the Bride of Christ and enjoy the security of His love as she both submits to Him and rules and reigns with her Beloved. Love and submission are no longer mutually exclusive. Men who have abused women over the millennia (in word, act, or attitude) have done violence not only to women, but to themselves and to Christ. This wound will be finally healed in the Marriage of Christ and His Church. It is the resurrection power of Jesus that returns shared power and authority to both men and women.

Perfected Mutual Intimacy between Bride and Bridegroom

To what degree these earthly metaphors of wedding, bride, bridegroom, and marriage can help us understand the heavenly realities that await us in the New Heaven and Earth is, by biblical definition, impossible to fully comprehend on this side of eternity. For now we see dimly. But Scripture from Genesis to Revelation refers to Christ's beloved human creation collectively as a wife and a bride. God chose intimacy with His Creation. We choose intimacy with God and enjoy the power of mutuality in relationships—not just in the Church, but in our homes, families, and friendships.

In fact, this kind of intimacy has the privilege of gathering all genders, races, and social distinctions into one integrated, whole, and beautiful being. We unite with the Creator of the universe, our Bridegroom, Jesus, having inherited all that is necessary from Him to co-rule and reign with Him in the New Heaven and New Earth Era. The words of the Triune God, "Let Us make humankind in Our image, male and female … and let them rule" have now even been surpassed in the New Heaven and Earth Era.

Women who love Christ have willingly seen themselves being made like the male Christ, as being referred to as a male son of God (John 1:12, KJV), and addressed dozens of times in the New Testament as "brethren" in letters to the Church. In the New Heaven and Earth Era, men willingly see themselves as part of the female Bride of Christ. Surely the unification of male and female believers into one body as the female Bride of Christ, even if just metaphorically speaking, is one of the most brilliant acts of gender reconciliation ever conceived, regardless of how this will be manifested in reality.

Conclusion of Part IV

The story of choosing intimacy does not end with simply restoring us to the pre-Fall design of male and female, husband and wife, ruling together in the world without knowledge of good and evil. As a result of the Fall and the need for God to become human and save the world from sin and its consequences, we see in Scripture that men and women actually surpass pre-Fall humanity and are elevated to be co-heirs, kings, and priests with God in Christ. At the end of time as we know it, we will be fellow heirs with Christ of God's redeemed and perfect universe. Redeemed human beings will trust, worship, and obey the God who alone safely wields the knowledge of good and evil. No longer immature children of God needing parental instruction, we will be mature adults and intimate friends with the Almighty. It is only by freely joining with Christ in the New Heaven and Earth Era that we can fully experience the perfected power of mutuality as we rule and reign as the beloved Bride with our beloved Bridegroom, Jesus, the Son of God.

In the Post-Fall Era of Isaiah 54:5a (NASB 1995), it was God who said, "For your husband is your Maker, whose name is the Lord of Hosts." In Isaiah 55:1 (NASB 1995, emphasis added) it was God who said, "Ho! Everyone who thirsts, *come* to the waters; and he who has no money, *come* buy and eat!" In the new-Creation era of the Gospel of Matthew, it was Jesus who gave the invitation and said, "*Come* to me, all who are weary and heavy-laden and I will give you rest" (Matthew 11:28, NASB 1995, emphasis added). The Messiah Jesus said, "I am the bread of life; he who *comes* to Me will not hunger, and he who believes in Me will never thirst" (John 6:35, NASB 1995, emphasis added). How perfectly appropriate it is then, in the New Heaven and Earth Era, for the mutuality of the Spirit and the exalted Bride to crescendo together with a triumphant and trinitarian invitation to the final "*Come*" (Revelation 22:17, NASB 1995, emphasis added).

As a woman, I cannot help but smile as I read again these final redemptive words of Revelation. It is none other than the Spirit and the exultant Bride who invite all to *come* and enter into a reciprocal and intimate love relationship with Jesus (Revelation 22:17). God's highest intention for his *ezer,* the creation of Eve for Adam, has now been fulfilled in the Bride of Christ. We often hear that Jesus is the Second Adam. Is it possible that the Bride of Christ is the second Eve?

There is no higher intention of God for humankind than to be invited to *come* as His Bride and be transfigured in the beauty of the Bridegroom's holiness. We are the love of His life, the apple of His eye, the delight of His existence. In the beginning, humankind, male and female, were created in God's image, in the likeness of our Triune God, to rule together as one. In the end, the Alpha and the Omega are united in Christ.

The Spirit and the Bride say, "*Come.*" We are the Bride of Christ, invited into the mutuality of sharing power and authority with the God of the universe in submission to Him alone who is safe to gloriously worship and adore. This, then, is choosing intimacy.

About The Author

A s long as Cindi J. Martin can remember, people have told her that she was an "old-soul"—someone who demonstrated an understanding and seriousness about life unusual for her age. Her desire to understand people—where they came from, and how their life histories shaped them—drew her into the world of counseling, theology, and psychology.

When she was 15 years old, Cindi chose to follow Jesus Christ as her Savior and Lord. God used the words of Isaiah 58 and Isaiah 61 to call her into a counseling ministry within the fields of psychology and social work. As a result, she studied Scripture, took classes in theology, and began her counseling career in the inner cities of Sacramento and Stockton, California.

Cindi and her college sweetheart, Keith, married in 1984 with a desire to study abroad and become missionaries in Europe. Cindi received a Fulbright research scholarship to study at the University of Stuttgart and the University of Tübingen in Germany as part of her graduate studies in Social Work and Psychology. This allowed them both to study at the German university and become lay missionaries abroad. She and Keith are both fluent in German and enjoy foreign languages and culture. Since then, she has integrated her work and family life to serve the needs of children and adults in schools, county mental health agencies, private practice, and non-profit missionary organizations here and abroad for nearly four decades.

Throughout her career as a licensed psychotherapist, she has integrated a strong, biblical faith with her clinical training and experience. She took courses in Greek at a local Bible college and studied Hebrew at a local Jewish synagogue to inform her work as Founder and Director of Wellspring Counseling Ministries,[126] which provides Christian counseling resources and referral services to the community. As a therapist, she specializes in working with faith-based couples healing from the wounds of sexual addiction as well as women and children healing from trauma, loss, depression, and anxiety. She is trained in equine-assisted psychotherapy and is passionate about the way animals facilitate emotional and spiritual healing.

Keith and Cindi live on a ranchette in the Central Valley of California. In 2010, Cindi was diagnosed with a rare bone disease that required three cervical spine surgeries and necessitated giving up her three beloved therapy horses. In 2016, their horse acreage was turned into Wellspring Charitable Gardens, a market garden that grows and harvests seasonal farm-to-table produce, educates the community about the value of nurturing healthy soil, soul, and body, and sells weekly produce boxes to local families, schools, and restaurants. One hundred percent of the proceeds are donated to the counseling program.

For fun, Cindi loves to bake, share, and eat German-style sourdough bread and has discovered the joy of making her own kombucha. Keith and Cindi enjoy being out in nature, conversing, reading, laughing, cooking, and eating harvest-fresh meals with friends and family at kitchen and garden tables. Cindi is most fulfilled when she succeeds at creating intimate spaces for people with or without faith to express honest questions, doubts, feelings, thoughts, and experiences about the complexities of life.

Keith and Cindi have been married for 39 years, have an adult daughter, numerous daughters and sons of their hearts, two cats, 20 chickens, an unknown number of gophers, racoons, lizards, snakes, insects, and even the occasional peacock or peacock hen.

---

126 A program of United Charitable, a 501.c(3) not-for-profit organization

A free ebook edition is available with the purchase of this book.

To claim your free ebook edition:

1. Visit MorganJamesBOGO.com
2. Sign your name CLEARLY in the space
3. Complete the form and submit a photo of the entire copyright page
4. You or your friend can download the ebook to your preferred device

MorganJames BOGO™

A **FREE** ebook edition is available for you or a friend with the purchase of this print book.

CLEARLY SIGN YOUR NAME ABOVE

Instructions to claim your free ebook edition:
1. Visit MorganJamesBOGO.com
2. Sign your name CLEARLY in the space above
3. Complete the form and submit a photo of this entire page
4. You or your friend can download the ebook to your preferred device

Print & Digital Together Forever.

Snap a photo

Free ebook

Read anywhere